BECOMING A SPORTS COACH

A 'coach' is more than just somebody who leads in the organisation and delivery of structured sport. The role of a coach goes beyond leadership, requiring an understanding of theories of teaching and learning. To become a coach you must know how people learn.

Becoming a Sports Coach aims to introduce the multi-dimensional and interlocking knowledge bases that any aspiring coach will need to develop, and that any established coach needs to master in order to improve their professional practice. While traditional coach education pathways have focused on *what* to coach, this book argues that understanding *how* knowledge can be communicated to learners is just as important. Asking *why* we coach, through critical reflection and self-knowledge, is also an essential part of the process of becoming a sports coach. The book explores three types of knowledge – content knowledge, pedagogic knowledge and self-knowledge – challenging the reader to reflect on their own coaching experiences and to develop a personal philosophy of coaching. It explores key pedagogic themes in contemporary coaching studies, such as humanistic coaching, inclusive practice, coaching for understanding and the athlete–coach relationship. Real case studies are used to illuminate the ways – transferrable across sports – in which coaches can apply theory to practice and ultimately enhance their work.

With contributions from leading coaching researchers and practitioners, combining practical guidance with important theoretical insights, this book will help any coaching student or developing professional to better understand the journey to becoming an effective sports coach.

James Wallis is a Principal Lecturer in Sport Coaching and Physical Education at the University of Brighton, UK, where he is course leader of the BSc(Hons) Sport Coaching programme. He has extensive applied experience in coaching and coach education in both performance and sport for development contexts. He is currently contributing to coach education in professional cricket.

John Lambert is a Principal Lecturer in Sport Coaching and Physical Education at the School of Sport and Service Management, University of Brighton, UK. He is a UEFA A licence football coach and works in the match analysis and talent identification department of a Premier League football club. He has been engaged in coaching and coach education for many years, including tutoring FA courses. John is Visiting Lecturer at the German Sport University, Cologne, and has worked on a major international sport for development project for over ten years. He is co-editor of *Values in Youth Sport and Physical Education* (Routledge, 2014).

BECOMING A SPORTS COACH

Edited by
James Wallis and John Lambert

Routledge
Taylor & Francis Group

LONDON AND NEW YORK

First published 2016
by Routledge
2 Park Square, Milton Park, Abingdon, Oxon OX14 4RN

and by Routledge
711 Third Avenue, New York, NY 10017

Routledge is an imprint of the Taylor & Francis Group, an informa business

British Library Cataloguing-in-Publication Data
A catalogue record for this book is available from the British Library

Library of Congress Cataloging in Publication Data
Becoming a sports coach / edited by James Wallis and John Lambert.
pages cm
Includes bibliographical references and index.
1. Coaching (Athletics) 2. Coaches (Athletics)–Training of. I. Wallis, James, 1973- editor of compilation. II. Lambert, John, 1956- editor of compilation.
GV711.B36 2016
796.07'7–dc23
2015020575

ISBN: 978-1-138-79345-3 (hbk)
ISBN: 978-1-138-79346-0 (pbk)
ISBN: 978-1-315-76111-4 (ebk)

Typeset in Bembo
by Cenveo Publisher Services

Printed and bound in the United States of America by Publishers Graphics, LLC on sustainably sourced paper.

CONTENTS

ILLUSTRATIONS

Figures

Tables

CONTRIBUTORS

James Beale, University of East London, UK

Dr Gary Brickley, University of Brighton, UK

Dr Brendan Cropley, Cardiff Metropolitan University, UK

Adriano de Souza, Louisiana University of Technology, USA

Cathy Devine, University of Cumbria, UK

Professor Joan L. Duda, University of Birmingham, UK

Bill Filby, University of Brighton, UK

Sid Hayes, University of Brighton, UK

Dr Marc Keech, University of Brighton, UK

Dr Lynn Kidman, Auckland University of Technology, New Zealand

Tracy Killingley, University of Brighton, UK

Dr Zoe Knowles, Liverpool John Moores University, UK

John Lambert, University of Brighton, UK

Jim Lawlor, Manchester United Football Club, UK

Dr Andy Miles, Cardiff Metropolitan University, UK

Dr Steve Mitchell, Kent State University, USA

Toby Nichols, Cardiff Metropolitan University, UK

Floris Pietzsch, University of Brighton, UK

Dr Hamish Telfer, retired, formerly University of Cumbria, UK

Dr Andrew Theodoulides, University of Brighton, UK

Dr James Wallis, University of Brighton, UK

Dr Simon Walters, Aukland University of Technology, New Zealand

Heather Watson, professional tennis player, UK

Dr Jean Whitehead, University of Brighton, UK

ACKNOWLEDGEMENTS

Professional acknowledgements

We would like to thank our colleagues who have authored chapters within this book. We are grateful for their insight and expertise but also their openness and willingness to share their own experiences. We would also like to thank the team at Routledge, in particular Simon Whitmore for his guidance in the early stages of conceptualising and planning the direction of the book.

Personal acknowledgements

To Carol, Connie and Freddie for the unconditional time, space and support in completing this project. (James)

To my father, Charlie Lambert, who, despite having limited educational and sporting opportunities himself, always understood the benefits of acquiring knowledge and playing sport, and encouraged his children to enjoy learning and physical activity. (John)

INTRODUCTION

James Wallis

I thought I became a coach when I completed my Football Association (FA) preliminary coaching award. I took pride in using the label and wearing the badge. I practised as I had been directed, reproducing 'coaching' sessions from the standardised curriculum. My Physical Education teacher training, with its emphasis on pedagogic process and child-centred learning, ran simultaneously with collecting numerous National Governing Body 'coaching' awards. These contrasting experiences highlighted how far one 'new' profession had evolved and exposed how far the other would have to travel.

James Wallis on becoming a sport coach

1979 was a significant year for me as it was then that I qualified both as a teacher and a coach. These vocations have followed parallel paths ever since and have influenced each other. I have never behaved any differently whether teaching in my school or at my football club. It seemed intuitively right to apply an holistic approach and adopt the humanistic outlook that I was using in PE lessons to my coaching. The difference was that, unlike my fellow teachers, many of the coaches that I worked alongside did not share my philosophy, preferring to take a narrow technocratic view of their role.

John Lambert on becoming a sport coach

In essence we are all still *becoming* sports coaches, regardless of experience, qualifications or status. As a result this book speaks directly to sport coaches from all levels. It draws on the accumulated experience of practitioners and academics who offer insights into their developmental journey to becoming a sports coach. Sport coaching is undergoing a significant period of change and evolution, even revolution, from a workforce largely made up of volunteers to a more 'professional' accredited vocation. This book focuses on enhancing coach practice and further supporting the continuing professional development of coaches at all levels.

A new era of sport coaching

'Coach' is a label liberally applied to categorise people who assist individuals or groups in enhancing their performance, fulfilling potential or the achievement of goals. Its literal meaning is the movement of people from one place to another, implying advancement or progression. In sport it is often used as an umbrella term to capture anyone who takes the lead in the organisation and delivery of structured sessions in discrete activities. The spectrum is wide, ranging from high performance coaches in Olympic disciplines, to highly paid coaches of Premier League footballers, to the life blood of organised sport in many countries across the globe, the voluntary sector. Traditionally, the label also applies to anyone who has received formal accreditation through one of a growing number of certificated pathways to *becoming* a coach. Many have questioned this exclusive view of what it means to be a coach as it elevates the importance of National Governing Body (NGB) coach education courses and diminishes the importance of alternative routes to coaching competence. Consequently, discourse has increasingly focused on issues surrounding the conceptualisation of coaching as a profession, how to achieve professional status and what this would mean to the existing coaching workforce.

One significant area of debate has focused on what constitutes a *profession*. The emergence of other 'new professions' such as nursing, midwifery and physiotherapy (Salvage, 2002) has led to discussion about what aspects of these vocations make them eligible to be regarded as such. An endpoint or unanimous agreement is never likely, given the very public status of each of these roles and the level of political, social and cultural expectations they are subjected to. Sport coaching is exposed to both internal (for example from athletes, participants and clubs) as well as external expectations (from politicians, sponsors, media) and is unlikely to enjoy a linear pathway into a new professional era. Whilst how one conceptualises what constitutes a profession can be contested, it is considered here that the following five characteristics, adapted from Carr (1999), may be used by readers of this book to add shape to their own views on sport coaching as a profession.

Professions provide an important public service

Importance is clearly a relative term. Viewed in the context of sport providing significant income generation to governments, as a tool for multi-million pound media coverage, advancing the health status of the nation and contributing to various societal needs, it would appear that sport coaching is of value as a public service. The degree to which current coaching and coach education can meet these diverse demands is a feature of ongoing debate.

Professions involve appropriate theoretical as well as practical knowledge

Coaching is predominantly a practical pursuit. However, this should not be to the exclusion of an appreciation of an evidence base that informs our practice. Being able to theoretically underpin practice is a crucial concern for an emerging profession, as is the ongoing need for at least minimal engagement with research and new approaches in the field. The area of sport pedagogy has benefitted from significant academic attention over the last 20 years, much of which contains accessible applied messages to practitioners. It is considered here that there is an expectation that members of a profession access recent advances in their area of work and seek to apply these as appropriate. Similarly, it should be expected that entrants to a profession are effectively supported in all required knowledge bases to fulfil their role. It has previously been suggested that UK NGBs have been overly technocratic in the education of coaches, to the exclusion of other required knowledge (Jones *et al.*, 2004).

Professions have ethical expectations and a code of practice

Practising within a set of universally agreed ethical principles may be the most important of these five criteria. Whilst the nature of the activity, contextual traditions and social norms may play a role in the specific parameters of a code of practice, it should be recognised that a profession requires guiding principles to advise, inform and regulate activity, particularly in the case of sport with its need for inclusivity, equity and fairness as desirable aspirations. Whilst higher order ethical expectations may be deferred to a higher authority (e.g. the law of the land), most ethical guidelines are set by the relevant sporting body.

Professions require organisation and regulation for recruitment and discipline

Linked to the point above is the need for a profession to be centrally organised and have a structure for governance, for example in the creation, communication and regulation of ethical guidelines or codes of practice. Recruitment to a profession should be dependent upon minimum standards of qualification, evidence of sustained standards of practice and examples of continuing professional development resulting in registration and de-registration of members. These are examples of roles for an over-arching professional body.

Professions should encourage a high degree of autonomy and individual judgement

This criterion is perhaps the most challenging to apply, and may even appear to contradict the pursuit of standardisation. Professionals require professional knowledge, which it may be the obligation of the profession to supply. There is a point at which formal training should be merged with personal judgement to meet the specific demands of the context. Received wisdom should only be considered to go so far. Coach education programmes may typically impose standardised content and principles of practice that are routinely reproduced by coaches. A profession may require practitioners to be capable of exercising a degree of autonomy, adopting personalised approaches and even developing their own philosophy of practice.

This book seeks to encourage readers to be conversant with the evolving status of coaching as a profession and the dimensions of professional practice that this may soon demand. The structure and content of this book are designed to provide coaches with further support in their own advancement against these broad headings. Specific chapters will pick up on many of these principles. As in many other developed countries, the coaching infrastructure in the UK has been under ongoing scrutiny for a number of years. Whilst the next section focuses on key developments in the UK and discussions either side of hosting the 2012 Olympic and Paralympic Games in London, the central arguments concerning any moves towards the professionalisation of coaching are relevant to multiple international contexts.

The UK coaching context

The previous section wrestled with some of the substantive issues pertaining to the advance of sport coaching into a new era and this section will seek to apply some of these issues to the UK coaching context. Sport coaching in the UK has traditionally been seen as a grass-roots activity, underpinned by the goodwill of a predominantly volunteer workforce (Taylor and Garratt, 2008; 2010). To provide a sense of scale, there were 2.75 million guided sport hours in 2008 with over 1.1 million adults taking part in the delivery of sport. Over 611,000 individuals considered themselves as 'coaches' by virtue of training through an NGB award (sports coach UK, 2009). The vast majority of these hours were delivered on a voluntary basis. Here lies one of the most significant challenges to the professionalisation of sport coaching in the UK: how to instil the characteristics of professionalism without losing sight of the significant historical and cultural foundations built on volunteerism.

Professionalising sport coaching in the UK is not a new issue. Earlier writing on the subject by Lyle (1986) and Woodman (1993) was followed by UK Sport's *UK Vision For Coaching* in 2001, which stated that

> By 2012, the practice of coaching in the UK will be elevated to a profession acknowledged as central to the development of sport and the fulfilment of potential.
>
> *(p. 5)*

This report, along with the purposeful statements contained within it, catalysed further discussion on the pathway to professionalisation, including factors that could enable and factors that could inhibit the emergence of coaching into a new era. These discussions were captured by Taylor and Garratt (2008) on behalf of sports coach UK in a prelude to the *UK Coaching Framework*, the blueprint for coaching in the UK to create a coaching system that is 'world-leading by 2016' (sports coach UK, 2008a: p. 11). The Framework's 11-year life span was divided into three phases:

building the foundations from 2006 to 2008, delivering the goals from 2006 to 2012 and ultimately transforming the system from 2006 to 2016 (sports coach UK, 2008a). The role played by the *Framework* in mapping the future of coaching in the UK should not be underestimated. It has provided focus, strategic direction and intention to the field. It has attempted to galvanise diverse and sometimes disparate bodies with a shared vision for the future. Specific outcomes are to

- enhance the quality of coaching at all stages
- provide active, skilled and qualified coaches to meet demand

Leading to

- sustained and increased participation
- improved performances in sport underpinned by clear career structures for coaches within a professionally regulated profession.

(sports coach UK, 2008b: p.6)

Since the publication of the Framework further academic debate has ensued, drawing together national and international perspectives on the existence of sport coaching as a profession (Taylor and Garratt, 2010; Lyle and Cushion, 2010; Duffy *et al.*, 2011). A strong contention is that there is little quantifiable evidence that sport coaching is any closer to achieving professional status. It is not, however, the intention of this book to add to the discussion, or evaluate the extent to which the *UK Coaching Framework* impacted on the national picture. The overview provided here is intended to inform front-line coaches of the wider picture outside of their immediate coaching context and to raise awareness of wider debates that are likely to re-shape coaching in the not too distant future.

How to use this text

This book is written to generate dialogue between author and reader. Each chapter contains a merging of theoretical principles with practical examples and case studies, many of which are based on real-life experiences of the authors. Common to each chapter is the embedding of the authors' reflexive voice along with signposted opportunities for readers to reflect on concepts raised and to interrogate content against their own practice settings. Whilst chapters exist as stand-alone elements offering readers the opportunity to dip in and out of the book at their own discretion, readers are encouraged to visit Chapter 1 as their starting point, which provides a conceptual overview of reflection for coaches. A solid grounding in this concept will increase the likelihood that the themes raised through subsequent reading can be internalised, and learning maximised. Using reflection as a constant motif throughout the text we ask readers to question their own coaching conventions and the assumptions they may hold, and ultimately to review and advance their practice. It should also not go unnoticed that chapters may overlap with each other in many places, in some cases cross-referencing has been made explicit. In other places readers may be able to identify inter-connecting sections of the book, demonstrating the complexity of coaching along with our attempt to present a 'joined-up' account of the coaching process.

The organisation of this book

The book is organised into three sections which focus on addressing three key considerations for coaches. The first is understanding *why* you coach the way you do, and Section 1 sets the scene for the rest of the book by asking readers to interrogate the personal and contextual factors that influence their philosophy and shape their practice. Chapter 1 (by Miles, Cropley and Nichols) is central to the rest of the text as it presents a conceptualisation of reflective practice in coaching. In order to fully utilise the reflective thread running through each chapter of the book it is recommended that readers come to terms with what constitutes reflective practice, how it is applied and how it can facilitate learning from experience. In Chapter 2, Devine, Telfer and Knowles introduce the concept of a personal coaching philosophy and how the involvement of different interested parties with varied value systems can lead to conflicting pressures on coaches. Examples of coach conflicts and dilemmas are provided to enable readers to consider their own position relative to those around them. Chapter 3 focuses on moral issues for coaches. In this chapter, Theodoulides presents arguments that coaching is an inherently moral activity, suggesting that coaches should be aware of the importance of adding moral and ethical dimensions to their work in the interest of developing positive values as well as enhancing athletic performance. Chapter 4 concludes the section as Keech considers the political and policy context surrounding coaching. Central to this chapter is a historical appreciation of the development of the policy landscape within which coaches operate.

Section 2 seeks to add to coaches' appreciation of *how* to coach using discussion of selected pedagogic themes pertinent to coaches at all levels of practice. Building on the reflective foundation of Section 1, this section asks coaches to critique their own coaching processes and to consider a range of alternative strategies and methodologies which may enhance their work. Inclusion in sport coaching is the focus of Chapter 5, where Hayes and Killingley present an overview of issues facing coaches who aspire to offer fully inclusive coaching environments. The authors use case study examples relating to gender and disability to further contextualise their writing. The next two chapters discuss approaches to coaching which break from traditional autocratic styles of delivery. Chapter 6 (by Walters and Kidman) considers the adoption of a more humanistic approach to coaching which places the athlete at the centre of the coaching environment. In Chapter 7 Mitchell and de Souza present an adaptation of the Games for Understanding methodology as a means to encourage greater player autonomy and decision making than afforded by traditional coach-dominated coaching styles. Both chapters offer applied examples to provide readers with further clarification of these two approaches. In Chapter 8

Duda and Whitehead focus on the perspectives of Achievement Goal Theory and the implication of task-involved and ego-involved motivational climates created by coaches. This chapter includes an explanation of the Empowering Coaching programme which has been tested via the Europe-wide PAPA (Promoting Adolescent Physical Activity) project. Chapter 9, by Pietzsch and Watson, the final chapter of the section, draws on a case study of a long-standing coach–athlete relationship within the context of elite, professional tennis, discussing how the relationship flourished through application of evidence-based principles of power relations.

Section 3 seeks to broaden understanding of *what* to coach, using contemporary views of what constitutes required knowledge for coaches. This section presents content knowledge that is transferable across a range of sports and goes beyond the technical and tactical. In Chapter 10 Brickley offers insight into the integration and application of sport science into coaching using a case study of his work within British Cycling. The diversity of knowledge required in order to support athlete needs is at the core of this chapter. In Chapter 11 Filby, Beale and Wallis illustrate features of their work in applied sport psychology settings, within professional cricket, which are applicable to the work of any coach. The authors argue that a move away from practitioner-led, content-driven psychological skills, as exemplified in this chapter, can enhance athlete performance. Chapter 12, by Lambert, considers the coaching of values through sport. This chapter presents key theoretical and applied perspectives for anyone working within community coaching and sport for development programmes. Chapter 13, by Lawlor and Lambert is written in the form of a reflective narrative focusing on key issues in the identification and nurturing of potential. Both authors utilise their extensive experience within professional football to support coaches in this contested area of youth sport.

The final chapter of the book is written by the editors and is presented as a plenary of the most salient themes emanating out of the whole text. This is intended to summarise and support coaches as they move forward with their careers. Included there are further thoughts about possible future directions and some critical questions for readers to ponder as coaching enters a new era.

References

Carr, D. (1999) Professional education and professional ethics. *Journal of Applied Philosophy*, 16(1), 33–54.

Duffy, P., Hartley, H., Bales, J., Crespo, M., Dick, F., Vardhan, D., Nordmann, L. and Curado, J. (2011) Sport coaching as a 'profession' – challenges and future directions. *International Journal of Coaching Science*, 5(2), 93–123.

Jones, R., Armour, K. and Potrac, P. (Eds) (2004) *Sport Coaching Cultures: From Theory to Practice*. London: Routledge.

Lyle, J. (1986) Coach education: Preparation for a profession. In *Proceedings from the VIII Commonwealth and International Conference on Sport, Physical Education, Dance, Recreation*. London: E and FN Spon.

Lyle, J. and Cushion, C. (Eds) (2010) *Sports Coaching: Professionalisation and Practice*. Edinburgh: Churchill Livingstone, Elsevier.

Salvage, J. (2002) *Rethinking Professionalism: The First Step for Patient-focused Care*. London: Allen and Unwin.

sports coach UK (2008a) *The UK Coaching Framework*. Leeds: The National Coaching Foundation.

sports coach UK (2008b) *The UK Coaching Framework: Executive Summary Booklet*. Leeds: The National Coaching Foundation.

sports coach UK (2009) *The UK Coaching Framework: The Coaching Workforce 2009–2016*. Leeds: The National Coaching Foundation.

Taylor, B. and Garratt, D. (2008) *The Professionalization of Sport Coaching in the UK: Issues and Conceptualisation*. Leeds: sports coach UK.

Taylor, B. and Garratt, D. (2010) The professionalization of sports coaching: definitions, challenges and critique. In J. Lyle and J.C. Cushion (Eds) *Sports Coaching: Professionalisation and Practice*. Edinburgh: Churchill Livingstone, Elsevier.

UK Sport (2001) *The UK Vision for Coaching*. London: UK Sport.

Woodman, L. (1993) Coaching: A science, an art, an emerging profession. *Sports Science Review*, 2(2), 1–13.

SECTION 1

'Why' you coach the way you do

This first section sets the scene by asking you to interrogate the personal and contextual factors that influence your philosophy of coaching and shape your practice.

1

LEARNING TO LEARN

The coach as a reflective practitioner

Brendan Cropley, Andy Miles and Toby Nichols

A reflection in a mirror is an exact replica of what is in front of it. Reflection in professional practice gives back not what is, *but what might be,* an improvement on the original.

Biggs, 1999: 6

Introduction

The exploration of reflective practice as an approach to the education and ongoing development of sports coaches has developed significantly in recent years (for a review see Huntley *et al.*, 2014). Emanating from this has been an increasing recognition of the benefits of helping coaches to learn from their practical experiences in a meaningful and productive manner (Gilbourne *et al.*, 2013). However, despite the empirical and anecdotal evidence that supports the efficacy of reflective practice, a number of issues remain that have arguably stunted the integration and development of reflective practices within the field of sports coaching (Marshall *et al.*, 2014). A lack of conceptual understanding, for example, appears to still surround the process and pedagogy of reflective practice, which in some cases has led to misinterpretation and misrepresentation, which is somewhat represented in the quote by Biggs (1999) at the start of this chapter.

This chapter will attempt to help readers develop a better understanding of some of the principles of reflective practice. It will discuss some of the misconceptions around what constitutes reflective practice within sports coaching in order to help readers consider the ways in which they might interrogate their own practice in the interest of enhancing the effectiveness of their work. In accord with these aims, we would like to establish from the outset that as coaches we need to view reflective practice as an approach and disposition to:

a) examining and better understanding the self and the agency that we have to impact on goal achievement;
b) understanding the connection and interplay between theory and practice in order to question the established traditions in the field;
c) transforming our experiences, and those of others, into learning; and
d) ensuring that learning is translated into improved practice.

As a result, we would like the reader to question whether the reflective practices they engage with will achieve these aims and, irrespective of the answer, challenge them to improve their current practice. Indeed, if we constantly ask our athletes to strive for continuous improvement then we have a social responsibility to ensure we ask the same of ourselves.

Situating reflective practice within the nature of sports coaching

A conversation between Brendan (author) and Becky (pseudonym), a sport coaching student:

Brendan: Hi Becky, how was the coach education course?
Becky: OK thanks … it was alright.
Brendan: [sensing a tone of trepidation] Only 'alright'?
Becky: Well I've really started to question (as a result of the course) how I learn best and what knowledge I value most, which has been confusing.
Brendan: What do you mean?
Becky: Well the course led me to believe that there's a 'right and wrong' way to do things, a 'black and white' approach to coaching, but many of the ideas presented were overly technical and they don't sit well with me as they wouldn't transfer to the context of my coaching … they're too rational.
Brendan: That's interesting; I appreciate the frustration. This resonates with my understanding that coaches have to know themselves, their athletes and the specific environment in which they are working, above other types of knowledge, if they want to be effective.
Becky: Yeah … I would have appreciated the opportunity on the course to gain an understanding of how to explore those things and how they shape each other.
Brendan: This reminds me of an analogy that I think is relevant here, and something to think about – 'the map is not the territory'!

The nature of sports coaching and the process inherent within the field has become widely contested territory (Chesterfield *et al.*, 2010; North, 2013). Traditionally, the process of coaching has been considered as something that can be modelled and taught through formal methods; a conceptualisation that has emerged from the positivistic roots of the field located within the sports sciences (Abrahams & Collins, 2011). However, more recently such notions have been brought into question by those who have suggested that the traditional views oversimplify what is an innately complex and ambiguous process (e.g. Bowes & Jones, 2006; Jones *et al.*, 2014). Specifically, researchers and practitioners have posited that coaching is characterised by a complex social system underpinned by human-to-human interaction and is thus better understood through the epistemologies of constructionism[1] and interpretivism[2] (North, 2013; Peel *et al.*, 2013).

From an individual perspective, this notion of complexity appears to hold credence (Jones & Wallace, 2005). For example, the interplay between intrapersonal emotions, thoughts, and behaviours that become socially and contextually dependent offers clear support for the notion that understanding why coaches 'do' and 'say' certain things is a compound endeavour. From a wider, interpersonal perspective, the micro-political environments that are constructed by the coach–athlete, coach–organisation and coach–stakeholder (e.g. parents, chairpersons, club officials) relationships offer further backing for the constructivist view due to the dynamic construction of the environments in which coaches operate. Such ideas have been supported within the empirical literature, which has indicated that practitioners do not find simplistic (rational) interpretations of the coaching process of much value in supporting or informing their work (e.g. Chesterfield *et al.*, 2010; Potrac *et al.*, 2013).

A consequence of re-conceptualising the nature of coaching in this way is that traditional approaches to coach education and development have been criticised for being too decontextualised and focused on developing technical–rational purveyors of coaching knowledge (Cushion *et al.*, 2010). If we agree with Cushion, Armour and Jones' (2006) contention that coach effectiveness is not dependent upon the efficient application of a sequential, rationalistic process but on the quality of the interactions between coach, athlete and context, then we have to accept and value the different approaches to learning and development that elicit the forms of *knowing* required to effectively manage the complex, and often chaotic, milieu of the coaching environment. In light of this, and drawing on the work of Schön (1983; 1987), we have to consider the varied typography of professional (coaching) practice in order to question how valuable traditional approaches to evidence-based (technical rationality) practice are and whether these have actually resulted in the oppression of coaching practice (cf. Johns, 2009).

The map is not the territory: the importance of reflective practice for coaches

'The map is not the territory' is a concept that has been used to consider the nature and value of different forms of knowing (Andersen, 2006; Devonport & Lane, 2014). In the analogy, the 'map' is seen to represent the theoretical or professional knowledge (knowledge about things) associated with a field (e.g. the efficacy of certain training protocols on the development of athlete performance); the types of knowledge often placed at the centre of formal education programmes. Here the map is thought to offer 'some form of *terra firma*, a land where things are known, where A precedes B, which leads to C, and the navigation is clear' (Andersen, 2006: 10). For many coaches this form of knowing offers stability because it provides an approach to practice that is uncomplicated. These maps, however, are thought to rarely represent the territory (the lived experience, craft knowledge) and as such those who place sole focus on developing this knowledge often feel unprepared for real-world practice issues (e.g. managing power relations in the coach–athlete relationship). Thus, in agreement with Devonport and Lane (2014), we argue that coaches must appreciate that learning needs to move beyond the development of professional knowledge and accept the responsibility that in order to progress from being competent towards being effective we need to continually draw meaning from events that occur across professional (coaching) and personal (life) contexts. This supports the contention of Saury and Durand (1998) that effective elite coaching practice is based on appropriate use of tacit, experiential knowledge and not just formal theoretical knowledge.

By presenting this argument we are not attempting to devalue professional, theoretical knowledge but to simply question the place it has within the hierarchical structure of importance for effective coaching practice. Certainly, in sports coaching there are solutions to some problems that tend to 'ring true' in many different situations and, as a result, we contend that the application of theory to practice may be suitable for well-defined and recognisable issues (Cropley *et al.*, 2012). Problems associated with coaching practice, however, rarely present themselves in easily definable and resolvable form (Peel *et al.*, 2013). This does not mean that in order to deal with, and potentially prevent such complex problems, technical knowledge should be overlooked or ignored. Instead, it is important for trainees and professionals to transform their experiences through reflective practice in order to bridge the gap between theory and practice. Integrating prior beliefs, values, prejudices and social norms with theory and practice in this reflective process is thought to help reconstruct professional knowledge and develop a way of *knowing-in-action* (Anderson *et al.*, 2004).

In summary, coaches have to acknowledge that the field in which they operate is socially derived and inherently complex. In order to learn how to better manage the coaching process, coaches need to develop different forms of knowledge (the map and the territory) and thus engage in ongoing approaches to learning that centre on understanding and learning from the lived experience. However, we cannot assume that learning is an automatic process associated with merely having an experience (Cropley & Hanton, 2011). Research has highlighted, for example, that for experiential learning to be obtained, learners must actively engage in processes that result in the excavation of knowledge embedded within the experience itself (Hanton, Cropley *et al.*, 2007). One such process is that of reflective practice (Cushion *et al.*, 2010).

Exploring reflective practice within sports coaching

A conversation between Andy (author) and Lee (pseudonym), an NGB Level 3 coaching course candidate:

Andy: So Lee, what have you been doing to learn from your coaching experiences?

Lee: Well I've been completing the log book straight after my sessions.

Andy: Great, so you've been engaging in reflective practice?

Lee: Oh yeah, I reflect all of the time anyway so this log book is pretty straightforward. I'm always looking back and thinking about the good and bad things from my session.

Andy: Can you give me a couple of examples?

Lee: Well, after my last session I thought that I gave good feedback and that my practice was realistic, but I thought that the area was too big.

Andy: That's interesting, but isn't that just an evaluation of your practice? What separates that evaluation from reflection?

What is reflective practice?

The way in which reflective practice is understood within sports coaching, and in the wider sports science literature, has come under some criticism. This has largely been founded upon the adoption of narrow interpretations and in some cases misrepresentations of reflective practice (Huntley *et al.*, 2014). Indeed, Dixon, Lee and Ghaye (2013) argued that much of what is currently regarded as reflective practice in sports coaching and coach education could be called a '*pedagogy of scarcity*' due to the 'somewhat anaemic and skeletal conceptions of reflection and its practices' implemented by coaches and those responsible for delivering coach education programmes (p. 588). In support of this, Cropley *et al.* (2012), who investigated issues currently associated with reflective practice within coach education, found that participants reported a lack of confidence in their understanding of reflective practice, which contributed to limited engagement with the process.

The issues presented here are likely to be a result of the number of definitions that are available, which are often accepted at face value despite them being borrowed from other fields (e.g. nursing and education) and frequently make it difficult for coaches to distinguish between reflective practice and other modes of thinking (e.g. evaluation). Additionally, the timing of reflective practice adds to the confusion due to the different considerations inherent within *reflection-in-, -on-,* and *-for-action*.[3] These issues are supported by Thompson and Thompson (2008), who indicated that a number of myths and misunderstandings have grown around reflective practice, including the tendency to take reflective practice too literally; that is, to see it as simply a matter of pausing for thought. We contend that it is important to go beyond this literalism to recognise that reflection is not simply thinking about practice in a general, loosely defined way. Indeed, it has been suggested that coach education has suffered from focusing on a type of reflection that links retrospection and review to projection, differing very little from the concept of performance evaluation (Dixon *et al.*, 2013).

One definition that has emerged from the sporting literature has attempted to assimilate a range of ideas in a way that helps readers begin to understand what actually constitutes reflective practice, and thus overcome the aforementioned issues; and is one with which we consider appropriate for practising coaches:

[Reflective practice is] a purposeful and complex process that facilitates the examination of experience by questioning the whole self and our agency within the context of practice. This examination transforms experience into learning, which helps us to access, make sense of and develop our knowledge-in-action in order to better understand and/or improve practice and the situation in which it occurs.

(Knowles et al., 2014: 10)

In order to make sense of this definition it is important to unpick its component parts and examine what they mean for the reflective practices of sports coaches. Indeed, by examining the process and outcome elements inherent within this definition we can better explicate the landscape of reflective practice (Knowles *et al.*, 2014) (see Table 1.1).

Although reflective practice is thought to occur at different levels of insight (e.g. technical, practical and critical), with each having its own characteristics (see Anderson *et al.*, 2004), here we contend that for reflective practice to occur at any level the process must involve all the characteristics presented in Table 1.1.

Presenting reflective practice in the way that we have done here moves understanding away from the traditional roots of reflective practice where reflection is thought to be initiated when individuals become aware of or concerned with an incident or problem (Cropley & Hanton, 2011). It could be argued that this is also the view of reflection adopted by those responsible for educating and developing coaches; one where reflection is used solely to solve problems and improve weaknesses (Miles, 2011). Dixon *et al.* (2013) argued that this view of reflection is based on the 'assumption that by fixing and getting rid of performance problems, weaknesses and undesirable aspects of practice, individuals, teams and squads, for example, will get better, perform better and get more fulfilment and enjoyment from what they do' (p. 589). Although we contend that reflecting on problems is important, it is equally beneficial to reflect on experiences where behaviour has been effective. Focusing on the positives, on our strengths, is likely to encourage the consideration of how we might better use these, and how we create opportunities to use these more often, and is likely to result in more appreciative action associated with a 'need to achieve' (Ghaye, 2011). By engaging in more appreciative action it could be argued that certain issues, problems, and/or weaknesses may begin to dissipate and thus we may take a more proactive approach to problem solving.

In the introduction to this chapter we challenged the reader to consider their reflective practices and we highlight this challenge again here. Does your reflective practice embody the concepts presented here? Are the characteristics in Table 1.1 embedded within your reflective practice? If not, then you have to question whether you are actually engaged in reflective practice at all, and thus could understand why the reported benefits of reflective practice may not be elicited from your endeavours. If they are, then how can you make more of reflective practice to help you to move your coaching and experience of coaching forward?

TABLE 1.1 Constituents of reflective practice and their application

Characteristic	Meaning	Application
Purposeful	Reflective practice is something that we consciously decide to engage in, which distinguishes reflection from the subconscious processes of day-dreaming and navel-gazing.	Many believe that they reflect 'all of the time' usually through some subconscious, implicit process that they cannot explain. However, in order to really make sense of and examine practice in a meaningful way reflective practice has to be purposeful. It has to be about something (e.g. a coaching experience) and for something (e.g. questioning taken-for-granted practice).
Complex, involves the whole self	Reflective practice has to consider personal cognitions, emotions and behaviours, their interaction and impact on the situation, as well as the impact of the context on these.	We have to excavate beneath the surface of our observable behaviours (e.g. the use of different forms of feedback) and examine why these behaviours occur, how they have come to be that way, and what impact they have. For example, adopting autocratic principles as a coach may not be as a result of your beliefs about what is effective but as a result of the confidence you have in engaging athletes in shared leadership.
Instigated through questioning	Thinking in an unstructured way about experience is complicated. Trying to process and make sense of a series of connected but random thoughts often leads to more confusion.	Using a series of questions through a reflective conversation (either with yourself or with other(s)) helps to guide the reflective process and encourage coaches to examine aspects of practice that they might overlook (e.g. Why do I react as I do to certain athlete behaviours? What impact do my values have on my practice?).
It's about you and your practice	Through reflective practice coaches need to consider the 'self' as an agent of change. Reflective practice is therefore about who you are, what you do, why you do it, and how it has come to be that way.	Many coaches focus too much on the external (e.g. the athletes, the environment) without considering themselves and the way in which they have impacted on the 'external'. Coaches have to question their own practice and the values that underpin it. Place yourself at the centre of your reflective practice.
Results in change	Change represents: (a) a change in behaviour, values or beliefs; (b) confirmation or rejection of a particular theory or practice; and/or (c) a change in knowledge of the self, the context of practice or the environment in which the practitioner is working.	The outcome of reflective practice is vital. It should result in a form of learning or understanding depending on the nature and purpose for reflection. This 'learning' should be articulated and sense should be made about how this will impact on future practice. Goal setting and goal striving (action planning) are good ways to consider how learning can be integrated into practice and evaluated for efficacy.

Adapted from Knowles *et al.*, 2014

What does it mean to be a reflective practitioner?

Sport coaching is seen as an 'emerging profession' and as such coaches have to accept the responsibilities that a profession brings with it (SCUK, 2009). These responsibilities include the notion of ongoing learning and development as well as a willingness to strive for effective coaching practice. Reflective practice and professional practice are therefore symbiotic in that one cannot exist without the other. Consequently, coaches must consider their development as a *reflective practitioner*. It is important to recognise, however, that becoming a reflective practitioner is more than a collection of techniques, and instead involves an all-encompassing attitude to practice that requires the coach to commit to professional and personal development (Anderson *et al.*, 2004). This requires coaches to develop a disposition that embraces reflective practice (and learning) through the integration of reflection-in-action (to assist decision making and intuitive action during practice), reflection-on-action (to make sense of the self and critically examine experience) and reflection-for-action (to strive for the integration of learning into practice).

Schön (1987) believed that the development of reflective practitioners was more likely to occur in an environment that prioritises flexibility, acknowledges that there are multiple views on issues, appreciates the complexity of issues and is non-hierarchical (e.g. opinions of all members of the organisation, such as the coach, the performance director and the athlete are valued equally). The consideration for coaches, therefore, is whether the environment in which they work, and within which they have agency to shape it, meets these criteria and how willing they are to alter their environment if they do not. In addition, coaches have to consider the personal characteristics and skills required to create such an environment (Cropley *et al.*, 2012). Dewey (1916), for example, suggested that before a person can develop as a reflective practitioner three personal attitudes are necessary: (1) open-mindedness; (2) whole heartedness; and (3) responsibility. *Open-mindedness* refers to a willingness to listen and accept alternative beliefs, attitudes and approaches to practice that may contrast with what we think is 'right'. It involves, therefore, a questioning of those things that we take for granted. *Whole heartedness* refers to being thoroughly interested in a subject, in this case personal and professional development (Cassidy *et al.*, 2009). Finally, *responsibility* requires us to consider and accept the consequences of our actions so as to enhance the congruence between our beliefs and actions. The challenge for coaches then is to consider whether these attitudes reside in them and whether they are able (and prepared) to develop and foster them through their continual professional development. In addition, coaches have to question 'how much' of these attitudes they are willing to adopt (e.g. *how* open-minded they are keen to be). Undoubtedly, these attitudes will help to facilitate reflective practice, and conversely, without them it is likely that our reflective practices will be inhibited.

Finally, we contend that a reflective practitioner works to develop an appreciation and acceptance of the social power they have within their role as a sports coach and how they might use this to oppress or liberate athlete potential and to dictate the type of experience that their athletes gain. Essentially, this idea focuses on the importance of moving towards a critical self-awareness that allows us to ruminate on the centrality of values in coaching practice, the tensions and conflicts created by them and the consequent impact on our attitudes, behaviours and emotions (Peel et al., 2013). Becoming a reflective practitioner is, therefore, not an easy endeavour. It requires a nurturing environment, appropriate personal attitudes, and the development of skills associated with effective reflective practice (e.g. problem-solving, critical thinking). For the field of sports coaching to progress, these requirements should be integrated into all coach education and development programmes so that reflective practice becomes a part of who we are (the reflective practitioner) rather than something that we simply do.

Facilitating reflective practices

For reflective practice to occur in a meaningful and effective way we have to move our understanding of *how to do* reflective practice beyond those approaches that might constrict the artistry of reflection. We need to embrace, therefore, approaches that facilitate the consideration of personal cognitions, emotions and behaviours, their interaction and impact on the situation, as well as the impact of the context on these. Further, any evocative outcome of questioning the taken-for-granted practices in the field will be hindered by reflective practices that only facilitate the consideration of the obvious (Dixon et al., 2013). Whilst practices that facilitate the consideration of the whole self may be avoided by coaches due to the degree of challenge, discomfort or vulnerability that is created through their engagement, if coaches are truly dedicated to improvement and to their professional responsibilities then such challenge should be embraced (Anderson et al., 2004; Cassidy et al., 2009).

For reflective practice to occur we require a number of 'elements' to be present: (a) something to reflect on or about (an experience); (b) something to reflect with (knowledge); (c) a purpose for reflection; and (d) a medium for reflection. It is easy to get consumed with procrastinating over *what to reflect on*, especially in situations where we might not have the time and space to reflect in a critical way (Gilbourne et al., 2013). In answer to this, some have advocated the use of subjectively determined critical incidents as a catalyst (Cropley & Hanton, 2011; Miles, 2011). Critical incidents are generally considered as those that are most likely to elicit significant learning about the self, the context and/or the profession. Consequently, coaches need to feel confident to reflect on any situation that is important to them (regardless of whether it is positive or negative), rather than being concerned with the potential significance of the situation for others. We also have to consider what we are actually *reflecting with*. It has been argued, for example, that without sufficient professional knowledge or day-to-day experience of the field (coaching) our reflections are likely to be limited (Moon, 1999). In these situations it is likely that we reflect only with what we currently know and are influenced by personal values and beliefs, making progression in practice problematic. Whilst reflective practice should be about you and your practice, without different forms of knowledge it is difficult to make sense of our cognitions and actions or their potential impact on those with whom we are working and the context in which our practice takes place. Coaches should, therefore, go about evolving their knowledge (and embracing new theoretical fields of knowledge such as pedagogy and social theory) through conversations, mentoring, and/or personal research as well as through ongoing reflection. It may also be beneficial to use a *critical friend* or *facilitator* at any stage of learning as research has indicated that shared approaches allow the reflector to examine their experiences in different, less prejudiced, and more meaningful ways (Cropley *et al.*, 2012; Knowles *et al.*, 2001).

Identifying a *purpose for reflection* is an important consideration as it should impact the approach to, and content of, reflective practice (Cropley & Hanton, 2011). For example, Anderson *et al.* (2004) suggested that reflective practice could be used to: (a) explore the intricacies of actually 'doing'; (b) make better sense of the self; (c) address issues experienced in practice; and (d) demonstrate accountability to the profession. In light of the work of Ghaye (2011), we would also add 'to explore ways in which we can make more and better use of our strengths'. The purpose for reflection might include one, a number, or all of these, but in any instance the practitioner should be clear that appropriate considerations can be made about the appropriateness of a specific *reflective medium*. Some approaches to reflective practice (e.g. paper-and-pencil-based activities that are structured through models borrowed from other fields) have come under recent criticism for being too mechanistic and outdated (e.g. Dixon *et al.*, 2013). We urge caution about some of this critique, however, as there are a number of instances in the literature where coaches have advocated the value of more structured reflective mediums that are facilitated through borrowed models, such as Gibbs' cyclical model (e.g. Knowles *et al.*, 2001; Peel *et al.*, 2013). Whilst we do agree with Dixon *et al.*'s (2013) contention that approaches to reflection that emphasise participation and facilitate innovative explorations, experimentations and purposeful alterations should be encouraged (e.g. blogs, wikis, social networks), we advise that individuals should be free to adopt a strategy that best suits them and their learning needs, with no one particular approach being valued over another. Placing the *constituents* (see Table 1.1) for reflective practice at the centre of any approach is imperative as is the recording of our reflections. In doing this we are more likely to actually engage in 'reflective practice' in a critical and meaningful way as well as commit to learning from our experiences and implementing that learning in future practice. Additionally, any approach should adopt three fundamental processes: *retrospection* (making sense of the experience); *self-analysis* (critically analysing and evaluating the actions and feelings associated with the experience, using theoretical perspectives); and *reorientation* (using learning emanating from the process to influence future approaches) (cf. Quinn, 2000). Building on the work of Knowles *et al.* (2014), descriptions of a number of approaches to reflective practice are presented in Table 1.2. These are thought to offer an insight into how reflective practice may be captured as part of ongoing professional training and development, and whilst it is appreciated that this is not an exhaustive list it is thought that the range of options indicates the need for people to develop their own approach that may or may not be formed through a combination of those presented. By doing this, coaches should be empowered to direct their own reflective practices in a way that allows them to be more critical and move practice forward in a way that is personally significant, rather than becoming standardised – the *norm* (Knowles *et al.*, 2014).

Finally, all of the approaches presented in Table 1.2 would benefit from the integration of a series of questions that help the coach to engage in purposeful reflection (Cropley & Hanton, 2011). Certainly, ineffective reflective practice emanates from self-absorbed navel gazing, and by guiding reflection through

TABLE 1.2 Approaches to and methods of capturing reflective practice

Approach	Description
Journals	Written journals can be structured with specific frameworks and questions to guide the reflective writing process. This approach can help to make sense of the experience by examining the minutiae of the situation, offering a cathartic release through writing, and considering the symbiotic nature of the self, practice and context.
Mind maps	Provide a more visual representation of reflective practice through the construction of interrelated factors that may have shaped the experience. This approach can help to unpick the relational nature of practice and learning in order to make better sense of practice, self and context.
Visual sociology	The use of photographs, still video images and drawings can provide the focus and stimulation for reflective practice and reflective conversation. These images help to remind, represent and reconstruct experiences from which new meanings and understandings can be created.
Recorded narrative	The use of digital voice recording media can help to capture thoughts, feelings and behavioural outcomes both *in-action* and immediately post-action. Such procedures help to 'bank' these things for consideration at a later date.
Communities of practice	Reflecting with others in homogeneous groups in both a non-structured (conversational) or a structured (framework of questions) manner can help to generate creative and innovative thinking. This is done by adding new knowledge from different experiences and discussing the potential for the development of practice.
Reflective conversations	Usually focused and structured conversations with 'critical friends' that help to challenge self-perceptions by examining the 'how' and 'why' of practice. Conversations are designed to stimulate thought by adding new knowledge and exploring practice more critically through the use of interview techniques.
Blogs	Blogs allow individuals a fast and easy way to share thoughts with others. Blogs have been seen as a beneficial approach to facilitating reflective practice by allowing people to 'post' personal commentaries about practice, concerns, traditions and developments within the field. Additionally, they allow individuals to receive greater feedback on their reflections and encourage ongoing dialogue.

Adapted from Knowles *et al.*, 2014

well-prepared and situationally specific questions we are more able to overcome this issue. Appropriate questions are often inherent within certain reflective models and established throughout the reflective practice literature (see Ghaye, 2011; Gilbourne *et al.*, 2013), but we must be wary of using these models or questions in mechanical or routinised ways. Doing so may result in us engaging neither with critical thought nor with emotions, resulting in reflective practice that is bland and self-descriptive.

Conclusion: Moving our reflective practices forward

In this chapter we have attempted to highlight and discuss some of the main issues that have emerged in relation to integrating reflective practice into the field of sports coaching. We have also offered conceptualisations of reflective practice and what it means for coaches to be reflective practitioners, in the hope that the discussion begins the process of overcoming the issues related to the practical importance that is placed on the concept, how reflective practice is located within sports coaching, and the approaches to reflection that are traditionally adopted within the field (cf. Dixon *et al.*, 2013). We do appreciate, however, that more research and debate is required before these problems can be fully solved.

It is clear that reflective practice should be firmly embedded within our 'emerging profession' simply due to the types of knowledge that we need in order to be able to cope better with the inherent complexity and ambiguity brought about by the human–human nature of the field (Marshall *et al.*, 2014). Moving beyond this, reflective practices are imperative for sports coaches due to the responsibility that they have to critically examine and question their practice and the context of their work in a way that facilitates better practice (Cropley *et al.*, 2012). In doing this it is more likely that they are able to manage a more positive experience of sport for themselves, their athletes and those with whom they work. In light of this discussion, coaches and those responsible for delivering coach education programmes must consider a number of factors. First, they have to foster a facilitative environment where reflective practices are encouraged and nurtured. Second, they have to identify and access the resources required to cultivate reflective skills. Third, more critical interpretations of reflective practice must be adopted to move practices away from mere evaluative forms of thinking. Finally, reflective practice cannot be seen as an 'add-on' to coaching practice, or simply as a part of NGB coaching qualifications, but as an inherent part of who we are as professionals.

In summary, we would like sports coaches to consider and reflect upon a number of key messages emanating from this chapter:

1. Reflective practice should be embedded within coaching practice, as it should be a fundamental part of what we do and who we are as coaches. Indeed, being a coach is about planning, delivering, reflecting-on-action and reflecting-for-action, and without the different stages of this cycle we are at risk of doing the profession a disservice.

2.   Reflective practice involves the 'self' and is about your practice. In this sense, reflective practice should be about challenging who we are, what/how we think, what we do and why these things have come to be this way.

3.   The skills and attributes required for reflective practice should be developed and nurtured. Those who do not see immediate 'results' from adopting reflective practices tend to place blame on the concept itself. These people are; however, probably better off questioning their own approaches to reflective practice as well as examining whether they have actually developed the skills and attributes required for reflection. Unfortunately, reflective practice is not like riding a bicycle in that once you have learned how to ride you will never forget. In the first instance we have to learn and develop the skills required for reflection. Over time we then have to develop and nurture the attributes for reflection in a way that allows our reflective practice to evolve with the context in which we are working. This requires a long-term commitment to the concept.

4.   We have to consider what we are reflecting 'on' and what we are reflecting 'with'. Understanding the professional knowledge (e.g. pedagogy, social theory) that is valued within the field (this can be done through conversations, mentoring and/or personal research) provides a lens through which we can begin to make sense out of our experiences and move our practice forward. If we do not constantly develop this knowledge then we are at risk of reflecting only on what we currently know, which may limit the significance of our learning.

5.   Reflective practices are varied, the value of them should be subjectively and situationally determined. There are many ways to reflect on your practice and, although it is easy to get carried away with those prescribed in other fields, we have to question the efficacy of any approach we take and its suitability for purpose, both in terms of outcome and in relation to what works best for us. Thus, we should embrace new or different approaches to reflection (e.g. reflective blogs, communities of practice, mind mapping) that encourage more critical and consistent engagement.

Notes

1   Constructionism is a theory of learning that is built on the understanding that knowledge is generated through experience and observation as well as through engagement and interaction with the socio-cultural environment in which we work.

2   Interpretivism is a theory relating to the nature of knowledge that emphasises the importance of understanding the differences between people and the way they interpret the world in which they live and work. It focuses on understanding how people's beliefs impact on the way in which they value knowledge.

3   In this chapter we are primarily concerned with reflection-on-action (a process of reflecting back on what we've done to make sense of our experiences and learn from them to improve future action). This is due to the aims outlined at the start and the potential we believe that this form of reflection has for generating the knowledge and understanding required for effective reflection-in- (a process of thoughtful 'in action' decision making in order to direct what we are currently doing) and -for-action (a process of reflecting forwards to explore the potential impact of our actions in future endeavours). For further discussion on these other modes see Cassidy *et al.* (2009).

References

Abrahams, A. & Collins, D. (2011) Taking the next step: Ways forward for coaching science. *Quest, 63*, 366–384.

Andersen, M. (2006) What's it like out there? Making the terra incognita more firma. *The Sport and Exercise Scientist, 9*, 10–11.

Anderson, A., Knowles, Z. & Gilbourne, D. (2004) Reflective practice for applied sport psychologists: A review of concepts, models, practical implications and thoughts on dissemination. *The Sport Psychologist, 18*, 188–203.

Biggs, J. (1999) *Teaching for quality learning at university*. Buckingham: Open University Press.

Bowes, I. & Jones, R.L. (2006) Working at the edge of chaos: Understanding coaching as a complex interpersonal system. *The Sport Psychologist, 20*, 235–245.

Cassidy, T., Jones, R.L. & Potrac, P. (2009) *Understanding sports coaching*. Second edition. London: Routledge.

Chesterfield, G., Potrac, P. & Jones, R. (2010) Studentship and impression management in an advanced soccer coach education award. *Sport, Education & Society, 15*, 299–314.

Cropley, B. & Hanton, S. (2011) The role of reflective practice in applied sport psychology: Contemporary issues for professional practice. In S. Hanton & S.D. Mellalieu (Eds) *Professional practice in sport psychology: A review* (pp. 307–336). London: Routledge.

Cropley, B., Miles, A. & Peel, J. (2012) *Reflective practice: Value of, issues, and developments within sports coaching*. Sports Coach UK Research Paper.

Cushion, C., Armour, K. & Jones, R.L. (2006) Locating the coaching process in practice: Models for and of coaching. *Physical Education and Sport Pedagogy, 11*, 83–99.

Cushion, C., Nelson, L., Armour, K., Lyle, J., Jones, R., Sandford, R. & O'Callaghan, C. (2010) *Coach learning and development: A review of literature*. Sports Coach UK Project Paper.

Devonport, L. & Lane, A. (2014) The utility of reflective practice during the provision of sport psychology support. In Z. Knowles, D. Gilbourne, B. Cropley & L. Dugdill (Eds) *Reflective practice in the sport and exercise sciences* (pp. 160–168). London: Routledge.

Dewey, J. (1916) *Democracy and education: An introduction to the philosophy of education*. New York: Macmillan.

Dixon, M., Lee, S. & Ghaye, T. (2013) Reflective practices for better sports coaches and coach education: Shifting from a pedagogy of scarcity to abundance in the run-up to Rio 2016. *Reflective Practice, 14*, 585–599.

Ghaye, T. (2011) *Teaching and learning through reflective practice: A practical guide for positive action*. Abingdon: David Fulton Publishers.

Gilbourne, D., Marshall, P. & Knowles, Z. (2013) Reflective practice in sports coaching: Thoughts on processes and pedagogy. In R.L. Jones & K. Kingston (Eds) *An introduction to sports coaching: Connecting theory to practice* (pp. 3–11). London: Routledge.

Hanton, S., Cropley, B., Neil, R., Mellalieu, S. & Miles, A. (2007) Experience in sport and its relationship with competitive anxiety. *International Journal of Sport & Exercise Psychology, 5*, 28–53.

Huntley, E., Cropley, B., Gilbourne, G., Sparkes, A. & Knowles, Z. (2014) Reflecting back and forwards: An evaluation of peer-reviewed reflective practice research in sport. *Reflective Practice: International and Multidisciplinary Perspectives, 15*, 863–876.

Johns, C. (2009) *Becoming a reflective practitioner*. Third edition. Chichester: Wiley-Blackwell.

Jones, R.L. & Wallace, M. (2005) Another bad day at the training ground: Coping with ambiguity in the coaching context. *Sport, Education & Society, 10*, 119–134.

Jones, R. L., Edwards, C. & Viotto, F. (2014) Activity theory, complexity and sports coaching: An epistemology for a discipline. *Sport, Education and Society*. http://dx.doi.org/10.1080/13573322.2014.895713.

Knowles, Z., Gilbourne, D., Borrie, A. & Neville, A. (2001) Developing the reflective sports coach: A study exploring the processes of reflection within a higher education coaching programme. *Reflective Practice*, *2*, 185–207.

Knowles, Z., Gilbourne, D., Cropley, B. & Dugdill, L. (2014) Reflecting on reflection and journeys. In Z. Knowles, D. Gilbourne, B. Cropley & L. Dugdill (Eds) *Reflective practice in the sport and exercise sciences* (pp. 3–15). London: Routledge.

Marshall, P., Nelson, L., Toner, J. & Potrac, P. (2014) Reflections on reflection. Some personal experiences of delivering higher education coach education. In Z. Knowles, D. Gilbourne, B. Cropley & L. Dugdill (Eds) *Reflective practice in the sport and exercise sciences* (pp. 80–90). London: Routledge.

Miles, A. (2011) The reflective coach. In I. Stafford (Ed.), *Coaching children in sport* (pp. 109–121). London: Routledge.

Moon, J. (1999) *Reflection in learning and professional development*. London: Routledge Falmer.

North, J. (2013) Philosophical underpinnings of coaching practice research. *Quest*, *65*, 278–299.

Peel, J., Cropley, B., Hanton, S. & Fleming, S. (2013) Learning through reflection: Values, conflicts, and role interactions of a youth sport coach. *Reflective Practice*, *14*, 729–742.

Potrac, P., Jones, R.L., Gilbourne, D. & Nelson, L. (2013) Handshakes, BBQs and bullets: Self-interest, shame and regret in football coaching. *Sports Coaching Review*, *1*, 79–92.

Quinn, F. (2000) Reflection and reflective practice. In C. Davies, L. Finlay & A. Bulman (Eds) *Changing practice in health and social care* (pp. 81–91). London: Sage.

Saury, J. & Durand, M. (1998) Practical knowledge in expert coaches: On-site study of coaching in sailing. *Research Quarterly for Exercise & Sport*, *69*, 254–266.

Schön, D. (1983) *The reflective practitioner*. Aldershot: Ashgate Publishing.

Schön, D. (1987) *Educating the reflective practitioner*. San Francisco: Jossey-Bass.

SCUK (2009) *Code of practice for sports coaches*. Leeds: The National Coaching Foundation.

Thompson, S. & Thompson, N. (2008) *The critically reflective practitioner*. Basingstoke: Palgrave Macmillan.

2

PHILOSOPHY OF PRACTICE AND PRACTICE CONFLICT

Coaching dilemmas and the performance spectrum

Cathy Devine, Hamish Telfer and Zoe Knowles

We wish to have a conversation with you so please don't skip this chapter. Usually the word philosophy has woolly connotations and yet it is usually the factor amongst practice dilemmas that is brought into sharp focus when issues relating to practice come into conflict. Discussion about 'a philosophy of coaching' is often mentioned in the training and education of coaches but seldom discussed or developed as a fundamental part of what the coach, their practice and coaching more generally is about. The coach is assumed to be able to grasp all the salient issues and get on with the process of coaching by the simple process of being reminded that having a 'philosophy of coaching' (whatever that may be) is necessary. To compound matters, the literature *on* and *about* coaching usually starts with either the 'role of the coach', or a model of the 'coaching process' and not with the coach themselves. Given that novice coaches tend to coach the way they themselves were coached as well as absorbing, often unwittingly, the values and approaches of their immediate coaching environment, the development of a 'philosophy of practice' is often subconscious and rarely articulated and discussed. Embarking on the road to becoming a coach typically boils down to taking up a coaching role when one's own playing career is ending or ends, embarking upon 'helping out' at a particular club or entering into the world of coaching through various levels of professional and academic courses aimed at providing the various 'markets' for coach deployment with an 'oven ready' workforce.

TASK 1

Reflect on the reasons or circumstances as to how you first engaged in coaching and what you thought it was about and what you would be doing as a coach, and then reflect on the changes (if any) that have occurred and what the triggers were for these changes.

This chapter deals with 'why' we do 'what' we do (which in turn may help us as coaches with 'how' we do things), and also the vexed and increasingly complex situations that sport now claims within the realm of what is called physical activity and recreation. It is important at the outset to state that it is our view that many of the dilemmas facing coaches relate to difficulties in matching what they think coaching *is about*; what they believe *is their duty* or obligation based on something they believe (e.g. developing winning individuals or teams); and *the context* in which they often find themselves. Put simply, individuals tend to come into coaching through avenues and routes that are usually to do with some internal mechanism and influenced by others who enthuse them enough to 'have a go'.

Fundamental to the issue of having or developing a philosophy of coaching is the parallel issue (at least in most of the literature) of coaching style. In other words, what you think you are about or believe will define in some way how you go about it. Lyle (2002) locates coaching practice and behaviour within a set of values. Jenkins (2010) sets out a useful starting point with regard to this as follows:

> Your coaching philosophy is a set of *beliefs* and *principles* that guide your behaviour. It helps you remain true to your *values* while handling the hundreds of choices you must make as a coach.
>
> *(234)*

If our values are based on our beliefs and define the way we engage with what we perceive as being true or false, good or bad and indeed whether actions are rooted in means or are ends in themselves then our practice will likely reflect this. These principles, beliefs and values will be shaped by ideology, prevailing discourses, knowledge and experience, to a greater or lesser extent.

Our values also determine our attitudes. However, it is also important to note that our values can shift over time based on exposure to differing evidence about things we believe in. Lyle (1999) alludes to this in discussing personal conflicts that may arise in coaching practice through the interface between stated beliefs, actual practice and personal values. Thus the 'aspirational' in coaching may be at odds with the reality, leading to conflict and dilemma (Lyle, 1999: 30–31).

TASK 2

Lyle poses the question: is it possible to have a philosophy about coaching if one is not a practising coach (an uncontextualised aspiration)? How has your experience of coaching to date allowed you to develop a coaching philosophy? Is this based on any preconceived notions of what a coach is and does? Have you noticed any changes in your approach as a coach over time?

We now turn our attention towards the various value systems at play in the coaching process. Figure 2.1 shows some examples of what one might call underpinning

Self-enhancement	Self-transcendence	Stability and tradition	Openess to change and agency	Personal well-being
Merit (talent or ranking)	Diversity	Discipline	Honesty	Happiness
Freedom	Honesty	Authority	Freedom	Companionship
Choice	Respect	Duty	Autonomy	Pleasure
Participation	Caring	Autocracy	Voice	Enjoyment
Winning	Equality		Individualism	Included
Competition	Justice		Courage	Empowerment
	Co-operation		Democracy	Amity
	Fairness		Trust	
	Truth			
	Pluralism			
	Responsibility			
	'Sportsmanship'			
	Tolerance			

FIGURE 2.1 Examples of core values categorised according to motivational goals

core values. If we accept that there are values that are both personal and stated (to simplify things), how do they then articulate with the values of the performer, the organisation within which the coach sits (usually a club and governing body of sport) and social values more broadly? This is important when considering practice dilemmas that may arise.

Generally, dilemmas and conflict arise when a sense of commitment or conviction is challenged. For example, a coach may hold the view that, particularly in the development of the young performer, there needs to be a clearly held understanding that all in the group or squad will get an opportunity to perform, as opposed to simply picking the best team or individuals to win on every competitive occasion. Thus, means and ends may be seen as at odds here in the immediate sense, but in the context of the long-term development of the performer this may be an appropriate action. However, sport by its very nature defines winners as 'good' and by implication those that coach them are also part of this 'good'. Nevertheless, to judge coaches as good or bad based on whether their performers win is tenuous ethical ground, as all sorts of factors come into play here, not least of which is the issue of early maturation of the young performer and of course 'natural talent', whatever that may be. Chapter 6 includes some case studies showing the pressure that can be exerted on a coach to prioritise winning at an early age over long-term player development.

Having set out this landscape, it is also important to state what philosophy should *not* be about. It should not be about 'rules' to be followed at all costs. There is perhaps a tendency with coaches and within coaching to seek some formula from which more certainty can be gained in the production and realisation of talent, and the seeking of a set of 'rules' that logically guide us through the process of engaging with the performer is a constant within coach education, specifically in the context of skill(s) development. The temptation here is that we reduce the performer as someone, or worse still *something*, that is part of a 'system' rather than an autonomous being. In this regard, one of the key questions relating to the various coach education and training programmes is whether they better serve those who design them (the system designers, e.g. sport governing bodies) or the coaches themselves (for whom they should be designed).

There are many ways of articulating your coaching philosophy, but often these fall along a spectrum from person-centred to sport-centred. It is not straightforward to attach a discrete set of values to each coaching philosophy. Nevertheless, a person-centred philosophy is likely to prioritise enjoyment, caring, voice and equality, whereas a sport-centred philosophy might value competition, winning and ranking, more highly. Within a physical education or school setting, a child-centred approach would generally be considered appropriate, whereas within a performance sport setting the philosophy will be more about competition and winning. However, coaches of performance and elite athletes may have a person-centred coaching philosophy, and conversely, coaches working in physical education settings often have a sport-centred approach. These two scenarios can then lead to value conflicts. For example, the requirement of elite sporting success might conflict with what the performance coach considers to be best for the athlete. Alternatively, the coach delivering physical education sessions could be more interested in winning inter-school competitions than in enabling all children in the class to find a sport or physical activity they enjoy and with which they are more likely to continue, which may be the greater priority for the physical education teacher.

In reality, your coaching philosophy is probably best viewed as a process and is likely to shift and change in relation to knowledge, experience and context. Further, what you regard as your coaching philosophy and underpinning values may not be reflected in your coaching practice (e.g. a coach may claim to have an inclusive philosophy but this may be abandoned when they know that by bringing on their bench players it is likely to lead to defeat). Finally, values are open to interpretation and the same value may be interpreted in many ways, so it is useful to reflect on what we mean by the things we value. A coach may have a value for long-term development but select physically big and strong players to win games at a young age without due regard for late developers.

TASK 3 YOUR COACHING PHILOSOPHY

Two significant issues need to be considered now. What is the purpose of what I do as a coach and who is it for? Is it person-centred or sport-centred? In answering the questions below, keep both of these issues foremost in your mind.

a)   Summarise the principles and beliefs that guide your coaching (try to give at least three examples).
b)   List and rank a set of core values you believe are important in your coaching (you may wish to refer to Figure 2.1).
c)   Are these values reflected in your answer to question a)?

To explore these issues, it is useful to articulate an embryonic coaching philosophy and identify a set of values which you feel guide your coaching. You will then be able to reflect on these within the context of practical coaching scenarios. This can help to develop your skill in integrating your values into your coaching with practice, knowledge and experience.

Coaching frameworks and where sport is 'experienced'

In gathering some momentum now in relation to asking you to reflect on your experiences of coaching, it is necessary to open up the terrain in which, and upon which, coaching exists. Two particular areas of strategic importance with their own inherent philosophical underpinnings and required outcomes need to be addressed here: 1) coaching frameworks, and 2) the varied nature of where sport is played and practised.

It is usual that coaches will be designated in some way or another, and the structure of coaching within the UK determines that the *UK Coaching Framework* matches a set of coaching competencies in four principle domains: children, participation, performance development and high performance. The neatness of these areas is further emphasised by a burgeoning literature on the technical and pedagogical development of the performers 'imprisoned' within them. Our language is deliberate here and explained below. The ability to equitably fit performers into notional boxes is often not the reality of the coaching environment for most coaches at club or beginner level. Often within the same group lie several abilities and competencies, thus demanding of most coaches the competency to design sessions that suit and relate to all those they coach in a particular session. This can be a significant challenge for any experienced coach, never mind those new to coaching. The ability to 'differentiate' within their sessions is a sophisticated pedagogical skill that relies upon what Lyle (2010) calls 'expertise'. The reality, currently, for most coaches is that they coach across an ability spectrum in conditions that are usually rudimentary in terms of resources and may even have more than one group in any one particular session. This presents most coaches with inherent dilemmas relating to session structure, organisation and management of sometimes large numbers of performers, and skill and technical development.

However, balanced against this is the fact that coaching at both development and high performance levels means that often the coaching resource is supplemented in the form of support coaches or the coaching is undertaken by teams of coaches, and therefore the coach is often surrounded by coaching support personnel. Thus the paradox emerges that as numbers become more manageable and the participants more uniform in abilities, the staffing tends to increase and support mechanisms are more often in place. The everyday world of coaching children and participation-level performers is less structured and less uniform in approach. Coaches actually need to possess numerous and sophisticated skills to cope with this.

What is called sport (and that debate would be too long to engage in here) is located within a number of places. For convenience we have grouped them broadly into three areas: sport as we commonly understand it in clubs which are usually attached to a particular sport's governing body; sport used within something called sports development which can be used to serve a variety of ends such as 'getting people active', getting children to take up an 'activity' and for health reasons; and finally physical education within school settings (also accepting that within the private, fee-paying school sector they often dispense with the notion of education and just have sport).

Coaches are increasingly becoming engaged in one or more of these sectors. The underpinning principles of each may vary significantly, with each having their own ethos and philosophical basis. Children and participation-level performers may exist in all of these three broad areas. As we move up the performance spectrum, however, coaches of performance development and elite performers are usually focused on competition with more developed performers, and are more engaged with the development of competitive advantage. Thus, while their broader expertise may shrink, their depth of expertise becomes more enhanced. This broad spectrum of the reality of coaching presents significant challenges to coaches in terms of their education and training in relation to the development of their craft skills or expertise. Coach education and training is usually the responsibility of sport governing bodies who regulate the content of coaching qualifications and determine who is able and ready to coach. We deliberately avoided the use of the word 'competent' here since there are few sports governing bodies who would enthusiastically benchmark competence on the evidence of a coaching course. The point we make here is the need to develop expertise in tandem with pedagogical and technical skills.

Different coaching settings may require coaches to 'fit' into an ethos. For example, coaches are increasingly recruited to work within education settings which have at their heart an ethos and philosophy for the teaching of physical education, which is significantly different from the coaching of sport. Notwithstanding this, coaches may find that with increased centralised intervention, what we have in schools is more akin to sport education, thus the physical education ethos may become more in tune with that of the sports coach.

Within sports development there is an increasingly more robust upskilling of coaches to undertake the diverse tasks which they will usually be employed to address with particular 'target groups'. Nevertheless, what is at stake here is a potential dissonance between what coaches think they are 'about', what they are trained to do, and what the expectations are of those they engage with.

Coaching 'cultures' and contexts

Although many coaches may explicitly espouse a person-centred philosophy of coaching, this is not always evident in coaching practice ('values in use'). This may be because coaches 'absorb' the prevailing coaching 'culture' even though in fact this differs from their underlying values. On the other hand, it may be because of a difference between belief systems and behaviours which might become apparent with some self-reflection. Alternatively, it could be that coaches are not aware of relevant research relating to coaching and sport and would benefit from 'unpacking' beliefs in the light of empirical evidence from academic research. Finally, the values of coaches may be different from those of other stakeholders (e.g. children, parents, teachers) or coaching contexts (such as schools, sports clubs, governing bodies of sport, government agencies). Whatever the reason, a conflict of values is problematic for coaches and warrants further exploration, and Task 3 above starts this exploration of coaching practice in differing coaching contexts.

Person-centred and sport-centred philosophies

Person-centred approaches link closely to the concepts of rights and respect which are central to the Convention on the Rights of the Child, equality legislation and human rights in general. The IOC, for example, states that sport is a human right and the *Code of Practice for Sports Coaches* (sports coach UK, 2005) asserts that 'Coaches must respect and champion the rights of every individual to participate in sport'. A person-centred philosophy is often known as child-centred or athlete-centred in the relevant contexts. It might be considered to encompass the values of: enjoyment, fairness, voice, democracy, equality, caring and respect. Further, it is likely to result in valuing a broad range of physical activities and a plural sport and physical activity culture.

Sport-centred philosophies tend to normalise the importance of competition in sport and society in general and view winning and losing, performance ranking and talent spotting as a 'natural' and even desirable part of sport and life. Unsurprisingly, a sport-centred philosophy would then highly value competition, winning and performance ranking, and regard sports or systems that encompass these activities as more valuable than those that do not. This may mean that competitive team sports are valued more highly than other sports and physical activities. It is also reflected in the belief that an element of competition should be introduced to all forms of sport and physical activity.

Value conflicts

An exploration of all the values listed above is beyond the scope of this chapter; however, many coaches, whether working at a participation or elite level, will want to sign up to the importance of enjoyment, fairness and respect.

TASK 4

Enjoyment, fairness and respect are deemed important qualities in good coaching practice. Can you think of examples within your own practice of where these are embedded and are therefore 'visible' to those you coach? How do you weave these qualities into other aspects of competitive training such as skill, technical, tactical and physiological development?

Since developing a coaching philosophy is a process, we will consider enjoyment, fairness and respect and some value conflicts around them in greater depth. Coaches are increasingly working with physical education professionals in the delivery of the physical education curriculum and the extended curriculum. These are useful contexts with which to explore any value conflicts that may arise as a consequence of potential differences in ideologies in relation to engaging children in physical activity.

Enjoyment vs winning

Research tells us that children value enjoyment and fun over winning and competition. Lee's classic research (2004b) showed that in sport, out of 18 values, children rank enjoyment (1), personal achievement (2) and 'sportsmanship' (3) much more highly than winning (18). This ranking is even more pronounced for girls. More recently, the Chance to Shine cricket charity (Cricket Foundation, 2011) found that '64 per cent of children would be relieved, not bothered or happier if the competitive element of school sport was removed' and that 'Overall parents and children agree that teamwork (43 per cent of parents and 36 per cent of children) and exercise (34 per cent and 37 per cent) are the two most important aspects of sport'. In a previous survey (Cricket Foundation, 2011) the charity found that 'Nine in 10 kids think that their teammates feel under pressure to win and nearly two-thirds (64 per cent) feel this pressure leads them to cheat' and that 'Three-quarters (75 per cent) think that their teammates would cheat if they had the chance to get away with it'. The Child Protection in Sport Unit (n.d.) also emphasises the importance of enjoyment and for coaches and parents to celebrate successes more widely than simply through winning (e.g. learning a new skill, playing well, trying hard).

TASK 5

a)   How do you balance the needs of those you coach, through opportunities to participate and compete, against the need to address a winning ethos which may involve only your better performers, thus creating potential conflict in selection and opportunity?

b)   Given your answer to a), how do you engage others (e.g. parents) in working with you to ensure that enjoyment, fairness and respect are central in your coaching practice? How do you resolve potential conflict?

Fairness as equality vs fairness as merit

'Fairness' or 'fair play' is often considered to be central to sport. However, this is an excellent example of how a particular value can mean very different things to different coaches. For one coach fairness might mean allocating playing opportunities on the basis of merit, which links to talent spotting, performance ranking and competition. This could actually work against fairness as inclusion or equality, as required within a school setting. For another coach, fairness could be about equality. This might be equal playing time within a participation setting, which links to inclusion, or equal 'voice' regarding the range of sports and physical activities on offer. 'Voice' is linked to democracy and simply means allowing people/children to express their preferences.

The issue of 'preference' is further accentuated in relation to gender. Participation research tells us that most boys and young men favour competitive team games. Most girls, women and older men prefer a range of sport and physical activities, most of which are not competitive team games. For example, in Europe, men play more sports than women and this is particularly marked in the 15–24 age group. However, far more people get 'informal' physical exercise (in such forms as cycling, walking, dancing or gardening) than play organised sport and 67 per cent are not members of any sports clubs or centres (TNS Opinion and Social, 2010).

In the UK, the UK's Women's Sport and Fitness Foundation (WSFF) and the Institute of Youth Sport set out in detail the different sport preferences of girls and boys (Gorely *et al.*, 2011) the summary of which suggests that many girls progressively reject 'sport' and are attracted to activities such as dance, exercise and fitness, with this decline being evident by the end of primary school. This research raises important questions as to the role and place of competition in physical education, which is perceived by many pupils as lacking fun, enjoyment and choice (Sport Wales, 2013). Table 2.1 sets out figures for demand and participation, which support the theory that girls gravitate towards 'individual' activities and away from team sport.

TABLE 2.1 Primary top five rankings for girls and boys: latent demand and club sport

Rank: Girls	Latent demand	%	Club sport	%	Rank: Boys	Latent demand	%	Club sport	%
1	Swimming	67	Dance	42	1	Football	60	Football	54
2	Dance	59	Swimming	41	2	Swimming	48	Swimming	37
3	Horse riding	47	Gymnastics	22	3	Rugby	44	Rugby	30
4	Cycling	45	Tennis	18	4	Cricket	40	Tennis	23
5	Gymnastics	43	Horse riding	16	5	Cycling	40	Cricket	18
			Football	16		Tennis	40	Martial arts	18

Source: Sport Wales (2013)

TASK 6 VALUING FAIRNESS AS EQUALITY

Given the differences outlined above, how would you as a coach approach working within an educational environment with its own sets of philosophical values and expectations emphasising equality and inclusion, especially with children for whom the activity may not be a preference? How do you take account of 'voice' and reconcile this with your own philosophy of practice?

Respect vs autocracy

Respect links closely to rights, autonomy, empowerment and equality. The Child Protection in Sport Unit (n.d.) and the University of Edinburgh (Alexander *et al.*, 2011) found that, while organised sport is generally a positive experience for many children and young people, 'a negative sporting culture exists, (and) is accepted as "the norm". Further, that this is perpetuated by peers, coaches and other adults' and is more prevalent at higher performance levels. For example, 75 per cent of the children questioned reported that they had experienced emotional harm (which includes being criticised disproportionately about performance, being humiliated, teased, sworn at or bullied) and that although this was mainly between team mates and peers, 'a third of those reporting it said coaches were involved, either participating directly, or indirectly by creating an ethos where such behaviour was condoned or not effectively dealt with'. In addition, 34 per cent of females reported experiences of sexual harassment (primarily non-physical: sexist jokes, being whistled or leered at) and 21 per cent of this was by coaches. The research reports that in general this was not dealt with effectively by coaches and other adults. Experience of physical harm was reported by 24 per cent of the sample and most of this involved being forced to train, whilst injured or exhausted, by a coach who regarded it as just a normal part of sport.

TASK 7 VALUING RESPECT

a) In your own practice as a coach (and possibly as a performer) can you think of situations where the coach 'power position' both wittingly and unwittingly may mask the legitimate right of the performer to opinion, and reduce opportunity to ask questions?

b) As part of the safeguarding requirement of the coach how do you balance the need to respect a confidence with that of the need to protect, if that confidence reveals a risk to the performer?

In answering these questions can you discern your rationale for your choice of answer, and can you identify the origins of knowledge that allowed you to make your decision?

Physical education vs sport

The juxtaposition of physical education (PE) and sport has been the subject of ongoing debate. At government decision-making level, discussion has largely focused on the contribution of sport to the 'national good' and the role of sport therefore within a school curriculum. However, these brief final paragraphs focus on the work of Martin Lee. Lee (2004b) identified the potential conflict of values between PE and sport. He explained that as a teacher he was 'concerned with helping all students find an activity that would engage them and perhaps provide an interest during adult life' as distinct from his role as a coach which was concerned with 'helping those with talent to excel' (Lee, 2004b: 7). However, as recently as 2013 OFSTED has found that

> Traditional team games tended to dominate the curriculum at the expense of aesthetic and athletic activities. For example, it was not unusual for the schools to allocate more than two thirds of the PE programme in Key Stages 3 and 4 to games … it left only minimal time for activities such as gymnastics, swimming, dance and athletics.
>
> *(OFSTED, 2013: 38)*

This is problematic in relation to fairness as equal 'voice', and also the aspirations of PE. Further, PE teachers and coaches, as we have mentioned, may well have competing philosophies. The nuanced differences, without necessarily being mutually exclusive, do however create tensions in the 'sport for all' versus 'sport for sport's sake' debate. Consequently, if schools outsource PE and sport to coaches, then 'sport for sport's sake' rather than physical education or 'sport for all' as evidenced by OFSTED may be the result.

Conclusion

Your coaching philosophy reflects your underlying beliefs and values, which may or may not conflict with those of other stakeholders or a range of coaching settings, and may to a greater or lesser extent be informed by discussion with others as well as research. Coaching philosophies will develop over time and to some extent will always be a 'work in progress'. This chapter has provided some opportunities to unpick some of the commonly stated values and, through reflection, coaches can consider the implications and impacts on their practice as well as any ability to articulate a philosophy of practice. Professionalisation of coaching now often involves working outside traditional coaching settings. This makes it even more important for coaches to reflect on the appropriate philosophy for the context in which they are coaching. In compulsory and universal contexts such as PE and participation settings, a child-centred coaching philosophy is certainly appropriate, whereas in voluntary settings, such as performance and elite sport clubs, a sport-centred philosophy may be more acceptable.

References and further reading

Books and book chapters

Devine, C. and Telfer, H. (2013) Why are sport and physical education valuable? In Whitehead, J., Telfer, H. and Lambert, J. (eds) *Values in Youth Sport*. London: Routledge.
Hardman, A. and Jones, C. (2008) Philosophy for coaches. In Jones, R.L. and Kingston, K. (eds) *An Introduction to Sports Coaching: Connecting theory to practice*. Oxford: Routledge.

Jenkins, S. (2010) Coaching philosophy. In Lyle, J. and Cushion, C. (eds) *Sports Coaching: Professionalisation and Practice*. Edinburgh: Churchill Livingstone, Elsevier.

Knowles, Z. and Telfer, H. (2009) The where, what and why of reflective practice. In Heaney, C., Oakley, B. and Rea, S. (eds) *Exploring Sport and Fitness: Work Based Practice*. London: The Open University/Routledge.

Telfer, H. and Knowles, Z. (2009) The 'how-to' of reflection. In Heaney, C., Oakley, B. and Rea, S. (eds) *Exploring Sport and Fitness: Work Based Practice*. London: The Open University/Routledge.

Lee, M.J. (2004a) The importance of values in the coaching process. In Silva, M. and Malina, R. (eds) *Children and Youth in Organized Sports*. Coimbra: Coimbra University Press.

Lyle, J. (1999) Coaching philosophy and coaching behaviour. In Cross, N. and Lyle, J. (eds) *The Coaching Process*. Edinburgh: Butterworth-Heinemann.

Lyle, J. (2002). *Sports Coaching Concepts. A Framework for Coaches' Behaviour*. Routledge: London.

Lyle, J. (2010) Coaches' decision making: a naturalistic decision making analysis. In Lyle, J. and Cushion, C. (eds) *Sports Coaching: Professionalisation and Practice*. Edinburgh: Churchill Livingstone, Elsevier.

Journal articles

Carless, D. and Douglas, K. (2011) Stories as personal coaching philosophy. *International Journal of Sports Science and Coaching*, 6(1): 1–12.

Dowling, F. and Kårhus, S. (2011) An analysis of the ideological work of the discourses of 'fair play' and moral education in perpetuating inequitable gender practices in PETE. *Physical Education and Sport Pedagogy*, 16(2): 197–211.

Green, K. (2000) Exploring the everyday 'philosophies' of physical education teachers from a sociological perspective. *Sport, Education and Society*, 5(2): 109–129, DOI: 10.1080/713696029, http://dx.doi.org/10.1080/713696029.

Green, K. (2002) Physical education teachers in their figurations: a sociological analysis of everyday 'philosophies'. *Sport, Education and Society*, 7(1), 65–83.

Lee, M.J. (2004b) Values in physical education and sport: a conflict of interests? *The British Journal of Teaching Physical Education*, 35(1): 6–10.

Nash, C., Sproule, J. and Horton, P. (2008) Sports coaches' perceived role frames and philosophies. *International Journal of Sports Science and Coaching*, 3(4): 538–554.

Other

Alexander, K., Stafford A. and Lewis, R. (2011) *The Experiences of Children Participating in Organised Sport in the UK*. The University of Edinburgh/NSPCC Child Protection Research Centre, www.childprotection.ed.ac.uk/publications/database/k201102.

Child Protection in Sport Unit (n.d.) https://thecpsu.org.uk.

Cricket Foundation (2011) *A Chance to Shine*, www.chancetoshine.org/media/press-releases.

Gorely, T., Sandford, R., Duncombe, R., Musson, H., Edwardson, C., Kay, T. and Jeanes, R. (2011) *Understanding Psycho-Social Attitudes towards Sport and Activity in Girls: Final Research Report*. Loughborough: Institute of Youth Sport, www.lboro.ac.uk/microsites/ssehs/youth-sport/research/physical-activity/wsff.html.

OFSTED (2013) *Beyond 2012 – Outstanding Physical Education for All*, www.gov.uk/government/publications/beyond-2012-outstanding-physical-education-for-all.

Rhind, D., Murphy, C. and Giles, M. (2013) *Young Athletes' Perceptions on Promoting Positive Parental Behaviour in Sport: Executive Summary*. London: Brunel University, https://thecpsu. org.uk/resource-library/?type=1174.

sports coach UK (2005) *Code of Practice for Sports Coaches*. Leeds: National Coaching Foundation.

Sport Wales (2013) *School Sport Survey 2011 – Primary School Participation Data*, www.sportwales. org.uk/research--policy/surveys-and-statistics/statistics.aspx.

TNS Opinion and Social (2010) *The Citizens of the European Union and Sport Special Eurobarometer 334, Sport and Physical Activity*. Brussels: European Commission.

United Nations (1989) *Convention on the Rights of the Child*. New York: UN Office of Public Information, www.unicef.org.uk/Documents/Publication-pdfs/UNCRC_PRESS 200910web.pdf.

3

MORAL ISSUES IN SPORT COACHING

Andrew Theodoulides

Introduction

An effective coach is thought to have many personal attributes and skills. Such attributes and skills include, but are not limited to, possessing technical knowledge appropriate to the sport they are coaching, having the ability to analyse technical and tactical elements and, prior to transmitting that knowledge effectively to athletes, an understanding of how they learn; that is, knowing and using the most effective coaching strategies and an awareness of how to motivate athletes. For many new coaches, and probably many experienced coaches too, the attraction of coaching generally lies in a desire to improve athletes' performance and so their attention is focused on this element of their work. It is the elements of coaching listed above which form the basis of most coach education programmes. In addition, however, an effective coach is a mentor to their athletes, setting standards of behaviour and conduct, both in and out of competition, and is a role model to the athletes they coach. Therefore, coaching makes it incumbent upon coaches to reflect upon, consider and address moral issues within their work. As Hardman *et al.* (2010) point out, a good coach is required not only to develop athletes' technical ability but also to support their moral development.[1] For many coaches, particularly those at the point of entry to coaching, if the notion of enhancing athletes' moral development figures on their agenda it probably does so well down the list of priorities. Nevertheless, coaching is an inherently moral activity, making it incumbent upon coaches to give attention to the athletes' moral development. In addition to seeing their role as an 'opportunity to realise a range of technical, physical and moral competencies', a coach is required to take a proactive role in promoting the moral development of the athletes they coach. Put another way, coaching goes beyond merely passing on technical information, or as Carr (1998: 131) puts it, 'expert instruction in a range of practical skills', to include 'the promotion and acquisition of values and virtues' (ibid.). Therefore, coaching takes on moral significance.

At first sight the impact a coach might have on athletes' moral development might appear difficult to ascertain, particularly if one sees professional sport as a blueprint for sport at other levels. In his powerful analysis of the state of American sports (but what he writes applies equally to many sports outside of America), Morgan (2006: 25) argues that as a result of self-interest and chasing financial rewards, modern sports 'are in dire moral straits today'. The relevance of this, Morgan (ibid.: 26) reminds us, is that professional sports 'generally set the tone, morally and otherwise, for what goes on in sports at all other levels'. However, money is not necessarily the route of moral decline in sports at lower levels, as other factors play a part. For example, an over-emphasis on winning is thought be an antecedent for cheating and over-aggression. Winning is an inherent part of sport but, as Morgan (ibid.) argues, it is winning which provides much of the impetus for cheating. So at all levels of sport, one of the most demanding of the challenges faced by a coach who is concerned with the moral development of players is how to balance winning, and the pressure and expectations that accompany this, with how to offer athletes and players a worthwhile experience.

Despite concerns regarding the impact of professional sport on moral matters such as fair play, and respect for rules, opponents and referees, there is still an enduring belief that sport has a significant role to play in developing sportsmanship and moral attributes. It seems that inherent within sport are numerous opportunities to promote athletes' moral learning. On this subject however, as Jones (2005: 140) so accurately comments, '[t]here is a long and rich tradition of moral philosophical debate in which sophisticated arguments and counter arguments, theory and counter theory have been applied to the problems, but apparently to no avail'. Upon further scrutiny it becomes clear that moral education is complex. One of the challenges for those concerned with promoting athletes' moral development is that at times it can look like there is no consensus as to what constitutes moral action within sport. Consequently, determining actions that are guided by moral principles is very difficult, as is determining the impact of the coach and coaching on athletes' moral values and actions.

Many of the studies that have been carried out into how participants in sport reason about moral issues such as breaking the rules have drawn upon quantitative research methods and have focused on children.[2] One study which employed qualitative research methods to explore athletes' understanding of moral dilemmas was that by Drewe (1999). Based on her research Drewe found that the moral reasoning of university athletes fell into six categories, all of which were consistent with the three theories of moral philosophy which she argues are traditional within that field of study.[3] Drewe summarises these three theories in the following way: 1) deontological, based on the notion that people have a duty towards others (and she cites Kant's theory based upon his categorical imperatives as the main example of this theory); 2) teleological, focused on the nature of being a particular type of person through the cultivation of the virtues; 3) consequential, whereby moral action is judged by what achieves the greatest good, an example of which is universalism. The relevance of this for coaches, she argues, is that 'reviewing the categories of reasons cited and their reflection of moral theory can help teachers and coaches facilitate the development of moral reasoning skills in their students and athletes' (Drewe, 1999: 125). She concludes that to be effective in this, coaches should be familiar with more than one of these moral theories.

Drewe's (ibid.) study was valuable in highlighting university athletes' perceptions of moral dilemmas within sport. In another study, Stuart (2003) has shown that younger athletes identify different moral issues. For example, Stuart found that 11–12 year old athletes identified favouritism, poor decision-making and pressure to play well as moral issues pertinent to them. What this shows is that factors such as age mediate the way in which athletes identify moral issues salient to them. Put another way, it highlights the contextual nature of moral reasoning and action (Jones and McNamee, 2000; Jones, 2008). More recently Camiré and Trudel (2010) used qualitative methods, and more specifically interviews, to understand how participants reason about, interpret and reconcile moral issues. Camiré and Trudel (2010: 205) concluded that to promote children's moral learning more effectively, 'practitioners should work with specific values and define the meaning of those values to the athletes since young athletes have a limited understanding of broad concepts such as character and moral development'. Therefore, to be most effective in promoting athletes' moral development, coaches ought to take a proactive role in employing learning strategies to address moral issues.

TASK 1

In order to help you determine where moral issues might arise when coaching, make a list of possible moral issues that you might come across in your coaching. Compare this to the list at the end of the chapter. Bear in mind that neither your list nor that at the end of the chapter is definitive and complete.

Learning theories relating to moral development

When exploring how moral development might be enhanced through sport, writers often conclude their analysis by setting out for coaches certain conditions or requirements under which moral learning ought to take place (Drewe, 1999; Jones, 2008; Hardman *et al.*, 2010). One popular theory of moral learning is that put forward by those who believe in a virtue ethics approach to moral learning. The main thrust of a virtue ethics approach is that sport develops moral virtues such as courage, honesty, fairness and determination. Central to the development of virtues is the coach as a role model. These arguments suggest that one way in which moral attributes are developed is as a result of the coach setting a good (moral) example and guiding the athletes in their charge to behave appropriately. Proponents of this theory argue that the coach should 'embody fairness, compassion, understanding, even-handedness, care and trust ... reward good behaviour and discourage bad behaviour' (Jones, 2005: 146). In this context, moral attributes are developed through modelling and habituation.

Another approach to moral learning involves coaches adopting direct teaching strategies, that is, planning and implementing learning scenarios which are targeted at promoting moral values. Generally studies of this have adopted quantitative methodologies centred around measuring the effectiveness of the intervention strategy on moral attributes. Where they have been used, these intervention strategies have been shown to have a positive impact in promoting moral reasoning (Gibbons et al., 1995; Miller et al., 1997; Mouratidou et al., 2007; Vidoni and Ward, 2009). Intervention strategies have been used mainly in children's sport programmes. Typically, learning experiences involve discussion and problem solving (Mouratidou et al., 2007), praise and reinforcement of moral actions, and explicit discussion of learning outcomes in the moral domain (Vidoni and Ward, 2009). In this context, the use of intervention strategies is thought to have a much greater and more explicit focus on promoting moral attributes than the strategies put forward by those who argue for a virtue ethics approach to moral learning. However, both strategies used in combination would seem to provide the most powerful learning opportunities for players. What is clear is that strategies employed by coaches have been shown to have an impact on the extent to which athletes' learning in the moral domain is enhanced.

Addressing moral dilemmas as a coach

In order to examine moral issues in coaching, a number of 'real life' scenarios are presented for you to consider. Each of these examples is taken from a different sport and requires you to decide upon what you think you would do in the same situation. Whilst these examples are drawn from sport and hence are 'real' scenarios (in the sense that you might well come across the same situation) they are in fact hypothetical. This is because you do not find yourself in the situation at this time. Hence the course of action you think you will take is precisely that: what you think. Should you ever find yourself in the same situation for real you might find you react differently. The use of hypothetical dilemmas to determine moral action has been criticised by some writers (Jones and McNamee, 2000). One criticism is that until you actually find yourself in the situation (for real), you will not know for sure what course of action you will take. In a hypothetical situation our moral reasoning might tell us what we *ought* to do, but it is our moral action that reflects the outcome of our reasoning, i.e. what we actually do. Another way of putting it is what we *say* and *do* are not always the same. We might claim that we would not cheat when playing sport but that is no guarantee of whether or not we would deliberately break the rules. As the saying goes, 'actions speak louder than words'.

EXAMPLE 1

Kelly is the coach of an under-13 basketball team. The father of a promising new player who joins the team regularly attends matches. For the first few games of the season he is an enthusiastic and supportive parent, cheering and groaning as most parents and spectators do with the ebb and flow of the match. But as the season progresses his demeanour changes. He starts to shout instructions at his daughter, cajoling her to 'get forward', 'get back' and shouting at her when to dribble and pass the ball. This continues for a few weeks and it becomes apparent to Kelly that something is wrong; the young player is not as enthusiastic as she was at the start of the season. Kelly asks the player what is wrong and the player responds by telling Kelly that her father is putting too much pressure on her both during the match with his instructions and afterwards at home. She is not enjoying playing basketball and thinking of quitting the team. Soon the father is berating officials and not long after that he starts yelling instructions at other players in the team.

Take a few minutes to reflect upon how you would handle this situation. Would you speak to the player or her father or both? At what point would you speak to either or both of them? What would you say?

Like many situations of this nature this example presents the coach with some difficult moral decisions relating to what course of action to follow. To explore the moral issues inherent in this example, a good starting point is to identify some of the moral issues faced by Kelly. As a coach you might object to parents and spectators shouting instructions to players, especially when those instructions undermine what you are trying to achieve in terms of the tactics you want your team to adopt. But is the shouting of instructions per se a moral issue? Not necessarily. For many spectators (including parents), one attraction of watching sport is their involvement in the events that happen. It is part of watching most sports, and arguably engages the emotions like no other activity to enhance the spectacle. Is it in the team's best interests for the player's father to be shouting instructions? Arguably no. So the dilemma here is what is the right thing to do? However, when comments from those watching become offensive or threatening, it is a different matter. The recent concern in football about racist chants from the terraces gives rise to a moral debate about the state of football. What ought to be of concern for the coach in this situation is the berating of match officials. Respect for others, in this case officials, has been acknowledged as an important moral issue within sport (Council of Europe, 1993; McFee, 2000). In order to set a good example for her players, in this situation the coach would be perfectly justified, and arguably obligated, to challenge the father about his behaviour.

Perhaps the most challenging moral issue for the coach to deal with here relates to the way in which she feels inclined to point out to the player's father the pressure he is putting upon his daughter. Should the coach say anything? Who has the responsibility to address the player's welfare and well-being in this situation? The coach or the parent? As a society we recognise the responsibility parents have in bringing up their children. Article 18 of The United Nations Convention on the Rights of the Child (UNICEF, 2004: 6) acknowledges this responsibly by stating that parents 'have the primary responsibility for the upbringing and development of the child. The best interests of the child will be their concern'. But is the player's father acting in her best interests here? David (2005) has highlighted the negative impact parents can have on their children's experience of sport through parental violence, cheating and emotional blackmail. In such cases Article 19 of The United Nations Convention on the Rights of the Child (UNICEF, 2004: 7) states that 'any other person who has the care of the child', has a responsibility 'to protect a child from all forms of physical or mental violence, injury or abuse, neglect or negligent treatment'. The issue here for the coach is whether or not the pressure the player's father is putting on her is having a negative impact on her well-being and participation, and the extent to which she feels she has a moral responsibility to discuss this with the father. Arguably she would have some justification for raising this issue with him; however, it might well call upon her to tread carefully and tactfully in any conversation.

EXAMPLE 2

During one evening training session Darren is coaching the attackers in his under-13 team on how to create space as an individual. He starts by telling his players that when marked tight by a defender to walk away from the ball and ensure that they keep their body between the defender and the ball. He then tells them that when they move to receive the ball, to lean into the defender and push him back and off balance by giving him a nudge. This will then enable the attacker to check back towards the ball into the space created, to receive and turn with the ball to run at the defender. As the practice progresses some defenders start complaining that they are being pushed and fouled. Darren responds by telling his player to get on with it, this is 'all part of the game'. As the practice session continues one defender starts pulling the shirt of the attacker. The attacker now complains to Darren about this and again Darren tells his players that this is 'all part of the game'.

Before reading on, how would you have handled these situations? Is nudging/pushing a defender off the ball to create space 'all part of the game', and therefore acceptable? Is it appropriate for Darren to coach his attackers to push a defender off the ball in order to create space? Before he started pulling the attacker's shirt, would you have said anything to the defender? If so, what would you have said? Does it make a difference that these players are playing in an under-13 team?

A good starting point for exploring this scenario is to analyse it from a moral standpoint. On the one hand one might accuse Darren of coaching his player to break the laws[4] of the game; after all, pushing an opponent and shirt-pulling is against the rules in football. So what part do rules play in moral issues within sport? Rules within sport are seen to serve two functions. On the one hand rules constitute a game; that is, they prescribe how a game is to be played (Reddiford, 1985). Some constitutive rules have no moral weight (such as how to score a goal in football), although they permit actions that can be held up to moral scrutiny. For example, in football the use of the hands by players other than the goalkeeper is prohibited. Therefore, players are not allowed to control or pass the ball using their hands. To do so would result in a free kick (or penalty to the other team if the offence occurred in the penalty area) and, potentially, expulsion from the game if the handball was deliberate and prevented a goal from being scored. As Reddiford (1985: 42) comments, it is the constitutive rules that 'give behaviour a significance in the context of the game' and it is the constitutive rules which guide our moral compass when making decisions about how a game is to be played. Moreover, as Loland (2005) points out, it is deliberate rule violations which cause moral indignation. Players who deliberately use their hand to gain an advantage run the risk of being branded a cheat. Thierry Henry's deliberate handball to set up William Gallas' winning goal that defeated Ireland in a World Cup play-off match in 2009 is one case in point.

> With cries of 'cheat' ringing in his ears from furious Irish fans, the Barcelona and former Arsenal forward emerged from the dressing room to say: 'I will be honest, it was a handball. But I'm not the ref. I played it, the ref allowed it. That's a question you should ask him'.
>
> (Ogden, 2009)

Whilst unintentional rule breaking can give rise to an advantage, this advantage is usually addressed by the referee or umpire penalising the offending player/team. When unintentional, penalising the offending player or team is deemed to be appropriate and the game continues. In Example 2 above, however, the attacker might be deemed guilty of what Loland (2005) calls a 'tactical foul', that is, deliberately pushing the defender in order to create time and space for him to receive the ball. By this account, if we consider the actions of the attacker in pushing the defender out of the way in order to create space, one might well claim that the player is guilty of deliberately breaking the rules. But Darren does not see it that way; he says pushing is 'all part of the game'.

To explain how some rule breaking is tolerated, D'Agostino (1981) points out how games have an *ethos*. According to D'Agostino (ibid.: 17) a game's ethos is 'that set of unofficial, implicit conventions which determine how the rules of that game are to be applied in concrete circumstances'. The idea that games have an ethos allows for scope and flexibility in the way in which rules are interpreted. As D'Agostino (ibid.: 14) writes:

> implicit in the ways in which basketball [and other games] are played and officiated [is], an unofficial *system* of conventions which determines how the official rules of the game will be applied in various concrete circumstances. Foul moves which deviate, not from the formal rules per se, but from the formal rules as these are interpreted in terms of a particular set of implicit conventions will, in fact, be penalised if detected. (original emphasis)

Russell (1999: 27) makes a similar point in his discussion of the 'untidiness of rules'. Russell argues that the meaning players and referees attach to some rules means rules are frequently modified or ignored. Specifically he claims that in baseball the interpretation of umpires as to what constitutes a fair pitch changes depending upon the level at which the game is played. A similar point can be made with regard to a wide in cricket. In a limited-overs match almost any delivery down the leg side would be deemed as not giving the batter a fair chance to hit the ball and so called wide. In a match not limited in overs some leg-side deliveries would be allowed, provided they were not too far down the leg side. The point at which a leg-side delivery is deemed wide is a matter of interpretation by the umpire.

As Loland and McNamee (2000: 67) point out,

> by attending to the ethos of an activity we can draw distinctions between permissible acts that are in accordance with the rules, acceptable acts in terms of rule violations that are 'part of the game', and rule violations that are considered unacceptable.

In this context, the notion of a game ethos provides a framework within which sporting actions can be deemed morally acceptable or unacceptable. Clearly some actions are not acceptable within sport. One would be hard pressed to condone a deliberate action that caused injury to an opponent, on the grounds that such an action is morally objectionable (Parry, 1998: 222). Interpreting rules within the context of the ethos of a game makes it incumbent upon a coach to reflect upon their moral values and beliefs about what is and is not acceptable within the sport in which they coach. One might agree with Darren that pushing a defender to gain an advantage or pulling the shirt of an attacker is indeed 'all part of the game'. The challenge for a coach in this is to reflect and decide upon where they draw the line between what is acceptable and what is not, and then communicate this to their athletes.

For the very reason that it is often difficult to determine where to draw the line between what is acceptable and what is not, the idea of a game ethos is subject to criticism. As Morgan (1987) points out, one weakness of game ethos is that some rule violations come to be seen as acceptable when in effect they are morally indefensible. Proponents of the game ethos have been unable to provide an adequate explanation of how this problem of deciding upon what is and is not socially acceptable can be adequately overcome. As Sheridan (2003: 172) puts it, 'there would be something unsettling, for example, if we were to recommend keeping to the ethos of a game if that ethos accepted cheating or causing harm to other players'.

But this is exactly how some games are played. As Drewe (1999) highlights, ice-hockey players (and to that add coaches and managers) see fighting amongst players as an acceptable part of the game. Thus, the notion of game ethos tells us how the game *is* played rather than how it *ought* to be played. All too often though, those involved in sport accept uncritically the practices, behaviour and values exhibited by others (often professional athletes). In determining where the line should be drawn between rule breaking that is 'all part of the game' and that which is unacceptable, what is important is a critically reflective coach who is aware of their own values and who has subjected these to moral scrutiny.

Promoting athletes' moral development through sport

The discussion to this point has focused on the need for a coach to consider their moral perspective on how the particular sport they coach is played. This chapter concludes with some thoughts on how a coach might effectively promote athletes' moral development through sport. For a coach to be most effective in promoting moral learning through sport they ought to recognise that this is part of their role, and some knowledge of how moral learning can be enhanced is needed. In terms of how a coach might then go about promoting their athletes' moral development more effectively, other considerations are important. Jones (2008: 340) writes, 'moral education must employ a range of strategies that target the variety of psychic processes that underpin virtuous action, which include sensitivity, emotion, understanding and action'. At first glance this might appear daunting. What are these psychic processes? Where will coaches develop this understanding? It seems unlikely that such knowledge will be developed through National Governing Body coach education programmes, as the content of these is predominantly focused on learning in the technical domain and change in this appears very unlikely. But some strategies are quite simple.

If a coach is to be able to promote moral values through sport then a first step is for a coach to show commitment to this end. The moral atmosphere of a sport, or alternatively, a sport's ethos, has been seen as a mediating factor in determining legitimate and illegitimate rule breaking (Jones and McNamee, 2000; Jones, 2005). As Jones (2005: 145) points out, '[t]he ethos of the sport is crucial in moulding children's behaviour in sport' and the standards set by a coach in terms of their expectations of athletes' behaviour and action plays a significant part in what athletes learn. Therefore, a coach's words and actions can have a positive or negative impact on their athletes' moral development. A coach, by the very nature of being a coach (Carr, 1998) is a role model for athletes and, as such, their actions are constantly subject to moral scrutiny. Consequently, a coach has a responsibility to ensure that his/her conduct is morally virtuous. This will include being aware of what they say and do, such as spur-of-the-moment comments to athletes, spectators, officials and other coaches. In addition, facial expressions and bodily gestures that might demonstrate non-sporting values can be transmitted to athletes. It is better to act honestly, fairly, with kindness and consideration. Being a role model requires a coach to embody the values of sportsmanship and fair play, and to show respect for opponents and for the rules of competition. In setting a moral example a coach will 'help their charges develop an articulate conception of what is valuable, a sense of what is worth striving for' (Hardman *et al.*, 2010: 351). Thus, a coach is a poor role model if they do not embody moral virtues and moral action. What this indicates is that athletes learn to act morally from being coached by significant others who act morally. Moral action is said to be 'caught'.

In addition to being 'caught' moral learning can be 'taught'. A coach ought to develop a number of effective learning strategies to enhance athletes' moral development. To do this, one step is to recognise how athletes and coaches can have different perceptions about what constitutes a moral dilemma within sport (Drewe, 1999). Therefore, whilst a coach might be well aware that some unsporting practices are of moral significance, an athlete or group of athletes might not. Thus a coach ought to take time to make clear to their athletes behaviours that relate to values in the moral domain. To do this effectively a coach might engage their athletes either individually or collectively in moral discussion and reflection. This requires coaches to create learning opportunities for athletes to discuss, explore and reflect upon moral matters. The most effective discussions are likely to be those that draw upon incidents that occurred in the training sessions, matches or competitions in which they have taken part (much like the 'real life' examples you were asked to reflect upon in this chapter). In light of this, revisit Example 2 above and reflect upon what, if anything, you would do or say that was different from your answer earlier. What learning strategies would you employ to enable players to consider and discuss these incidents? It would be unrealistic to expect an athlete to be able to consider fully all the moral implications of their actions, particularly during a fast-moving game or match. On the other hand, post-game or post-competition a coach might, where an athlete has acted in a non-sporting manner, discuss with their athletes alternative courses of action and give them an opportunity to discuss their actions and their consequences. A coach ought certainly to register their disapproval of the athlete's behaviour. Similarly, such discussions ought to occur in order to reinforce good sporting behaviour too. Give praise where praise is due.

Conclusion

Through their involvement in sport in their formative years, athletes and subsequently coaches internalise particular values and attitudes towards the sport in which they participate. These attitudes, beliefs and values become deeply embedded. To be effective in promoting athletes' moral development through sport a coach must demonstrate a commitment to moral sporting values. To do this more effectively a first step is for a coach to reflect upon their own moral sporting values, particularly in the context of the *ethos* of the sport in which they coach. Once a coach is clearer about their moral sporting values, then they ought to demonstrate a commitment towards developing those moral values in their athletes. Coach education programmes are generally silent on how such matters are effectively delivered so a coach will need to find strategies that work. Some have been presented here. There is no secret formula for doing this well. It can be challenging given the range of other influences, such as significant others (for example peers and family members), and the images athletes see from professional sport on TV and in the media. However, when a similar commitment, enthusiasm, energy and consideration of learning strategies are devoted to moral outcomes as with the physical, technical and tactical, then claims for moral learning within sport are more likely to be realised effectively.

POSSIBLE MORAL ISSUES FACED BY COACHES (TASK 1)

- Asking an injured athlete to compete/play and so risking exacerbating the injury
- Arguing with officials
- When coaching young children, giving more playing time to some players and less to others
- Promoting your own values and motives above those of the players
- Deciding whether to play a player who does not turn up to training
- Coaching rule-breaking/cheating
- Encouraging aggression or hurting opponents
- Having a relationship with an athlete
- Encouraging athletes to take performance-enhancing drugs, or turning a blind eye to drug taking
- Pushing athletes beyond physical and mental limits in order to improve performance
- Coaching a son or daughter
- Athletes and alcohol consumption
- What you write/publish on social media

Notes

1 For the purpose of this discussion moral relates to the development of a number of sportspersonship and fair play values such as respect for others (opponents, officials, team mates), abiding by the rules of the sport, being concerned about the welfare and well-being of others, equality, fairness and good competition.
2 See the work of Miller *et al.* (1997) and those mentioned below.
3 For a more detailed account of these theories see Drewe (1999).
4 Some sports refer to laws whilst others refer to rules to prescribe what constitutes how to play in a particular sport. In the literature on morality in sport, rules are typically used to refer to sports which have laws and for that reason rules will be used in the context of football.

References

Camiré, M. and Trudel, P. (2010) High school athletes' perspective on character development through sport participation, *Physical Education and Sport Pedagogy*, 15(2), 193–207.

Carr, D. (1998) What moral educational significance has physical education? A question in need of disambiguation, in McNamee, M.J. and Parry, S.J. (Eds) *Ethics and Sport*, London: E and FN Spon, pp. 119–133.

Council of Europe (1993) *The Council of Europe's Code for Sports Ethics.*

D'Agostino, F. (1981) The ethos of games, *Journal of Philosophy of Sport,* 8, 7–18.

David, P. (2005) *Human Rights in Youth Sport: A Critical Review of Children's Rights in Competitive Sport,* Abingdon: Routledge.

Drewe, S.B. (1999) Moral reasoning in sport: Implications for physical education, *Sport, Education and Society,* 4(2), 117–130.

Gibbons, S.L., Ebbeck, V. and Weiss, M.R. (1995) Fair play for kids: effects on the moral development of children in physical education, *Research Quarterly for Exercise and Sport,* 66(3), 247–255.

Hardman, A., Jones, C. and Jones, R. (2010) Sports coaching, virtue ethics and emulation, *Physical Education and Sport Pedagogy,* 15(4), 345–359.

Jones, C. (2005) Character, virtue and physical education, *European Physical Education Review,* 11(2), 139–151.

Jones, C. (2008) Teaching virtue through physical education: some comments and reflections, *Sport, Education and Society,* 13(3), 337–349.

Jones, C. and McNamee, M. (2000) Moral reasoning, moral action, and the moral atmosphere of sport, *Sport, Education and Society,* 5(2), 131–146.

Loland, S. (2005) The varieties of cheating – comments on ethical analyses in sport, *Sport in Society,* 8(1), 11–26.

Loland, S. and McNamee, M. (2000) Fair play and the ethos of sports: an eclectic philosophical framework, *Journal of Philosophy of Sport,* 17, 63–80.

McFee, G. (2000) Spoiling: an indirect reflection on sports' moral imperative? in Tannsjo, T. and Tamburrini, C. (Eds) *Values in Sport,* London: E and FN Spon, pp. 172–182.

Miller, S.C., Bredemeier, B.J.L. and Shields, D.L.L. (1997) Socio-moral education through physical education with at-risk children, *Quest,* 49, 114–129.

Morgan, W. (1987) The logical incompatibility thesis and rules: a reconsideration of formalism as an account of games, *Journal of Philosophy of Sport,* 14, 1–20.

Morgan, W. (2006) *Why Sports Matter Morally,* Abingdon: Routledge.

Mouratidou, K., Goutza, S. and Chatzopoulos, D. (2007) Physical education and moral development: an intervention programme to promote moral reasoning through physical education in high school students, *European Physical Education Review,* 13(1), 41–54.

Ogden, M. (2009) *The Telegraph Online,* www.telegraph.co.uk/sport/football/teams/republic-of-ireland/6599687/Thierry-Henry-admits-to-handball-that-defeated-Ireland-in-World-Cup-play-off.html (accessed 18 July 2014).

Parry, J. (1998) Violence and aggression in contemporary sport, in McNamee, M.J. and Parry, S.J. (Eds) *Ethics and Sport.* London: E and FN Spon, pp. 205–224.

Reddiford, G. (1985) Constitutions, institutions, and games, *Journal of the Philosophy of Sport,* 12, 41–51.

Russell, J.S. (1999) Are rules all an umpire has to work with? *Journal of the Philosophy of Sport,* 26, 27–49.

Sheridan, H. (2003) Conceptualising 'fair play': a review of the literature, *European Physical Education Review,* 9(2), 163–182.

Stuart, M.E. (2003) Moral issues in sport: the child's perspective, *Research Quarterly for Exercise and Sport,* 10, 445–462.

UNICEF (2004) *The United Nations Convention on the Rights of the Child,* http://unicef.org.uk/UNICEFs-Work/UN-Convention (accessed 30 July 2015).

Vidoni, C. and Ward, P. (2009) Effects of fair play instruction on student social skills during a middle school sport education unit, *Physical Education and Sport Pedagogy,* 14(3), 285–310.

4

THE POLITICAL CONTEXT FOR COACHING

Marc Keech

The importance and profile of coaching in sport, since the early 1980s, has been one of the most significant and under-researched developments in sport policy. Coaching policy is located at the nexus of the three pillars of sport policy and development in the UK – elite sport, physical education (PE) and school sport, and community or 'grassroots' sport. This chapter provides an introduction to the development of coaching as a vocation and its emergence as a policy priority in sport. The chapter examines the structure and organisation of sport from a coach's perspective and analyses challenges presented by the historical development of policy in understanding the landscape and context in which sports coaches work, signposting those involved in 'becoming a sports coach' to further, more detailed sources. There are significant resources through which to see the developments in elite coaching but here the focus is placed on developments related to introductory levels of coaching and the process of 'becoming a sports coach'. The chapter provides background to the emergence of the social, political and policy context for coaching in sport, offering indicative examples as to why coaching has become such an important element of sport policy. The chapter concludes with author reflections on the policy context for sports coaching and asks readers to consider the significance of issues raised in their own coaching contexts. Whilst examples from the UK are used, it should be recognised that sport policy, driven by political influence, has an impact on the work of coaches throughout the world. In all countries, coaches need to understand the socio-political setting in which they practise and the associated constraints and opportunities.

Some landmarks in the developmental history of sports coaching

Sports coaching is not new. In Ancient Greece a sports coach was a person who exhibited wisdom in anatomy, heritage and nutrition (Bompa, 1983), whilst a '*gymnastes*' was a retired athlete who used the laws of heredity to understand sport performance. The 'paidotribes' was the athletic trainer, a practitioner who applied the knowledge of training to prevailing medical theories, whilst the 'gymnastes' was the theorist and the teacher. The history of sports coaching provides perspective on the complexities of the coaching context and the forces influencing the development of coaching. The antecedents for becoming a sports coach in the UK are found in the latter half of the nineteenth century (Holt, 1989; Maclean and Prichard, 2013: 85–88) and were situated within class-based debates surrounding participation in sport. In football, for example, there was no science of coaching. Instead the trainer, whose responsibility was to ensure the players were fit for the start of the season, was an experienced volunteer who provided guidance to players by concentrating on fundamental skills. Training began its evolution into what became known as coaching when the Old Carthusians, playing the more skilful Old Etonians in the 1881 FA Cup Final, departed from the practice of individual skills by successfully adopting a strategy of combined play which required planning and co-ordination (Keech, 2002: 63). The 1981 Oscar-winning film, *Chariots of Fire*, had as one of its sub-plots the relationship between athlete Harold Abrahams and his coach Sam Mussabini, prior to and during the 1924 Olympics. Mussabini coached athletes to 11 medals over five Olympic Games but became a pariah amongst athletic administrators due to his status as a 'professional' coach. The professionalisation of sports coaching was facilitated by increased commercialisation during the latter half of the twentieth century, whilst the use of drugs in sport during the 1960s served to focus attention on how athletes were supported (Green and Houlihan, 2005).

By the 1970s most National Governing Bodies (NGBs) of sport had introduced coaching schemes and in 1982 the Sports Council announced that, with the support of the British Association of National Coaches, it planned to set up a national coaching centre, which would run courses and co-ordinate information (Sports Council, 1982: 40). The policy context for sports coaching in the UK has developed since the establishment of the National Coaching Foundation in 1983. Since then, the importance of coaching to the aims of sport policy – increasing participation and developing technical skills from foundation to elite level – has become a critical element of policy development. As with a number of other countries, sports coaching in the UK follows a reasonably structured pattern, in principle at least, but is delivered by a workforce which is largely volunteer-based, essentially meaning that sports coaching has been, historically, largely confined to grassroots activity. Along with other support services such as sport science, sport medicine and performance lifestyle management, coaching is also a critical ingredient in the success of elite athletes at the highest levels of international competition. This diversity of coaching practice creates challenges for sport policy makers who must attempt to satisfy the diverse objectives of stakeholders involved at all levels. Young people's involvement in sport was identified as being heavily influenced by coaches (Kremer *et al.*, 1997) whilst most programmes aimed at coach education are designed to raise standards in coaching performance in practice. Champion Coaching was the first high-profile programme that brought these two areas of policy together. Champion Coaching was introduced in April 1991 when £700,000 was allocated to the National

Coaching Foundation, which was given the sole target of developing an after-school sports programme that would deliver good-quality sporting opportunities for children (Collins and Buller, 2000). Its original mission was 'to promote quality assured youth sports coaching for performance motivated children within a co-ordinated community structure' (National Coaching Foundation, 1996: 3) and involved four clear objectives:

- to recruit and support the development of coaches working with young performers;
- to create quality coaching opportunities to enable keen and interested 11- to 16-year-olds to become more competent and confident;
- to support the development of junior clubs and their coaches; and
- to raise the national and local profile of coaching and youth sport development.

Studies of the Champion Coaching programme (e.g. Collins and Buller, 2000; Bell, 2010) have indicated that the benefits for coaches were long-term for coaching practice; but also, importantly, the programme enabled contact between coaches and other key local agents of provision, illustrating the importance of situating coaches and coaching practice as integral elements of co-ordinated provision to enhance local sporting opportunities.

REFLECTIVE QUESTIONS 1

A topic for readers of this book to reflect upon is the level they are working at and the requirements for developing a coaching career. In particular, consider the needs of those you are coaching and:

- What do they require to continue their sporting development or enjoyment?
- What and where are you coaching?
- What are your objectives and how can current policy frameworks shape what you do?
- Reflect on your development as a coach to date and consider how policy has influenced your practice.

The emergence of coaching policy and the development of specific programmes

Although the Sports Council (now Sport England) produced strategy documents from 1972 to the mid-1990s, including the review of coaching, *Coaching Matters* (Sports Council, 1991), the first formal government sport policy in the UK, *Sport: Raising the Game*, was only published in 1995 (DNH, 1995). Not unexpectedly, specific policy for sports coaching took further time to emerge and develop in its own right. In 2001, the *UK Vision for Coaching* proclaimed:

By 2012 the practice of coaching in the UK will be elevated to a profession acknowledged as central to the development of sport and the fulfilment of individual potential. Coaching will have:

- Professional and ethical values and inclusive and equitable practice.
- Agreed national standards of competencies as a benchmark at all levels.
- A regulated and licensed structure.
- Recognition, value and appropriate funding and reward.
- A culture and structure of innovation, constant reward and continuing professional development.

(UK Sport, 2001: 5)

The statement offered a vision which demanded substantial change in sporting structures in the UK. Yet, becoming involved in coaching sport is not an accidental phenomenon. For the majority of coaches, initial involvement occurred at a relatively young age when, like most people, they simply became involved in helping out. Gradually, involvement in coaching becomes accredited as qualifications accrue. But, as a coach, one quickly learns that working in sport, even on a voluntary basis, is much more complex than people at first appreciate and that policy change, at club and voluntary level, can be an alien concept. Indeed, for many volunteers, the complexity of sport policy often leads them to complain about policy itself, the associated bureaucracy and the fact that they only got involved in coaching because of the sport itself, not the policies which underpin the sport's development. Coaching also has two additional issues which have not been (re-)iterated strongly enough: first, coaching is critical to elements at all levels of policy, from elite to grassroots, to PE and school sport; and, second, coaching is fundamental in all the settings for participation, including the community, sports clubs, schools, further and higher education, elite settings and the home. In a wide-ranging review, Taylor and Garrett (2008) noted that:

The occupation of sports coaching in the UK is undergoing a dramatic and far-reaching structural and cultural change. The particularities of a strong voluntary base, a diverse and fragmented sports club structure and the overarching ethos of 'volunteerism' and self-help mean that, while some parallels and lessons can, and will, be drawn from other professional sectors undergoing similar transformation, sports coaching finds itself in unique and relatively uncertain territory, whose landscape defines an exciting period of change.

(Taylor and Garratt, 2008: 5).

The *UK Vision for Coaching* has not been realised. As argued previously, until practitioners develop a greater strategic awareness of the complex policy context within which they operate, they will not be fully able to realise why policy does not always work in practice (Keech, 2003: 211). As volunteers, however, coaches (and many other volunteers in sport) have little interest in the policy context within which they operate, despite the significant contribution coaches make to community sport (Griffiths and Armour, 2011; 2013). Griffiths and Armour (2011) also noted:

> The tradition of sports clubs in the UK is one with a strong sense of independence, autonomy and resilience (Taylor *et al.*, 2003). Yet, sports clubs operate in a crowded organisational space where their function is impacted upon by a number of external organisations (National Governing Bodies of Sport, Health & Safety Executive, County Sports Partnerships, and Financial Institutions). Haugh & Kitson (2007) argued that this has led to an increasing 'marketisation' of voluntary organisations (such as sports clubs) which are forced to adopt the language and practices of the market (e.g. attract financial resources) ... Importantly, authors wonder whether the voluntary sector can deliver a service agreement without jeopardising the trust and support between coach and participant.
>
> *(Griffiths and Armour, 2011: 5)*

Lyle (2013: 240–241) noted that the role of the sports coach has been highlighted in successive policy documents. The multitude of ways in which policy has been interpreted and developed at a local level is indicative of the confusion surrounding the place of coaching within sport policy in the UK. Table 4.1 is illustrative and indicative rather than exhaustive, but selectively traces and highlights a range of policy documents and the key messages which affected coaching policy. It was a slow process, but the responsibility for policy development for coaching gradually became one of the primary responsibilities of sports coach UK (scUK).

Unlike Champion Coaching, a number of coach education programmes for specific sports have been organised centrally by the NGBs and delivered locally to meet the needs of volunteer coaches. The policy process through which coaching became central to developing grassroots sport has been intricately constructed without much media coverage or contextual writing. Two short case studies illustrate how coaching developed within such a complex framework, situated at the centre of sport policy development but which provided a challenge to those for whom coaching has always been the domain of the sport and the local club.

In the first case study, the headline objective for the Community Sports Coach (CSC) scheme (2003–2006) was to establish 3,000 paid, qualified Community Sports Coaches working at local level to increase the number and range of coaching opportunities by 2006. The Coaching Task Force Final Report (DCMS, 2002) identified issues relating to the employment of coaches in England, including: the limited opportunities for coaches to develop coaching as a career; the lack of active, professional coaches; and a lack of professional development of coaches. It was intended that the scheme would result in a step change in developing a career structure for coaching, addressing the dearth of career paths for coaches and enabling the provision of high-quality coaching with a focus on young people. CSCs were qualified NGB coaches with relevant experience for the role. Employed on a full- or part-time basis, CSCs were deployed to work across schools, clubs and local authorities to:

TABLE 4.1 A selective history of the development of sport coaching policy

Year	Policy document	Author	Coaching
1995	*Sport: Raising the Game*	DNH (Department of National Heritage) (now Department of Culture, Media and Sport) (Conservative Party)	Coaching mentioned briefly, specifically in agenda item 13, 'coaching support to be targeted on schools where sporting commitment is below average' (p. 4) and as an element in the development of excellence along with high standards of sports science and medicine (p. 37)
2000	*A Sporting Future for All*	DCMS (Department of Culture, Media and Sport) (Labour Party)	Coaching linked to talent development for sport in schools and seen as central to elite sport development throughout the document, illustrating some continuity from the proposals in *Sport: Raising the Game*
2001	*The UK Vision for Coaching*	UK Sport	The first document to fully set out the policy challenges for a fully fledged coaching system at all levels of participation and performance
2002	*The Coaching Taskforce*	scUK (sports coach UK)	Responding to *The UK Vision for Coaching*, the document pledged specific proposals, including a national coaching certificate, regional talent development, coaching in 10 sports, a local coach employment scheme, locally deployed coaching development officers based at county sports partnerships and a 'Come into Coaching' recruitment campaign
2002	*The Game Plan: A strategy for delivering the Government's sport and physical activity objectives*	DCMS/The Strategy Unit[1]/	Emphasis on coaching sport in schools through School Sport Partnerships and the School Sport Coordinator (SSCO) programme; funding for coaching a central element of policy development at all levels of participation
2003	*PE, School Sport and Club Links (PESSCL): Learning through PE and Sport*	DfES (Department for Education and Skills)	Focused on developing PE and sport in schools and in out-of-hours learning with three key goals: to improve the quality of teaching, coaching and learning in PE and school sport; to improve coaching standards and quality; and to ensure the Long Term Athlete Development model linked to policy and player pathways for NGBs
2004	*National Framework for Community Sport in England*	Sport England	Sport England's response to the challenges set out within *The Game Plan* using a comprehensive model for policy development and action. Coaching not seen as a key driver in developing community sport, although coaching was implicit in many of the statements regarding sustaining participation

Year	Policy/Document	Organisation	Content
2008	*Playing to Win: A new era of sport 2008*	DCMS (Labour Party)	'By 2017 there will be competition and coaching at the heart of the school sport system, world leading coaching infrastructure, a legacy of a world leading elite sport infrastructure including high quality coaching' (p. 4)
2008	*UK Coaching Framework (UKCF)*	spUK	Focal point of policy for sport coaching with three distinct time phases offering coherent reflection into future planning • Building the foundations – 2006–2008 • Delivering the goals – 2006–2012 • Transforming the system – 2006–2016
2008	*PE and School Sport Strategy (PESSYP)*	Youth Sport Trust/Sport England	Focused on sport in school-related settings The ambition of was: • To create a step change in the quantity and quality of coaching offered to young people • To ensure coaching within schools connects to competition, leadership and volunteering, and club links to enhance and strengthen pathways for young people • To ensure coaches are deployed effectively, and developed and valued by trained 'coach managers' • To create a culture of co-coaching and coach mentoring • To transform the coaching of children through the promotion of fundamental movement skills and fundamental sports skills by a multi-sport and multi-skill approach • To establish over time a network of coach development hubs within the education setting
2012	*Creating a Sporting Habit for Life*	DCMS (Conservative Party)	Coaching not mentioned – coaches viewed as an element of 'structured environments' for participation as evidenced in case studies from boxing, cycling and badminton

[1] The Strategy Unit, which operated under the premierships of Tony Blair and Gordon Brown, was based within the UK Cabinet Office and its purpose was to provide the Prime Minister with detailed advice and policy analysis of key issues and priorities.

- coach young people, predominantly outside of curriculum time, to develop core movement and sport skills across a number of sports or with a particular focus on one sport;
- coach at a local level with a focus on the fundamentals/learning to train (or equivalent) development phases of NGB player pathways; and
- retain young people in sport by ensuring a high-quality, enjoyable, young-person-centred experience and providing guidance on progression opportunities based on the young person's interests and abilities.

Much of this is highly laudable until one reads the third point. It is precisely that type of language, written in good faith but in practice sounding so vague as to render it meaningless, which volunteer and aspiring sports coaches reject immediately.

County Sports Partnerships (CSPs) acted as strategic co-ordinating agencies for the CSC scheme. In principle, working through CSPs should have ensured a co-ordinated, multi-agency approach to the identification of strategic and local need for coaching. In practice, the involvement of multiple agencies working at a local level proved too complex and the scheme reflected dominant ideologies in coaching at the time. A majority of CSCs were male (70%), British White (92%) and did not have a disability (98%). CSCs were younger, on average, than the UK coaching population. Additionally, ten sports and/or multi-sports/skills activities – football, rugby union, multi-skill, cricket, basketball, athletics, gymnastics, multi-sport, hockey, swimming – accounted for three quarters (76%) of all CSC roles. The coaches undertook more than one coaching 'role' – coaching different groups in the same sport; coaching different groups in different sports; coaching different groups in different contexts, such as clubs and schools – primarily because many of those community-based coaches who had good qualifications and local knowledge were appointed to the full-time posts (North, 2006). Thus, the coach with both a range of skills and at least a working knowledge of the local policy environment appeared to be at an advantage in applying for the posts available at the time. Two points emerge here: first, CSCs tended to embody the coaching workforce at the time and provided paid opportunities for existing, well-qualified coaches, and second, CSCs could cover a number of roles in communities due to their existing knowledge of both their sports and their communities. It is important, therefore, for aspiring coaches to reflect upon the networks they build up and the knowledge they demonstrate in order to progress their careers.

In the second case study, the School Sport Coaching Programme was identified in January 2008 as a strand within the PE and School Sport Strategy for Young People (PESSYP – Youth Sport Trust/Sport England, 2008) and aimed to improve the quantity and quality of coaching offered to young people. This programme was designed to drive up standards in the coaching of children and make a positive contribution to the 'five hour offer', a critical element of the Labour Government's aims to promote a legacy from London 2012 wherein all young people in state schools would be able to access two hours of PE within the curriculum and three hours of sport or activity out of school time. The programme comprised four elements: a school sport coaching grant to every School Sport Partnership; training in coach management; local coach briefings; and School Sports Coaching Scholarships. According to Brown *et al.* (2012), in the first year of the programme there was a 70% increase in the number of hours of paid coaching. The main issues for consideration for the future of coaching in schools were that the most successful partnerships were: employing a coach manager to manage the team of salaried and volunteer coaches across the partnership; employing full-time or substantial hours part-time coaches by seeking joint funding with NGBs and other agencies; setting-up satellite clubs on school sites to assist the development of effective school club links; and enabling coaches to organise festivals and competitions for the young people. Although the PESSYP strategy was discontinued when Labour lost the 2010 General Election, the initial indications were that increased investment into coaching in schools, aligned with an appropriate structured PE curriculum provided the appropriate infrastructure to develop further participation amongst young people.

REFLECTIVE QUESTIONS 2

- Do volunteers need to consider the policy context in which they work and, if so, why is it important for them to do so?
- Do volunteers have the time and inclination to do so?
- Is this something that readers should consider more widely in order to recognise not just how much volunteering takes place through coaching but the *value* of that volunteering?
- Given a greater appreciation of the policy context surrounding your coaching, how might this awareness further enhance your context and your work?
- Have you set out a career path and do you actually know what is required to advance your coaching career?
- What actions are you taking to build up your network in the policy landscape you inhabit?

Policy development and sports coaching in communities

In June 2008, the home nation Sports Councils, together with NGBs, adopted the *UK Coaching Framework*. More than 40 sports now have their coach education programmes endorsed as meeting the standards of the UK Coaching Certificate (UKCC) as an indication of quality assurance (see Bolton and Smith, 2013). Typically, such programmes classify coaches within Levels 1–4, with Level 2 being the minimum standard for someone to coach unaccompanied. Written by sports coach UK (scUK) in collaboration with other agencies, the vision of the *UK Coaching Framework* (scUK, 2008b) was to create a cohesive, ethical, inclusive and valued coaching system where skilled coaches support children, players and athletes at all stages of development in sport. Essentially, this indicated that the UK would create 'a world-leading' coaching system which would be underpinned by five strategic action areas. To meet the targets in the *UK Coaching Framework*, however, there would need to be a 178% increase in coached hours. Such a change, whilst greatly needed, was almost immediately identified as being unlikely. A more pragmatic approach of 5% annual growth leading to 41% overall growth by 2016 was proposed. scUK adopted a 'mixed model' of coaching provision which continued to value a balance between full-time (paid) and volunteer coaches. It will be interesting to see the extent to which the *UK Coaching Framework* has met its targets should research be published in 2016 or soon after.

The roles of a sports coach include but are not confined to counsellor, instructor, teacher, trainer and mentor (Lyle, 2002). The *UK Coaching Framework* put significant emphasis (and indeed pressure) on the coaching profession to further develop its profile. As athletes are obviously such high-profile elements of policy, coaches, by necessity in an age of professionalisation, specialisation and technologisation, also gain such profiles. Whilst coaching is essential to developing levels of performance and can no longer be seen as just a grassroots product, coaching in local communities represents a fundamental element for increasing and sustaining participation in sport. Most readers of this book will be looking to develop their coaching practice in community-based settings, working in the broadly termed area of sport development. Whilst there are numerous definitions of sport development (see Collins, 2010; Hylton, 2013), it is argued that sport development must be 'used to describe processes, policies and practices that form an integral feature of the work involved in providing sport and sporting opportunities' (Hylton and Bramham, 2008: 1). As a central component of community sport development it is important to recognise that a coach's practice does not take place in isolation and, much to the chagrin of many volunteers, a sports coach is a key actor in the complex policy landscape in the UK.

The emergence of coaching as a sport policy priority has also witnessed the growth in the debate about the purpose of coaching in contributing to that priority. As North (2007) noted, there have been few studies which have examined the role of the coach in improving levels of participation and a majority of studies have been centred on psychological or environmental factors which induce sustained adherence to (exercise) participation. North's research offered six main conclusions, the most significant of which were that:

- first, there is a very strong case for increasing and sustaining participation coaching, associated with an increasing evidence base;
- second, many participants receive coaching but coaching itself is under-utilised as a means of increasing participation levels; and
- third, the emphasis on recruiting and training high-quality coaches is critical and the role of the coach and coaching in general needs to be more clearly thought through.

North concludes that coaching is an essential part of wider policies and interventions addressing sport participation (North, 2007), but the critical question the research raises is: what is the role of coaching and, subsequently, does coaching suffer from the long-held political context for sport in which sport is trying to meet the needs of both participation and elite requirements? For example, with the implementation by the coalition government of the PE and Sport Premium for primary schools, it should be noted that over £450 million was to be spent on improving PE and sport in primary schools between 2013 and 2016. This funding was directly allocated to primary head teachers, thus schools can choose how they use the funding, such as in hiring specialist teachers or qualified sports coaches to work with teachers during PE lessons or in the organisation of after-school and holiday clubs. Introduced as a partial replacement for the School Sport Partnership Programme, each primary school receives a set amount of money. As long ago as 1982 the Sports Council stated that a major task was to work with and through the education system, but it is only since 1990 that substantial staff and grant resources have been focused on schools, prompted by strong commitments from the Major and Blair governments (Collins and Buller, 2000: 201). It has long been recognised that the primary school age range is where the most significant periods of development take place for young people (Gallahue and Ozmun, 1995). If children are unable to efficiently perform basic physical competencies, such as throwing and catching a ball, they will find it difficult to participate successfully in physical activities that require the skills at a later time (Stidder and Griggs, 2012: 202). This is a significant problem when sports coaches are involved, as they tend only to be able to coach 'their sport' at a time when children need diverse movement education and fundamental sport skills rather than specialist/explicit tuition in single sports. These developments could be an example of policy being well meaning but practically flawed, and readers should reflect on their work within some of the policy frameworks discussed and ask critical questions about what they were expected to do if working with young people and how suitable the activities actually were.

What is evident is that whilst, historically, sports coaching has either been treated as a homogeneous activity or, at times, synonymous with high-performance coaching, specialisation has usually occurred within the process of professionalisation – i.e. coaches tend to predominantly focus on community activities or elite coaching and rarely exhibit an ability to do both. Duffy et al. (2013) considered sports coaches as a segmented workforce with four main roles identified – children's coaches, adult recreational coaches, performance development coaches and high-performance coaches – closely aligned to the specific requirements of performers and participants. Participation in sport is dependent to a greater or lesser extent on sport leadership, teaching, instruction or coaching. In so far as sport development is a process that is intended to lead to increased sport participation, more sustained participation or improved standards of performance, the sports coach (as a collective term) becomes an extremely important element of provision (Lyle, 2013: 232).

Table 4.2 is an excellent summary of the current purpose of the sports coach in local communities. Critically, however, there are very few coaches who are able to embrace the twin purposes of, first, coaching as a policy tool for grassroots development and elite success as an end in itself and, second, coaching's contribution to broader developmental and policy objectives, as this dichotomy remains a significant area for debate. Table 4.2 enables the aspiring sports coach to question their own role and prompts policy actors to reflect upon whether sufficient numbers of sports coaches see their role in the context of the bigger picture. There will be many in the

TABLE 4.2 Common goals between sport development and sport coaching

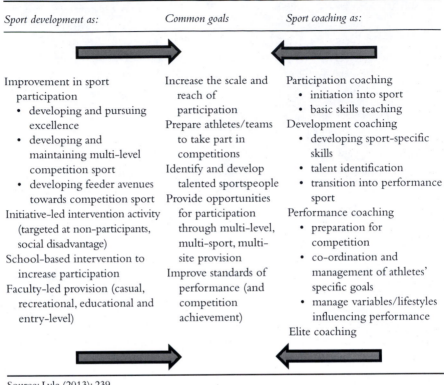

Sport development as:	Common goals	Sport coaching as:
Improvement in sport participation • developing and pursuing excellence • developing and maintaining multi-level competition sport • developing feeder avenues towards competition sport Initiative-led intervention activity (targeted at non-participants, social disadvantage) School-based intervention to increase participation Faculty-led provision (casual, recreational, educational and entry-level)	Increase the scale and reach of participation Prepare athletes/teams to take part in competitions Identify and develop talented sportspeople Provide opportunities for participation through multi-level, multi-sport, multi-site provision Improve standards of performance (and competition achievement)	Participation coaching • initiation into sport • basic skills teaching Development coaching • developing sport-specific skills • talent identification • transition into performance sport Performance coaching • preparation for competition • co-ordination and management of athletes' specific goals • manage variables/lifestyles influencing performance Elite coaching

Source: Lyle (2013): 239

coaching profession who would choose to ignore the contextual developments of recent years. However, if sport policy is to ever succeed in its twin goals of increasing participation and maintaining performance at elite level, the practice of sports coaching will be a prime determinant of relative success or failure.

REFLECTIVE QUESTIONS 3

• Do coaches feel completely confident with Level 2 qualifications as the minimum standard to coach unaccompanied – i.e. is Level 2 rigorous enough?
• Does it require coaches to engage with sufficient knowledge?
• Can those with Level 2 be rightfully given the name 'coach'? At what point have coaches been professionalised?
• When working with young people, how suitable are the activities within coaching sessions? To what extent is practice age-appropriate, meeting educational recommendations for youth sport development?
• Do sufficient numbers of sports coaches see their role in the context of the bigger policy picture? Should they?

Conclusion

In its 2013–2017 strategy scUK proclaims it will further champion and drive policy and investment in coaching. During this period, in 2016, the timescale for the *UK Coaching Framework* will conclude and offer an indication of the extent to which coaching has actually achieved the status of being a fully fledged profession. Coaching is historically grounded within the voluntary sector with little protection of the terms 'coach' or 'coaching'. The 'coach' is often one of many volunteers helping to keep people involved in sport. The commitment to the *UK Coaching Framework* objectives was exciting and encouraging but, if like me, readers became involved in sports coaching because of their fundamental love of sport, the policy context which has developed for sports coaching is very often rejected and not seen as relevant. Volunteers will continue to form the bulk of the coaching profession, but with a marked shift in qualifications and a shift to part-time and full-time paid positions. There has been dominance of established and powerful coaching pathways, but many sports are now being challenged to develop innovative coaching structures and improve coaching standards as a critical component of raising levels of participation and performance. A question for the evaluative research which must come from the *UK Coaching Framework* is to ask whether the *Framework* has forced sports to embrace change. Along with this practical expansion comes associated administration, management, budgeting and further resource implications. Coaches help participants to work towards achieving their potential and they operate on a variety of levels, from introductory participation with young people, to supporting community teams and groups, to working with elite athletes. As such, coaching roles within sport policy vary significantly according to context and, whilst some people are lucky to be full-time sports coaches, many who wish to become a sports coach work part-time and voluntarily, usually having to complete a set number of hours in order to achieve introductory and mid-level qualifications. At times job advertisements may require people who have also played sport to a high level, although in and of itself high-level participation does not make someone a good coach. Likewise, it is essential for aspiring sports coaches to recognise that they are not just a coach, but that they are an actor in key policy developments and that their practice can often be fundamental to whether others, especially young people, choose to enjoy sport and continue participating. Finally, the reflective opportunities in this chapter offer the aspiring sports coach a chance to consider where their place in the policy landscape currently lies and whether the coaching profession should pay more attention to such questions.

References

Bell, B. (2010) Building a legacy for youth and coaching: Champion Coaching on Merseyside, in Collins, M. (ed.) *Examining Sports Development*, London: Routledge, pp. 139–166.

Bolton, N. and Smith, B. (2013) Sports development for coaches, in Jones, R.L. and Kingston, K. (eds) *An Introduction to Sports Coaching: Connecting Theory to Practice* (second edition), London: Routledge, pp. 131–144.

Bompa, T.O. (1983). *Theory and Methodology: Training the Key to Athletic Performance*, Dubuque, IA: Kendall/Hunt Publishing Company.

Brown, S., Mason, C. and Nevill, M. (2012) Shifting policy in school sport coaching – an evaluation and implications for schools and coaches, in Spracklen, K. and Adams, A. (eds) *Sport, Leisure and Tourism Politics and Places*, Eastbourne: LSA Publications, pp. 85–95.

Collins, M. (2010) (ed.) *Examining Sports Development*, London: Routledge.

Collins, M. and Buller, J (2000) Bridging the post-school institutional gap in sport: evaluating Champion Coaching in Nottinghamshire, *Managing Leisure*, 5, 200–221.

DCMS (2000) *A Sporting Future for All*, London: Department of Culture Media and Sport.

DCMS (2002) *The Coaching Task Force: Final Report*, London: Department of Culture, Media and Sport.

DCMS (2008) *Playing To Win: A New Era for Sport*, London: Department of Culture, Media and Sport.

DCMS (2012) *Creating a Sporting Habit for Life*, London: Department of Culture, Media and Sport.

DCMS/The Strategy Unit (2002) *The Game Plan: A Strategy for Delivering Government's Sport and Physical Activity Objectives*, London: The Strategy Unit.

DfES (2003) *Learning through PE and Sport*, London: Department for Education and Skills.

DNH (1995) *Sport: Raising the Game*, London: Department of National Heritage.

Duffy, P., North, J. and Muir, B. (2013) Understanding the impact of sport coaching on legacy, *International Journal of Sport Policy and Politics*, 5(2), 165–182.

Gallahue, D. and Ozmun, J. (1995) *Understanding Motor Development: Infants Children, Adolescents, Adults* (third edition), Madison, WI: Brown and Benchmark.

Green, M. and Houlihan, B. (2005). *Elite Sport Development: Policy Learning and Political Priorities*, London: Routledge.

Griffiths, M. and Armour, K. (2011) *An Analysis of the Capacity of Volunteer Sports Coaches as Community Assets in the Big Society: A Scoping Review*, London: AHRC.

Griffiths, M. and Armour, K. (2013) Volunteer sports coaches as community assets? A realist review of the research evidence, *International Journal of Sports Policy and Politics*, DOI: 10.1080/19406940.2013.824496.

Holt, R. (1989) *Sport and the British: A Modern History*, Oxford: Oxford University Press.

Hylton, K. (ed.) (2013) *Sport Development; Policy, Process and Practice* (third edition), London: Routledge.

Hylton, K. and Bramham, P. (2008) *Sport Development: Policy, Process and Practice* (second edition), London: Routledge.

Keech, M. (2002) Coaching, in Cox, R., Russell, D. and Vamplew, W. (eds) *Encyclopaedia of British Football*, London: ABC Clio, pp. 62–65.

Keech, M. (2003) Sport through education? Issues for schools and sports development, in Hayes, S. and Stidder, G. (eds) *Social Inclusion and Exclusion in Physical Education*, London: Routledge, pp. 211–231.

Kremer, J., Trew, K. and Ogle, S. (eds) (1997) *Young People's Involvement in Sport*, London: Routledge.

Lyle, J. (2002) *Sport Coaching Concepts: A Framework for Coaches' Behaviour*, London: Routledge.

Lyle, J. (with Dowens, T.) (2013) Sport development and sport coaching, in Hylton, K. (ed.) *Sport Development: Policy, Process and Practice* (third edition), London: Routledge, pp. 231–252.

Maclean, M. and Prichard, I. (2013) History for coaches, in Jones, R.L. and Kingston, K. (eds) *An Introduction to Sports Coaching: Connecting Theory to Practice* (second edition), London: Routledge, pp. 83–97.

National Coaching Foundation (1996) *Champion Coaching – The Guide*, Leeds: Sports Council.

North, J. (2006) *Community Sports Coach Profile Survey Report*, Leeds: sports coach UK.

North, J. (2007) *Increasing Participation in Sport: The Role of the Coach*, www.sportscoachuk.org/sites/default/files/Coaching-and-participation.pdf (accessed 5 February 2014).

scUK (2008a) *The Coaching Workforce 2009–2016*, Leeds: The National Coaching Foundation.

scUK (2008b) *UK Coaching Framework*, Leeds: sports coach UK.

scUK (2013) *Putting Coaching at the Heart of Sport: sports coach UK Strategy 2013–2017*, Leeds: sports coach UK.

Sport England (2004) *The Framework for Sport in England: Making England an Active and Successful Sporting Nation, A Vision for 2020*, London: Sport England.

Sports Council (1982) *Sport in the Community: The Next Ten Years*, London: Sports Council.

Sports Council (1991) *Coaching Matters: A Review of Coaching and Coach Education in the United Kingdom*, London: Sports Council.

Stidder, G. and Griggs, G. (2012) Healthism and the obesity discourse, in Stidder, G. and Hayes, S. (eds) *Equity and Inclusion in Physical Education and Sport* (second edition), London: Routledge.

Taylor, B. and Garratt, D. (2008) *The Professionalisation of Sports Coaching in the UK: Issues and Conceptualisation*, Leeds: sports coach UK.

UK Sport (2001) *The UK Vision for Coaching*, London: UK Sport.

Youth Sport Trust/Sport England (2008) *The PE and Sport Strategy for Young People: A Guide to Delivering the Five Hour Offer*, Loughborough/London: Youth Sport Trust/Sport England.

SECTION 2

'How' to add value to your coaching

This second section asks you to critique your own coaching processes and to consider a range of alternative strategies and methodologies which may enhance your work.

5

INCLUSIVE PRACTICE IN SPORT COACHING

Sid Hayes and Tracy Killingley

Issues of inclusivity have been prevalent in many spheres of sporting involvement over recent decades and will be a significant area of interest for individuals wishing to become sports coaches. Increasing levels of scrutiny surrounding areas of sporting practice have led to significant debate in this area of study, with numerous scholars identifying exclusionary practice in relation to special educational needs and disability (SEND), gender, age, class, ethnicity and sexuality (Stidder and Hayes, 2013). Such issues have gained further prominence through the introduction of the Equality Act (2010) which has attempted to outlaw exclusionary practice in society. The Act sets out to end discrimination experienced by individuals within society in relation to education, employment and access to facilities, goods and services. In legal terms it covers four main areas, which are: direct discrimination, indirect discrimination, harassment and victimisation. Whilst generally speaking discrimination in any context is normally unlawful, there are some important exceptions within this area. There may be specific roles within society that have a vital physical requirement which may legitimately exclude some individuals. For example, having a major physical disability would mean that an individual could justifiably not be considered for the role of an active firefighter due to the nature of the work undertaken. There may be other examples of this nature, but it is also worth considering and challenging some pre-conceived ideas and stereotypes about what people can and cannot do. It is within this context that this chapter investigates the professional practice of a sports coach in relation to inclusivity and social inclusion. The importance of developing an awareness of these societal contexts of exclusionary practice can be highlighted through the recent experience of the England manager, Roy Hodgson, who was placed under the media spotlight for comments related to Andros Townsend in one of England's pre-World-Cup friendlies in 2014. Whilst Hodgson was eventually exonerated from having made comments which were racially offensive to the individual in question, it highlighted certain sensitivities around this issue and followed on from other high-profile incidents of alleged racial abuse in professional football. It is evident from this example that coaches will have the responsibility to develop awareness and an understanding of practices that particular groups in society may perceive as exclusionary. As we navigate through this chapter we aim to provide coaches with knowledge and understanding of inclusivity and how it can inform practice.

Social inclusion generally relates to processes through which people can be integrated into society. The Centre for Economic and Social Inclusion offers a definition of social inclusion, which refers to:

> the process by which efforts are made to ensure that everyone, regardless of their background, experiences and circumstances, can gain access to the services and facilities they need to achieve their own potential in life. To achieve inclusion, income and employment are necessary but not sufficient. An inclusive society is also characterised by a striving for reduced inequality, a balance between individuals' rights and duties and increased social cohesion.
>
> *(Britton and Casebourne, 2002: 14)*

This indicates that, for inclusion to be attained, striving to reduce inequality is fundamental and it is with this in mind, along with the earlier considerations, that we have framed this chapter. Sport has become an increasing focal point for achieving objectives in relation to social inclusion, hence the importance of being aware of this as a sports coach.

It has been suggested that sport and physical activity have the potential to improve employment opportunities, reduce crime, improve educational achievement and enhance a person's health through participation in competitive and non-competitive activities (Stidder and Hayes, 2013). The Youth Sport Trust (2002) reported that disadvantaged and under-represented young people who actively engaged in sport, such as pupils with disabilities, girls and those from ethnic minorities, would gain much personally from increased access to and opportunities in a range of activities in their local communities. In this context, sport aims to have an impact on improving the self-esteem and confidence of young people. Government ministers have previously made this link, including former UK Minister for Sport, Kate Hoey, who suggested that social inclusion highlights how sport programmes could contribute to wider societal issues relating to opportunity:

> Sport can make a unique contribution to tackling social exclusion in society. We recognise that this is not something that sport can tackle alone but by working with other agencies sport can play a significant part ... We must work together to promote the provision of high quality physical education by qualified personnel for all ages, regardless of sex, race, religious or ethnic background or ability.
>
> *(Hoey, 2001: 23)*

Inclusion is, however, more than a concern about any one group of people. Its scope is broad. It is about equal opportunities for all, irrespective of their background. Within this context inclusive practice can be likened to a journey with a function, its function being to develop a philosophy of identification and address the critical issue of who is included and who is excluded within society. This chapter will offer two case studies with examples for consideration by sports coaches. Whilst these two case studies will focus specifically on areas of inclusive/exclusive practice in relation to a particular group of individuals, it is hoped that the reader will be able to utilise the general concepts identified, reflect on their own practice and transfer these concepts into other social contexts not specifically discussed in any detail in this chapter. The two case studies will draw upon the areas of gender and special educational needs and disability.

Gender and inclusive practice

This section will focus on gender, and discuss ways in which coaching practice can contribute to, or challenge, gendered inequities (Flintoff and Scratton, 2005). There are numerous theories concerning the complexities of gendered practices. Essentially they are socially constructed, learned masculine or feminine behaviours which are dynamic and changeable. Through gender socialisation society constructs femininity and masculinity, and what gendered attributes, behaviours and practices constitute being a male or female.

It is appreciated here that boys, girls, young men and young women are not homogeneous groups that can be simplistically labelled and categorised, but are more complex conglomerations with interconnections of gender, race, disability, sexual orientation and social class. Despite their being the subject of widespread debate which has led to positive changes and some legislation around inclusivity, the arenas of sport and sport coaching are still largely a male preserve. Status and privilege in sport are ascribed to hegemonic forms of masculinity, further suggesting that sport is a male domain, steeped in tradition that generally reinforces gender stereotypes.

As coaches develop awareness and understanding of exclusionary practices it may be significant to consider your own gendered identity and whether you are perpetuating your own philosophical standpoint, values, beliefs and cultural stereotypes (Jones *et al.*, 2001). How might this impact on how you approach your practice and work with males and females, boys and girls? Within coaching practice you will need to consider:

1) *Who* is coaching?
2) *How* are they coaching?
3) *What* is being coached?

So it may be appropriate to question and reflect on your 'personal biases and assumptions' (Cassidy *et al.*, 2004: 56). It might be pertinent to ask how your practice may exacerbate potential barriers for some participants, and to look to facilitate equity and inclusive practice where it is possible and indeed appropriate.

When offering girls and boys different activities or tasks are you privileging one over another? Or are you providing equal access and opportunity to all across a range of activities? It would be prudent not to make assumptions about boys' or girls' sporting knowledge, ability and experience, or what is appropriate for males and females. Coaches could benefit from overt thinking about the activities, roles and responsibilities that are made accessible to all participants. It is important to avoid making girls (or indeed boys) the negative reference group; for example, 'you must pass to a girl' or 'each team must have at least two girls'. The focus of achievement should be equal for boys and girls and avoid setting girls an easier task than boys or assuming that boys are unable to perform certain activities. Furthermore, implicit as well as explicit communication may also impact negatively, so it would be judicious to avoid phrases such as 'playing like girls', 'throwing like a girl', 'man to man', 'sportsmanship', or overuse of '*he*' or '*she*' in examples.

Consideration of what participants want from sport and sport coaches, irrespective of their sex or the sex of the coach, has highlighted positive feedback and constructive interventions, enhancement of self-esteem and an appropriate coaching style as significant. It would be appropriate to reflect upon the interventions and feedback given in your sessions and consider who receives more feedback and why. Differing expectations of boys and girls can lead to preferential verbal interaction with some participants and it would seem logical to be equitable in your time with all participants.

Much research has been conducted within the area of mixed-gender coaching groups and, where appropriate, integrating girls and boys seems to be considered beneficial (Stidder and Hayes, 2013). Others suggest that mixed groups can limit and constrain girls' behaviour and confidence, therefore a coach needs to be mindful not to let any individuals dominate the game, practice or questioning. When working in a mixed-gender environment the coach needs to intervene to prevent such inequities before disinterest, disengagement and potential disaffection sets in. Co-educational coaching does not necessarily equate to equality of opportunity. Merely mixing girls and boys, without considering the pedagogy and approach, could simply reinforce masculine hegemony (male power and dominance). Some research suggests coaches struggle to develop effective co-educational practices and may therefore need to consider explicitly developing co-educational pedagogy and gender-equitable practice. For example, coaches may need to be critically reflective of the community in which they work (Navin, 2011) and ensure they value the contributions of both girls and boys equally, sharing key roles, such as captains, within coaching sessions, and using a range of demonstrations and resources which show both males and females as key role models (Flintoff and Scratton, 2005).

The impact of the media

Stereotypical expectations concerning what it is to be *female* and *male* pervade sport, reinforced through the mass media, and coaches may 'consciously or inadvertently either challenge or reaffirm these stereotypical views' (Jones, 2007: 31). The media is one way through which many participants and the wider public relate to sport. Developing an awareness of its influence, power and framing of events can be highlighted by the high-profile presenter John Inverdale and his inappropriate comments on the BBC with regard to the 2013 Ladies Wimbledon Champion Marion Bartoli as 'never going to be a looker' and that she would have to 'compensate for that' through her tennis. It further confirmed the importance of developing appropriate awareness and sensitivities. Indeed, some research suggests that gender equality efforts in sport may in fact maintain the existing gender order and further reinforce stereotypes, suggesting that a more 'holistic, critical approach to sport itself, its structures, norms, media practices and media representation is needed' (Svender *et al.*, 2011: 476). The media can have a very positive impact and role models may inspire young people to participate (Giuliano *et al.*, 2007), with high-level-performance sport providing some good examples, such as Jessica Ennis, Nicola Adams and Katherine Grainger amongst many female athletes at the London Olympic Games, 2012. The Games also saw the first female competitors from Saudi Arabia, Brunei and Qatar, which was perceived as either tokenism or strides towards equality. Coaches in their own practice can look to be representative and present equality of role models in providing demonstrations, in being used as technical examples, in leadership roles (e.g. a male choreographer in dance or a female coach in soccer) and in any visual materials, such as images or displays.

Whilst some girls can demonstrate a desire to participate in physical activity and be successful in sport (LeUnes, 2008), sport is still perceived by many as a hegemonic male domain perpetuating aggressive and competitive attitudes (ibid., 2008), which some girls perceive as unfeminine and some boys as undesirable. With elite sport dominant in our wider media-orientated society, participation that is recreational is often deemed less significant and its subsequent values and benefits can be undervalued. Whilst some young people do aspire to high performance and high status, others participate for sociability (peer relations), enjoyment, developing physical competence and the physical, social and emotional pleasure it can provide. An overemphasis on competition and elite performance can frequently be a barrier to participation for young people. The Physical Education National Curriculum 2014 places significant emphasis on competitive sport and developing elite performers, and these commonly dominate curriculum design and delivery in many schools which promote team games, competition and school teams to the exclusion of broader recreational and lifestyle-choice activities. The implication here for coaching practice is to know your participants, what they want, and develop a coaching environment which focuses on personalised holistic development

Gender and physical identity

Sport resides in a 'mass media culture where highly visible representations of the body are powerful and influential in constructing identities' (Garrett, 2004: 225) and can impact on young people, in particular adolescents. Body image and physical identity are important areas for consideration. It is easy to say that coaches should embrace the multiplicities of individual identities and challenge discourses around 'ideal' bodies for both males and females, but negotiating a physical identity for girls and boys is not straightforward. Young people can be 'complex creatures who are challenged by a myriad of different factors when engaging in sport and physical activity' (Garrett, 2004: 235). Media images of the sporting body can be limiting for girls and boys where:

> Dominant media-led sport narratives can create another source of pressure for young people by encouraging their desire to strive for unrealistic ideals of corporeal perfection, given young people's already shifting and contested identities.
>
> *(Azzarito and Katzew, 2010: 30)*

Some young people can be vulnerable to the embodiment of elitist sporting ideals (Azzarito, 2011), therefore coaches would be well advised to critically evaluate media and sporting representations of the body and show sensitivity and understanding around these areas.

For some participants the influential pressures of feminine and masculine concepts associated with fashion, such as kit, hair styling, jewellery, alongside changing facilities can provoke a rebellious reaction which needs to be handled with care. Kit can be perceived as unfashionable, unflattering, un-feminine/un-masculine, and coach interventions should be based on decency, enhancing self-esteem and developing positive body images. Coaches should try to avoid situations where participants feel intimidated, embarrassed and subject to ridicule. The changing room scene involving the character Billy Casper in the film *Kes*, or more recently John Farley being humiliated at that hands of his sadistic physical education teacher in *Mr Woodcock* or the ridicule of Billy Elliot are powerful images with overt messages about not conforming to the stereotypical forms of heterosexual masculinity and in some cases perpetuating forms of bullying. These behaviours are far removed from an understanding of 'progressive physicalities' (Garrett, 2004: 235) and practices which allow for multiple physical identities, challenging narrow and limiting conceptions of gender and the body.

Sport coaches might consider how their professional practice in various sport coaching contexts could promote or inhibit their participants. The research presented here is not conclusive; indeed, some research has posed the question whether seeking a perceived desirable appearance is creating potential barriers for full engagement in sport. Recently, Jennie Price (Chief Executive of Sport England) stated that young women who require cubicles, hairdryers and fifteen minutes to change need to 'reconstruct' themselves after physical exercise. The disparate responses to this statement caused some debate in the media.

Cassidy *et al.* (2009) suggest that:

> coaching practitioners should be sensitive to how notions of masculinity and femininity may be intimately linked to a participant's body, and the task for coaches is to challenge behaviours that threaten others' rights or identities.
>
> *(26)*

Moreover, perpetuating ideas that sport participation is un-feminine or un-masculine and making assumptions about preferences and ability based on gender stereotypes should be avoided. Sport coaches should refrain from creating a stage where heterosexual identity is measured. Deviance from the perceived norm can lead to perceptions of lesbianism or homosexuality resulting in possible alienation from social peers, family and significant others. Inappropriate language which is tacitly condoned such as gay, lesbo or similar, should be challenged (Meyer, 2008). What a coach says and what they allow their participants to say can have an impact and in some cases reinforce bias, stereotypes and prejudice. Unchallenged discourse could impact significantly on boys and girls', men and women's future intentions and engagement. Whilst it may well present a challenge for coaches, inclusive practice needs to focus on the learning and coaching that is taking place and the holistic development of individuals. Coaches will need to de-stabilise both stereotypical femininities and stereotypical masculinities, if physical empowerment of the individual is to be possible (Azzarito, 2011).

Women in coaching

Statistics presented on BBC Sports International Women's Day, 2014 showed only a quarter of coaches at the 2012 Paralympics were women; this figure was just 9 per cent at the Olympic Games, and in the UK male coaches outnumber female coaches 3:1. Clearly, there is more that can be done to allow women to access coaching roles, especially within perceived 'male' sports. Kilty (2006) considered some of the barriers for women in coaching, but we need to look more closely at why women are, or are perceived to be, less confident and motivated, and to identify how more non-elite women coaches can become elite coaches and why women feel undervalued and underrated. How many women hold high-ranking positions in the IOC, FIFA, FA, Premier League, NBA, National Governing Bodies? Structures, whether implicit or explicit, display a significant lack of women in positions in men's sport whereas men are represented in, and to a large extent, control women's sport. On a positive note, on 5 August 2014 an NBA team, the San Antonio Spurs, hired WNBA star Becky Hammon as the first full-time, paid female assistant coach in history on an NBA coaching staff. Whilst this is a sign of progress, advocates of equal opportunities may ask why it took so long.

To sum up the points made on gendered coaching practices in this section, the challenges of responding to the diverse needs of a range of participants in a coaching session should be an important aspect of coaching practice (Navin, 2011), with an emphasis on encouraging girls, boys, men and women to move out of their gender 'comfort' zones and attempt new activities which extend their perceptions of their own physicality (Stidder and Hayes, 2013). Overcoming stereotypes and negotiating narrow conceptions of masculinity and femininity could help coaches to maximise engagement in sport and physical activity settings. Practising gender neutrality in coaching, understanding the power and influence of the mass media and adopting coaching practices that allow for multiple physical identities, catering for a range of ways of being physical and challenging narrow conceptions of gender could be effective in valuing the participation of all and identifying the needs of individuals (Garrett, 2004).

Sport and disability

When considering issues of disability it is important initially to understand some of the theoretical framework in relation to how disability is socially constructed within society. Recent global events such as the London 2012 Paralympics and more recently the Commonwealth Games 2014 in Glasgow, which had a partially integrated approach to competition for disabled athletes, have significantly raised the profile of disability sport. To some extent these events challenged conceptual thinking surrounding the involvement of individuals who have disabilities in sporting activities. There are a number of different ways in which disability can be viewed and this will have a significant impact on how individuals coach. Traditionally disability has been defined through health and social services and such definitions have focused on medical constraints. In this context any disability is identified as either abnormal, different or special. The disability is allocated to an individual and the role of any professional interventions is to try to 'cure or care'. The disability is internalised to the individual and it is up to them to come to terms with this. However, it is appropriate to consider an alternative perspective which includes looking at any disability as the interaction between a person's physical, mental or sensory impairment and the way that the social environment is organised, constructed or perceived around them. In this context any disability is the result of environmental, social and personal obstacles/barriers which inhibit people from realising their potential. Barriers can include physical, structural, organisational and attitudinal perceptions. If this theoretical model is adopted it can be argued that disability belongs to society and not the individual, and therefore disability becomes a public issue rather than a private experience to be coped with by the individual. This is often referred to as the social model of disability and it is this theoretical approach that the authors of this chapter more readily align with.

Vickerman (2007) suggests there are some general guiding principles for including individuals with a disability in sporting activities. These encompass both the philosophy and practice of inclusion and should be considered as central to successful sports coaching. As in the physical education profession, entitlement and accessibility should be important considerations when undertaking a career in sport coaching. In relation to entitlement, the premise is to acknowledge the primary right of individuals to access sport, and this is of particular significance with the arrival of inclusive legislation as illustrated earlier in this chapter.

The concept of accessibility relates to the responsibility of the coach to try to plan strategies to ensure inclusion within a coaching session where possible. This involves coaches adopting flexible approaches to their work, recognising that it is their responsibility to modify and adapt activities. This view draws upon the social model of disability through which society should adapt provision to accommodate individual needs.

It is hoped that sport coaches will adopt a position of inclusive practice within their professional work. For some time now this has been a standard expectation for many professionals working in the school context of physical education and, whilst it has proved challenging, significant progress has been made in this area. As sport coaching moves towards an era of professionalisation, coaches should be prepared to interrogate their practice in order to enhance inclusivity. Whilst sport coaching clearly inhabits a different pedagogic domain, sport coaches and physical education teachers are increasingly occupying similar working environments which cover both school-related work and sport instruction outside of curriculum time. It will be beneficial to both professions if practitioners can have an inclusive attitude relating to individuals who wish to be involved in sport, and there is much to be gained through cooperative understanding and generic working practices. For the sport coach it is hoped that the principle of inclusion should start with the recognition that in most coaching sessions there will be a continuum of participant needs. As such, coaches should work upon the basis of planning for fully inclusive sessions where possible.

Working towards inclusion – theory into practice

In order to assist sport coaches to be inclusive they may wish to adopt a number of strategies which may include the use of specialised intervention approaches highlighted by the 'inclusion spectrum'. The work of Black and Stevenson (2012) identifies a valuable thought process with regards to inclusive practice for individuals with a disability, and indicates methodologies and considerations for a sports coach to consider when embarking upon practical work. This spectrum may assist coaches to adopt a range of strategies such as open, modified, parallel, disability sport and separate activities.

Open activities are where all individuals perform the task in the same way with no or minimal need for alteration. It is potentially good practice to start from the premise of being fully inclusive then work back towards separate activities if required. Modified activities may include changing the size of a court, ball or racquet to aid inclusion. Parallel activities involve streaming groups of performers in terms of abilities so they all may be involved in the same activity but compete at different degrees of complexity in relation to rules or conditions you place on a game. Disability sport activities are where those leading the session may introduce an activity such as Boccia or seated volleyball for all individuals to gain an appreciation of disability-oriented activities. A coach may also ultimately decide that separate activities may be more appropriate at particular points within a session (Vickerman and Hayes, 2012).

In conjunction with knowledge of the inclusive spectrum, the sports coach may wish to consider ways of altering how the activity is delivered to maximise inclusive opportunities. The STEP concept is a helpful set of considerations which coaches may wish to contemplate in order to be more inclusive, as long as the individual and not the activity is placed at the heart of the decision–making process. Figure 5.1 identifies some of the considerations identified by Black and Stevenson (2012).

It is also worth bearing in mind that there may be a need for sport coaches to work with other specialists with regards to intervention when working with individuals in sporting activities. This may involve developing networks of people, for example physiotherapists for movement advice, and/or contact with a disability sport association for links to life-long physical activity.

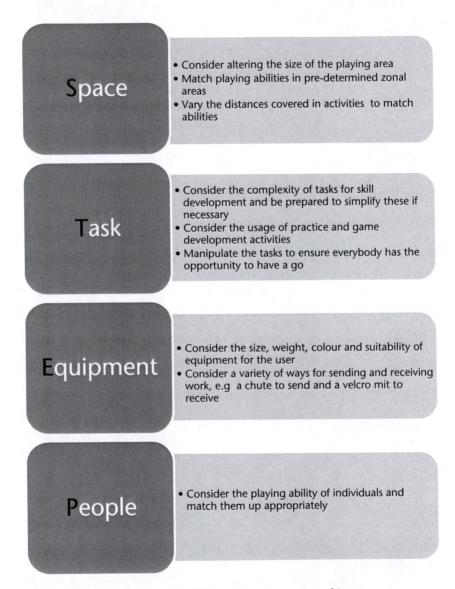

FIGURE 5.1 The STEP process for differentiation in sport coaching

Examples of inclusive practice

When planning inclusive activities for individuals with a disability it is helpful to start from the principle of full inclusion within the activity as indicated by Vickerman and Hayes (2012), and, where this may not be viable, to consider adaptation and/or modification of coaching strategies or activities. An example of this could be in games activities such as basketball, where individuals may require a lighter, larger or different coloured ball in order to access the activity. Variations to rules (modified activities) may need to be contemplated, such as allowing a player with movement restrictions five seconds to receive the ball and execute either a dribble or pass. In addition, if utilising such a strategy, it is vital that all members of the group comprehend the need for such an adjustment in order that they can play to this rule throughout a game. Another illustration of inclusive participation in athletic activities for physically disabled participants who use a wheelchair could include one or two pushes of their wheelchair to represent a jumping action for the long jump rather than a jump into the sandpit. Additionally, if there are individuals with visual impairments coaches can organise activities such as sprinting activities in which a guide runs alongside the participant, as seen at the Glasgow Commonwealth Games 2014.

Opportunities for individuals with disabilities

Coaches should be aware of the structure of sport in the UK when considering opportunities for involvement in sporting activities within society, as this may help to facilitate participation. As outlined by Vickerman and Hayes (2012) there are a number of organisations and initiatives aimed at providing activity for individuals who have a disability, and sport coaches may wish to develop a multidisciplinary approach and work in partnership with such organisations to facilitate participation. Sport England advocates the mainstreaming of disability sport into the work of National Governing Bodies. The English Federation of Disability Sport (EFDS) has aims to: expand sporting opportunities for people with disabilities, increase the numbers actively involved in sport, and work with mainstream governing bodies of sport. EFDS works closely with the National Disability Sports Organisations (NDSOs) recognised by Sport England to develop sporting opportunities for disabled people. In 2011 eight NDSOs were members of EFDS. Each of these organisations provided sporting opportunities for a specific impairment group. The organisations were:

- British Amputee & Les Autres Sports Association
- British Blind Sport
- Cerebral Palsy Sport (CP Sport)
- Dwarf Sports Association
- Special Olympics
- WheelPower – British Wheelchair Sport
- UK Deaf Sport
- Mencap Sport

Local opportunities

There are two key pathways that can be followed by disabled athletes locally: disability-specific sports clubs or mainstream sports clubs. Local authorities should have a sports/leisure development officer who will know where local sports clubs meet and how accessible they are to disabled people. Local authorities also produce directories of sports clubs that provide openings for disabled people. Sports Development Officers (SDOs) can also provide a valuable link between working professionals in the area of sport and the local community. Development work in disability sport is intent on delivering choices for individuals with disabilities, though clearly there is still some way to go before sport achieves total inclusion and mainstreaming of disability sport. It is easy to be critical but it should be recognised that inclusion is a reality and not just a possibility. Positive steps taken in recent international sporting events are strong evidence of this point.

A number of disability-specific activities have been developed over the years to enhance participation levels. These games are: Boccia (a bowls–type game), Table Cricket, Table Hockey, Polybat (an adapted version of table tennis) and Goalball (a game played by visually impaired people). Four of these games have pathways for young people to go on and progress from recreational level through to national, international and Paralympic competition, the exception being Table Hockey.

Although these activities may go some way towards addressing activity levels for people with disabilities, evidence suggests that there are still considerable improvements to be made. Research published by the Department for Work and Pensions indicates that:

> Disabled people remain significantly less likely to participate in cultural, leisure and sporting activities than non-disabled people.
>
> *(Department for Work and Pensions, 2014)*

Opportunities are being created for disabled people to participate either recreationally or competitively in sport. However, it is knowing where and how to access the network of provision available at both local and/or national level that can be problematic. The situation could be improved through a more dynamic, multidisciplinary approach between relevant partners both nationally and regionally, and it is hoped that forward-thinking sport coaches can play a significant role in this area of work.

Reflecting on inclusive practice

This chapter has outlined some of the many issues surrounding gender, SEND and inclusion in coaching. Opportunities for reflection have been permeated through the chapter and it is intended that readers will be able to recall occasions which resonate with some of the sentiments contained within. Readers are now invited to interrogate their *own* practice in response to some of the issues raised in the chapter.

To assist with this process, some pertinent reflective questions are presented that coaches can use to review their work in relation to the propagation of inclusive practice.

REFLECTIVE QUESTIONS

- To what extent are you conversant with the needs of different groups and to what extent are they catered for within coaching sessions?
- Consider your own level of confidence in including different groups within your coaching. Are there any areas for you to address?
- If sessions had broader appeal and more diverse membership, could you cater for all needs?
- What are your coach education needs and to what extent has your education to date fulfilled your needs to build towards inclusive practice?

References

Azzarito, L. (2011) Young people, sporting bodies, vulnerable identities. In Armour, K. (ed.) *Sport Pedagogy: An Introduction for Teaching and Coaching*. Harlow: Pearson.

Azzarito, L. and Katzew, A. (2010) Performing identities in physical education: (en)gendering fluid selves, *Research Quarterly for Exercise and Sport*, 81(1), 25–37.

Black, K. and Stevenson, P. (2012) www.sportdevelopment.info/index.php/browse-all-documents/748-the-inclusion-spectrum (accessed 11 August 2014).

Britton, L. and Casebourne, J. (2002) *Defining Social Inclusion*, Working Brief 136, July 2002, p. 14, www.cesi.org.uk (accessed 20 August 2002).

Cassidy, T., Jones, R. and Potrac, P. (2009) *Understanding Sports Coaching: The Social, Cultural and Pedagogical Foundations of Coaching Practice*, 2nd edition. London: Routledge.

Department for Work and Pensions (2014) www.gov.uk/government/organisations/office-for-disability-issues/about (accessed 11 August 2014).

Equality Act (2010) London: HMSO.

Flintoff, A. and Scratton, S. (2005) Gender and physical education. In Green, K. and Hardman, K. (eds) *Physical Education: Essential Issues*. London: Sage, pp. 161–179.

Garrett, R. (2004) Negotiating a physical identity: girls, bodies and physical education, *Sport, Education and Society*, 9(2), 223–237.

Giuliano, T., Knight, J., Lundquist, J. and Turner, K. (2007) Gender and the selection of public athletic role models, *Journal of Sport Behaviour*, 30(2), 161–198.

Hoey, K. (2001) The Prince Philip Lecture, *The British Journal of Teaching Physical Education*, 32(1), 20–23.

Jones, R.L. (2007) *The Sports Coach as an Educator*. London: Routledge.

Jones, R., Potrac, P., Cushion, C. and Ronglan, T.L. (eds) (2011) *The Sociology of Sport Coaching*. London: Routledge.

Kilty, K. (2006) Women in coaching, *The Sports Psychologist*, 20, 222–234.

LeUnes, A.D. (2008) *Sport Psychology*, 4th edition. New York: Psychology Press.

Meyer, E.J. (2008) A feminist reframing of bullying and harassment: transforming schools through critical pedagogy, *McGill Journal of Education*, 43(1), 33–48.

Navin, A. (2011) *A Reference Guide for Students, Coaches and Competitors*. Marlborough: Crowood Press.

Stidder, G. and Hayes, S. (eds) (2013) *Equity and Inclusion in Physical Education and Sport: Contemporary Issues for Teachers, Trainees and Practitioners*, 2nd edition. London: Routledge.

Svender, J., Larsson, H. and Redelius, K. (2011) Promoting girls' participation in sports: discursive constructions of girls in a sports initiative, *Sport, Education and Society*, 17(4), 463–478.

Vickerman, P. (2007) *Teaching Physical Education to Children with Special Educational Needs.* London: Routledge.

Vickerman, P. and Hayes, S. (2012) Special educational needs and disability in physical education. In Stidder, G. and Hayes, S. (eds) *Equity and Inclusion in Physical Education and Sport: Contemporary Issues for Teachers, Trainees and Practitioners*, 2nd edition. London: Routledge.

Youth Sport Trust (2002) *Building a Brighter Future for Young People through Sport: Annual Review 2001/2002.* Institute of Youth Sport, Loughborough University.

6

HUMANISTIC COACHING

Simon Walters and Lynn Kidman

[The most important thing about sport is] to have fun, it's not if you win or lose. My coach thinks it's if you win or lose, but it's if you have fun.

(Dave aged 10, as cited in Walters *et al.*, 2012a)

[I like sport] when you're all treated fairly and that's what I like about it. Our coach always treats us all fairly.

(Alec aged 9, as cited in Walters, 2011)

Children's construction of organised sport is heavily dependent upon adult influences, with arguably the most significant influence coming from the coach (Lombardo, 1987). To become a humanistic or athlete-centred coach (as noted by Kidman and Lombardo (2010b), the terms are interchangeable), it would seem to be fundamentally important that we consider the needs of athletes themselves. In this chapter, we draw upon the perspectives of three emerging coaches, who reflect upon their experiences of implementing a humanistic approach in their coaching.

Although coaching today encompasses a wide variety of approaches, concerns have been expressed about a traditional leadership style which is outcome-driven, and gives coaches a licence to 'exploit' their power by taking the choice and control away from the athlete (Tofler and Butterbaugh, 2005). There has also been a tendency for coaching to be presented simply as the art of imparting knowledge, with little regard for the significance of the complex human interactions that exist between coaches and athletes (Jones, 2009; Potrac *et al.*, 2000). A humanistic approach to coaching, however, focuses on the whole person and aims to nurture an environment where sport can play a part in enabling young individuals to reach their full potential as human beings (Kidman and Lombardo 2010a). As Lombardo (1987) points out:

> Coaches, as well as athletes, parents, and spectators, have, by and large, simply not paid much attention to humanistic approaches to sport. Humanism is flippantly dismissed as impossible, implausible, or inappropriate in terms of the current, real world (i.e. the professional model) of sport. Organized sport often encourages mindless conformism and a sense of pessimism related to the possibilities for (creative) play in the sport setting.
>
> *(18)*

Lombardo suggests that an athlete's experience in sport is about being authentic, true to oneself, human in every way. In practice, this means coaches need to understand and care about what their athletes want and need, which will promote athletes' sense of self-fulfilment and ultimately encourage that 'ah ha' moment that enhances learning and performance. The key features of humanistic coaching are understanding:

1. self (self-awareness)
2. the athletes (psychosocially, cognitively, physically, spiritually, emotionally)
3. that sport has educational intent
4. that if athletes gain and take ownership of knowledge, development and decision making that will help them to maximise their performance and their enjoyment.

What young athletes say they expect from sport has been documented as far back as the 1970s, when interviews conducted by Orlick and Botterill (1975) found that children and youths play sport primarily for excitement, enjoyment and fun. It is important to acknowledge that the concept of 'fun' is complex and can mean different things to different people, and children have indicated that the opportunities for competition offered by sport are also a key source of their enjoyment (Light and Curry, 2009). Light and Curry contend that there has been a tendency to be over-critical of the notion of competition, but what consistently emerges from studies is that an over-emphasis on winning adversely impacts children's enjoyment (Conroy and Coatsworth, 2007; Keegan *et al.*, 2009; Walters *et al.*, 2012a). In these studies, sport was found to be more enjoyable for children when the coaching environment was supportive, learning activities were age-appropriate and when achievable goals were set. However, as can be seen from 10-year-old Dave's comment in the first vignette, what athletes actually want from sport can often clash with their coaches' expectations (see Chapter 2 of this book).

Preparing our coaches

At Auckland University of Technology (AUT), through our sports coaching major, we aspire to meet the philosophy of the New Zealand Coach Development Framework (CDF) (Sport New Zealand, 2011), which according to Penney (2008) is informed by practices indicative of current research and understanding of how people learn. In New Zealand, coach development has moved from an accredited and certified, standardised programme approach to an on-going professional development process informed by a humanistic, athlete-centred coaching philosophy (Cassidy and Kidman, 2010). This process acknowledges that learning is non-linear and complex, and is not confined to formal institutions or situations (Light and Dixon, 2007). Some key principles underpinning the CDF are:

- Ownership – coach development will be owned by coaches and those responsible for supporting coaches.
- Holistic – coach development programmes will equip coaches to support the holistic development of their athletes to produce self-reliant athletes.
- Continuous improvement – the framework will enable and encourage coaches to participate in ongoing development opportunities.

(Sport New Zealand, 2011)

In our sport coaching major, through a student-centred learning approach, we promote and practise this philosophy. In their first year, students are introduced to theoretical principles of coaching. Over the next three years, these students are encouraged to engage with theory in an applied setting, develop their own coaching philosophy, engage in an ongoing process of critical self-reflection and analyse their own and their peers' coaching practice. As educators, we aim to facilitate an environment that enables all our students to be humanistic coaches who understand their athletes, focus on enhancing athlete self-awareness, and nurture the holistic growth and development of the individual (Kidman and Lombardo, 2010b; Lombardo, 2001; Cassidy *et al.*, 2009). Our coaches have a purpose of helping the athletes perform not only to the best of their ability, but to also develop as human beings. For example, in their final year, our students coach a team or an individual athlete, and conduct a holistic needs analysis of athlete needs. The focus of the analysis is moved away from the physical needs of the athlete, to try and encourage our students to become more aware of the athlete as a human being, to get to know them better as people, to find out what they want from sport and life in general, and to move away from simply viewing their athletes as performers.

From our observations, students embrace this philosophy to varying degrees. Using Mosston's spectrum of teaching styles (Mosston and Ashworth, 1994)[1] as a reference point, on enrolment the vast majority of our students would appear to have been exposed predominantly to a command style of coaching. Over the course of the next three years all students move some way along the teaching style continuum toward a more learner-led approach but it is probably fair to say that only a few fully embrace a humanistic coaching philosophy. Final-year classroom conversations reveal that what these few athlete-centred coaches find most difficult is putting theory into practice. This chapter focuses on the successes and challenges experienced by three recent coaching graduates and draws upon their perspectives to help other new coaches to become successful humanistic coaches.

Our graduates and their initial experiences of humanistic coaching

We deliberately selected three coaching graduates to interview (Ignacio Arellano, Lawrence Njenga and Nic Downes[2]), due to their passion for coaching and their commitment to putting athlete-centred, humanistic coaching philosophy into practice. The purpose of the interviews was to gather information about their experiences when trying to implement a humanistic approach in the very traditional environments we are aware these students work within. They are all actively coaching in their respective sports, predominantly at junior (ages 6 to 13 years) and youth (ages 14 to 19 years) level, and are also currently working in coach development environments involved in the delivery of coach education programmes.

In our initial question we attempted to gain an understanding of the processes they went through to fully appreciate what is actually meant by 'athlete-centred, humanistic coaching':

> *Ignacio:* It is really easy to jump immediately into what the book says, the standard definition. But you first need to learn how you see things yourself before you as a coach can create the conditions to empower athletes to actually achieve what they want to achieve. It is quite hard … in the first year, we started talking about the term 'athlete-centred', the concept and it didn't really make any sense. In the second year, you start developing the contextual situation and you go out and actually start coaching. So you start learning from those experiences and then through the whole reflection thing, it starts to make sense.

> *Lawrence:* I came into university thinking I had athlete-centred coaching experience from the coaching I had done within my sport. They push the athlete-centred philosophy, but it is just words. They encourage you to ask athletes questions, but I didn't really understand what I was trying to do. I was not really trying to get 'into' an athlete. All athlete-centred coaching meant to me when I came into university, was simply asking questions and using more games than drills, but it wasn't until I got to the third year I started to realise that it wasn't just about asking questions, it was about understanding yourself and then the athlete, and why they are the way they are and then how you can help them improve.

The assignments throughout the coaching major revolve around self-reflection. As has been found in research into the use of reflection in developing coaches (Cassidy et al., 2009; Dixon et al., 2013; Kidman and Lombardo, 2010b; see Chapter 1 of this book), self-reflection plays an important role in enabling coaches to become more humanistic. Each coach should take responsibility for evaluating the way he or she coaches, the way the athletes respond and the general team environment. As Ignacio and Lawrence highlight:

Ignacio: In my case, I didn't really understand why I was doing this whole reflection thing. But when we jump to the third year, somehow things are starting to make sense as you realise that you may go against what the establishment [traditional coaching environments] tells you how to coach, or how parents want their children to be coached. So theory started to make sense. In my case, I started reflecting on all my experiences, what happened to me when I was playing, how I started coaching, or doing my degree, what I had seen, and then that started making sense. It means that you are now confident about how you see the world, about the coaching philosophy and it is only then, that you can translate that into your actions. It is a really emotionally demanding experience, because you are technically going against how many people think you should coach. But when you create that self-confidence, that resilience, that internal personal character, and you actually believe that this is the way to go, that is when things start to make sense.

Lawrence: Reflection is important in our second year, in every session and every game: What did I do? What could I have done better? By the middle of the season, I was just doing it automatically, it became real, not just for an assessment. All of a sudden, I am going a bit deeper than just the context of the game, and at the end of the season looking back, I thought, oh, we just managed to get the focus of the players away from the score board to their individual goals.

These comments highlight some difficulties we face as educators. For the first two years of their education, these students tend not to see the relevance of becoming more self-aware, of engaging in the self-reflection process. It is only towards the end of their second year, or even as they move into their final year, that the theory becomes 'real' for them and they are enabled to apply it in practice. It is this increasing self-awareness, however, that gives them the strength to deal with the challenges they face when working in traditional outcome-focused environments.

Challenges of being athlete-centred

The reflection of these graduates highlighted some challenges about moving from the more commonly accepted 'traditional' coaching approach to a more humanistic approach. We often hear comments from our students that using this humanistic approach is not generally accepted by what Ignacio (and later Lawrence) refer to as the 'establishment': the parents, other coaches and administrators. As a result, students can find it difficult to have the faith and confidence to implement such an 'alternative' approach, where the focus is more on athlete learning and holistic growth than on outcomes:

Nic: It's really hard to be an athlete-centred coach. It's easy and it's safe to be command centred, and to make your session look organised. I know some of my sessions probably look terrible and parents will be thinking this is just chaos. And maybe that's because I have tried something new, experimenting with the guided direction philosophy and maybe gone too far and it's just a mess. So you are scared to try it again.

My first real season trying to be athlete-centred – there was one parent in particular at all the games. On game day I would let them warm up and they would do their activities and I would let them play – didn't do a lot of yelling from the sideline, and then at half time I would ask them what have we done well, what can we improve? Let them set the direction. One game, my wife was watching and this guy did not know who she was. She was just standing in the background. She said she heard him talking to another parent and he said that he thinks 'Nic is doing really well at motivating the players, but what we really need is a football coach, somebody who really knows what they are doing and knows about football'. When she told me that, it really hurt. I know football, but that athlete-centred style of coaching for him showed him that I did not really know what I was doing – so that hurt a lot. You have to really believe in what you are doing and just keep going. I saw some good results and even if the parents don't see it I am seeing it, and that keeps me going.

It is not only parents and administrators that are resistant to an alternative approach. Players themselves can also take time to adapt, as many are not used to being able to have choice and the freedom to solve problems for themselves in sport:

> *Nic:* There are challenges also with athletes at first in getting them used to the style. They really struggle with doing things for themselves, don't want to answer questions, and are used to being told what to do. That can be awkward for new coaches. You have to let the athletes come to a place where they know they are safe to be able to work something out for themselves and know that it is okay for them to ask questions.

It can clearly be extremely challenging for new coaches to introduce new ideas into traditional coaching environments. However, some resistance faced by our students can be excessive and highlights how seriously children's sport can be taken:

> *Lawrence:* You get a lot of resistance from the establishment and from people who just think this is different. I was coaching a representative Under-12 weight restricted (under 55 kg) team. We actually got physically threatened by two parents after we lost a game. These were ex-international players! It was absolutely unbelievable. The children were supportive and for us it was about the individual players. These parents couldn't see that. For them it was 'physically train them harder, make them run, make them do these drills'. We said that is not the way we want this team to be, it's about development, it's about these players in another few years, not just now. You get a lot of resistance. Some parents didn't like the way we coached and even came up to us with coaching plans they had written.

These types of extreme situations, unfortunately, are not uncommon for our students. At junior and youth levels, winning has become imperative for many parents and coaches. The construction of sport, as a consequence, moves from a developmental one to be predominantly outcome focused. Although there has been some criticism of the one-dimensional and linear nature of athlete development models (for examples see Ford *et al.*, 2011 and Light *et al.*, 2013), the developmental literature and models that exist are consistent in the assertion that the sporting environment for the age group Lawrence was working with (boys under 12 years of age), should be focused less on winning and more on athlete development (Balyi and Hamilton, 2004; Fraser-Thomas *et al.*, 2005).

Simon and Lynn reflect

What we have witnessed is how hard it can be for our students to introduce new ideas into their coaching environment. This is especially true when this approach challenges long-held traditional beliefs about the role of sport and coaching practice. In class discussion, this issue is constantly raised by students, and it is reinforced that they should not be over-zealous in their approach, especially when working in non-supportive environments. We recommend that they gradually introduce ideas for parents, or other coaches to consider, rather than telling people that this is the best way. These student vignettes show how strong our students have to be. It is our role and responsibility as educators to ensure we prepare our students to be able to face and deal with these challenges. All coaching texts talk about the importance of having your own coaching philosophy. This is fundamentally important for any new coach, especially when working in a challenging environment. It is what sustains you. Rather than simply teaching the theory and providing opportunities to reflect and practice, coaching educators need to include the development of skills such as resilience and conflict resolution to better equip our future coaches for their 'real world' experiences. To heighten their awareness of how to resolve and deal with some of these 'real world' experiences, our third-year students present to their peers examples of problems they have faced when coaching in the form of case studies. The group then debates, critiques and formulates strategies that can prepare them to be better equipped to deal with similar issues or challenges when they arise again.

Cultural and societal expectations

Rather than simply looking at the practice of coaching in isolation from broader influences, our students also reflected upon societal forces that may impact upon the development of coaching in the Western World:

> *Ignacio:* I think if you look back at the history of Western education, we have moved away from the focus on moral or character development, that humanistic approach. Somewhere along the way we have lost the ability to wonder about things and to be curious. We have this very linear, structured education

system, and you are told this is what you are supposed to know, this is how it works, so you need to do all these courses. It should be more about, how can we do this, how can we do things differently, what happens if things change? When you have this ability to wonder, in terms of coaching, you start realising that it is not just about learning the game, it's about the person. It's about getting them to think for themselves but that is quite difficult to achieve, but when you can create that environment, learning starts to happen. But when you start getting into it, going deeper and deeper and you start believing in what you do, you start making sense of why you do what you do, the benefits are greater, more effective and more meaningful in the long term. It is you changing and then helping other people change which is difficult. That is why it is so easy to revert to the traditional model of coaching.

Lawrence: In my opinion our society and our education system is very performance based. There are certificates for everything. If you do anything, you get a certificate. I can see what they are trying to do and encourage people, but it becomes more performance based. At the end of the day, everyone gets really conditioned to expect something.

Lawrence's feelings that we live in a rewards-based society were reinforced by Ignacio's experiences when implementing a new coach programme at a local school:

Ignacio: There is a difference between education and learning. I am seeing this in the work I do in the 'Growing Coaches programme'.[3] There is a difference between the traditional top-down education system, where the teacher tells you what to do, you work hard, you get a certificate. But are you learning? What is learning, what sort of things should you be focused on when it comes to learning? It may be informal, it may be through experiences, your ideas.

I am trying to target our 16- to 18-year-olds as new coaches. It was suggested to me that we should give these coaches NCEA[4] credits, which then means they have to be assessed. However, I said do you think that the students will like to be in a situation where they are going to be academically assessed? These children do this because they want to coach. The programme is structured in such a way that the workshop at the moment is really informal, you just need to attend and participate. We run role playing activities, good coach–bad coach, and we get them to talk about their experiences, and they design activities and coach each other. We then reflect afterwards, identify what was good, what was bad, what do you feel about the experience and we start raising awareness. That is what learning is about. There is no assessment. Why would you want to do that? It's supposed to be fun, and interesting. So, I think the school agreed with me.

The students here are critical of a society that is rewards based. In educational environments (including the sport industry), a structured, linear accreditation system is seen to stifle learning, creativity and imagination (Robinson, 2003). For us as educators, these comments gave us cause to reflect on the delivery of our own coaching major. We expect our students to develop a love for learning, a thirst for knowledge, and to be creative in their coaching. However, we attempt to do this constrained within what our students perceive as a traditional 'Western education, performance based' model of teaching and learning.

Meeting the challenges

Some of the scenarios relayed by our students reflected extremely challenging environments. In employing strategies discussed at university, Lawrence attempted to inform his team's parents about his coaching philosophy, to give them a chance to understand why his focus was more on the longer-term goal of athlete development rather than the shorter-term goal of having to win each and every game. In doing so, Lawrence emphasised that he was not saying that winning was not important, rather that evidence suggests that athlete learning, growth and development should be the foremost purpose of youth sport (Walters, 2011):

> *Lawrence:* After the initial selection of our Under-12 weight restricted (under 55 kg) representative team we had three meetings. We had an initial meeting with players and parents. We outlined our approach and talked about our athlete-centred coaching philosophy. We had a couple more meetings and there were a few parents who were really unhappy that we did not include strong overweight players in the team.[5] In previous seasons overweight players had been selected and put on diets and had saunas before weigh-ins to get their weight down. But overall, in that first meeting there was no resistance to our philosophy. But as soon as training started, we started noticing opposition from parents trying to interfere. They wanted us to do mainly fitness with them. That's when we called another meeting and restated our philosophy and our approach and that we wouldn't have the kids just running laps. We said 'Please let us do the job we have been appointed to do. This is actually not just for this year, we want them to play rugby even 5 or 6 years from now and be really good players, and grow from this experience'. After a couple of days, it still went on. Finally, the last meeting was to ask the parents not to come to training. We said we know you have to wait for your kids for training, but from now on it is going to be closed training. The Union was supportive of us and backed us up, even when one of the parents arranged a petition to get us removed, and in spite of the opposition we were offered the job again this year.

> *Nic:* I've talked to a few parents and tried to tell them what I am doing and this is my philosophy and this is the philosophy of the organisation and that I am trying to get the kids to engage to learn for themselves. Some are into it and some aren't. I recently had a parent who kept asking me every session

'When are we doing some REAL training?' I tell him it's the philosophy of this programme. He has stopped asking now – I am not sure if he has given up – he keeps sending his kids back. For me the most important thing is the environment. I am pretty much free to do what I want, my boss knows what I do and he is supportive and lets me get on with it ... This has been fantastic for my growth and development ... I also coach 13- and 14-year-old teams at school and they are seen as pathway teams so there is no real expectation about winning and therefore no pressure – yet. I think the environment can create the pressure. There is a lot of pressure around school 1st XI and I can imagine there being questions asked if you weren't getting results.

Although the organisations Nic (football) and Lawrence (rugby) were working for were supportive of their coaching approach and philosophy, they acknowledge that the immediate club or school environment can create significant pressure on coaches to achieve short-term results (this relates to the practice-conflict coach dilemmas discussed in Chapter 2). From our perspective, although difficult, there is a lot more work that the National and Regional Sporting organisations, and schools, need to do to create a safer coaching environment, both emotionally and physically, for young coaches. With reference to Lawrence's experience, it is disappointing but not surprising that a representative Under-12 tournament engendered the over-competitive behaviours that contrast with the developmental approach that he wishes to foster. One might question the wisdom of organising such competitions with young age groups.

Children's experiences

Parents clearly struggle with coming to terms with a new approach which may challenge what they traditionally perceive as the correct way to coach. However, in Ignacio's team, the children themselves started to enjoy this style of coaching and the parents started to be more receptive. Ultimately, however, although the parents' reactions indicated they were appreciative of the learning environment, in the end the over-riding focus for some was still related to winning:

> *Ignacio:* At first, the children, they enjoy it, they have fun, but they felt a little bit challenged from time to time because they realised that they had the chance to have a say. So at the beginning, it was interesting, the relationships and the foundations that we laid, like this is us, this is how we coach. Don't expect us to tell you what to do all the time. They found it challenging, they found it different. But some of them realised it was cool. But the thing is the team started doing really well. The parents were happy, they saw that their children were happy, and saw that 'wow, this new way of coaching works'. Traditionally this team had not done very well. We came to the end of the season undefeated. The parents realised that their children were actually learning. For us the important thing was the learning, but some of the parents

although they saw the learning, really liked the winning. The next year, we started losing some games and some parents started questioning and challenging this approach: 'Too many questions', 'This doesn't work', 'You need to go hard and get the best players'.

Advice for developing coaches

Our three students have clearly engaged in some in-depth, soul searching processes over their three years of studying. We asked what advice they might be able to offer new coaches:

Nic: If something does not work – keep trying. I really believe in the philosophy, especially working with the younger kids and you see how much fun they are having. I really enjoy it. I have been four terms on this programme and seeing the kids so much better at the end than when they started is great. It's really hard at the start but you just have to keep on trying.

Ignacio: Don't take the easy way out when the going gets tough. It's quite daunting, quite challenging. But at the end of the day, you need to create, facilitate an experience that cares for all these athletes. For me, that means focusing on the intangibles. I guess in a humanistic way, they are those things that you can't see but are aware of because your athlete tells you something, or you observe how he expresses himself in training. You have to have the internal belief that what you are doing is for a reason, even if it goes against the status quo. The process of reflection is crucial to actually understand and make sense about all these concepts. You have to take an integrated approach. By integrated I mean you cannot charge in like a bull and say this is the way to do things, because that doesn't work. You need to say that this is what I am proposing and I am more than happy to share what I know, I am inviting you to relook at how you do things. And you have to do it in a systematic way, it has to be done on an ongoing basis and you need to show you care. It doesn't happen straight away. It is very complicated telling parents, other coaches, and administrators that it is not about what happens now. Obviously I care what happens now, but the important thing is that in two or three years' time, we are creating a foundation for you the player, not to win a championship, but so you can be a champion. We are trying to create the conditions or the experience so you become independent, become aware, become resilient. We want you to be able to cope not because someone instructed you or directed you, but under your own terms.

Lawrence: In society today, there is that element of wanting to do something on your own for the love of doing it. For kids, a lot of that has been taken away. Kids are driven everywhere to do dancing, soccer, judo, whatever, but half of those things, they really don't want to do. It's the parents putting them in. So, what us as athlete-centred coaches can try to bring back, is nurturing that element of love in what you do and give the athlete the freedom to do what they would really like to do and enjoy it while they are doing it.

Simon and Lynn: summative reflections

New coaches have to go through a process of understanding themselves before they can become humanistic coaches (Humm, 2010). They need time, time to practise, and time to reflect on their practice. These students went through a process of increasing their self-awareness, to gain a better understanding of how they see the world, before they could truly be athlete-centred. Becoming a humanistic coach is not easy. It involves a strong belief in what one is doing. To get there, coaches need to engage in considerable critical self-reflection (Dixon *et al.*, 2013), and be prepared to experiment and make mistakes in often very unsupportive environments.

As coach educators we also need to be student-centred in our practice. We need to focus less on the transmission of knowledge, and more on creating an environment that enables students to learn more about themselves, and to develop their own philosophy. It is this philosophy which will underpin their practice and give them the strength to be resilient in the face of adversity.

Ultimately, the environment tends to be the key driver of the more inappropriate coaching and parental behaviours witnessed in sport (Walters *et al.*, 2012b). A number of sporting organisations in New Zealand now espouse guidelines and run courses for coaches that are underpinned by an athlete-centred philosophy. What these organisations need to do is to go beyond words, and facilitate a sporting environment that has an over-riding focus on longer-term athlete development and caters to the needs of athletes. The debate about the relative emphasis on winning or development tends to polarise views about a humanistic coaching approach, but it needs to occur as it goes to the heart of the issue. What provides us with cause for optimism is witnessing the work of passionate coaches like Ignacio, Lawrence and Nic. In spite of the challenging environments they sometimes operate within, they demonstrate the strength of character to stay true to their philosophies and, by doing so, effect real change.

Notes

1 The spectrum of teaching styles shifts through 11 teaching styles, from absolute control (command style) to facilitating complete freedom in learning for the student (self-teaching style).
2 The graduates opted to have their names used in this chapter.
3 Growing Coaches is a Sport NZ coach education programme for secondary school students.
4 The National Certificate of Educational Assessment which is used in New Zealand schools.
5 In New Zealand, junior rugby has strict guidelines relating to age and weight, to try to ensure that children play against other children of a similar age and size. For more specific information see North Harbour Rugby (2013).

References

Balyi, I. and Hamilton, A. (2004) *Long-Term Athlete Development: Trainability in childhood and adolescence.* Victoria, BC: National Coaching Institute British Columbia and Advanced Training and Performance Ltd.

Cassidy, T., Jones, R.L. and Potrac, P. (2009) *Understanding Sports Coaching: The social, cultural and pedagogical foundations of coaching practice.* London: Routledge.

Cassidy, T. and Kidman, L. (2010) Initiating a national coaching curriculum: A paradigmatic shift? *Physical Education and Sport Pedagogy* 15(3), 307–322.

Conroy, D.E. and Coatsworth, J.D. (2007) Assessing autonomy-supportive coaching strategies in youth sport. *Psychology of Sport and Exercise* [Online] 8. doi:10.1016/j.psychsport.2006.12.001.

Dixon, M., Lee, S. and Ghaye, T. (2013) Reflective practices for better sports coaches and coach education: Shifting from a pedagogy of scarcity to abundance in the run-up to Rio 2016. *Reflective Practice* 14(5), 585–599.

Ford, P., De Ste Croix, M., Lloyd, R., Meyers, R., Moosavi, M., Oliver, J., Till, K. and Williams, C. (2011) The long-term athlete development model: Physiological evidence and application. *Journal of Sports Sciences* [Online] 29: doi:10.1080/02640414.2010.536849.

Fraser-Thomas, J.L., Côté, J. and Deakin, J. (2005) Youth sport programs: An avenue to foster positive youth development. *Physical Education and Sport Pedagogy* 10(1), 19–40.

Humm, R. (2010) How's your coaching? In L. Kidman and B.J. Lombardo (Eds) *Athlete-centred Coaching: Developing decision makers.* Worcester: IPC Resources. pp. 256–275.

Jones, R.L. (2009) Coaching as caring (the smiling gallery): Accessing hidden knowledge. *Physical Education and Sport Pedagogy* [Online] 14. doi:10.1080/17408980801976551.

Keegan, R. J., Harwood, C.G., Spray, C.M. and Lavallee, D.E. (2009) A qualitative investigation exploring the motivational climate in early career sports participants: Coach, parent and peer influences on sport motivation. *Psychology of Sport and Exercise* [Online] 10. doi:10.1016/j.psychsport.2008.12.003.

Kidman, L. and Lombardo, B.J. (Eds) (2010a) *Athlete-centred Coaching: Developing decision makers.* 2nd edn. Worcester: IPC Resources.

Kidman, L. and Lombardo, B.J. (2010b) TGfU and humanistic coaching. In J.I. Butler and L.L. Griffin (Eds) *Teaching Games for Understanding: Moving globally.* Champaign: Human Kinetics. pp. 171–186.

Light, R. and Dixon, M.A. (2007) Contemporary developments in sport pedagogy and their implications for sport management education. *Sport Management Review* 10, 159–175.

Light, R. and Curry, C. (2009) Children's reasons for joining sport clubs and staying with them. A case study of a Sydney soccer club. *Healthy Lifestyle Journal* 56, 23–27.

Light, R.L., Harvey, S. and Memmert, D. (2013) Why children join and stay in sports clubs: Case studies in Australian, French and German swimming clubs. *Sport, Education and Society* [Online] 18, doi:10.1080/13573322.2011.594431.

Lombardo, B.J. (1987) *The Humanistic Coach: From theory to practice.* Springfield: Charles C. Thomas.

Lombardo, B.J. (2001) Humanistic coaching: A model for the new century. In B.J. Lombardo, T.J. Caravella-Nadeau, K.S. Castagono and V.H. Mancini (Eds) *Sport in the Twenty First Century: Alternatives for the new millennium.* Boston: Pearson. pp. 3–10.

Mosston, M. and Ashworth, S. (1994) *Teaching Physical Education.* 4th edn. Columbus: Merrill Publishing Company.

North Harbour Rugby (2013) *North Harbour Junior Club Rugby* [Online]. Available at: http://www.harbourrugby.co.nz/media/files/2015 Junior Club Rugby Rules.pdf [accessed: 14 March 2014].

Orlick, T. D. and Botterill, C. (1975) *Every Kid Can Win*. Chicago: Nelson-Hall.

Penney, D. (2008) *Curriculum as a Key Concept for Coaching*. Symposium conducted at the meeting of the Korean Coaching Development Center 10th anniversary global conference and International Council for Coach Education Asian Regional Coach conference, Hoseo University, Asan, South Korea.

Potrac, P., Brewer, C., Jones, R., Armour, K. and Hoff, J. (2000) Toward an holistic understanding of the coaching process. *Quest* 52, 186–199.

Robinson, K. (2003) Mind the gap: The creativity conundrum. *Critical Quarterly* 43(1), 41–45.

Sport New Zealand (2011) *Coach Development Framework* [Online]. Available at: http://www.sportnz.org.nz/Documents/Communities and Clubs/Coaching/coach-dev-framework.pdf [accessed: 14 March 2014].

Tofler, I.R. and Butterbaugh, G.J. (2005) Developmental overview of child and youth sports for the twenty-first century. *Clinics in Sports Medicine* [Online] 24. doi:10.1016/j.csm.2005.05.006.

Walters, S.R. (2011) 'Whose game are we playing? A study of the effects of adult involvement on children participating in organised team sports'. Unpublished doctoral thesis. AUT University, Auckland.

Walters, S.R., Payne, D., Schluter, P.J. and Thomson, R.W. (2012a) 'It just makes you feel invincible': A Foucauldian analysis of children's experiences of organised team sports. *Sport and Education in Society* [Online] doi:10.1080/13573322.2012.745844.

Walters, S.R., Schluter, P.J., Oldham, A.R.H., Thomson, R.W. and Payne, D. (2012b) The sideline behaviour of coaches at children's team sports games. *Psychology of Sport and Exercise* [Online] 13. doi:10.1016/j.psychsport.2011.11.008.

7

COACHING FOR UNDERSTANDING

Steve Mitchell and Adriano de Souza

The concept of 'Coaching for Understanding' derives from an approach to games teaching in physical education (PE) that became known as Teaching Games for Understanding (TGfU). This approach was conceptualized in 1982 at Loughborough University in the UK by David Bunker and Rod Thorpe who, in visiting schools and observing games lessons, saw instruction that was ineffective in developing game performance in children. Bunker and Thorpe (1982) believed that they were observing games instruction that had the following results: (1) a large percentage of children achieving little success due to the emphasis on performance, (2) the majority of school leavers 'knowing' very little about games, (3) the production of supposedly 'skilful' players who in fact possess inflexible techniques and poor decision-making capacity, (4) the development of teacher/coach-dependent performers, and (5) the failure to develop 'thinking' spectators and 'knowing' administrators at a time when games (and sport) were an important form of entertainment in the leisure industry.

What became TGfU has been used widely in PE and PE teacher education (Metzler, 2011; Mitchell *et al.*, 2013) but it has had limited impact on coaching and coach education in sport. Proponents of using TGfU in coaching aim to develop thinking players who are autonomous, rather than coach-dependent, in relation to their decision-making. This chapter will explain the conceptual development of the model, highlighting its strengths and limitations, and offer some applied examples of and personal reflections on its use in coaching different type of games, namely soccer and volleyball.

Teaching Games for Understanding: the conceptual model

Arguing for a different approach to teaching games, Bunker and Thorpe (1982) first proposed the instructional model in a physical education context which we know

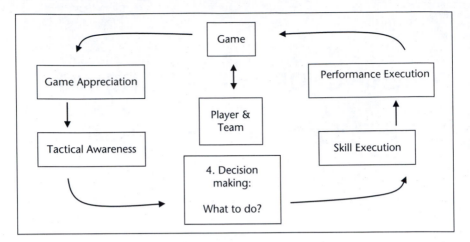

FIGURE 7.1 TGfU model (adapted from Bunker and Thorpe, 1982)

as Teaching Games for Understanding (see Figure 7.1). Its emphasis was on learning game principles in order to understand the tactical strategies most likely to lead to success. They argued that this approach would benefit the students because: (1) students would develop game awareness and become better decision-makers, (2) students would engage more in game play because they would understand more about the game, (3) students would attach greater value to skill development after they saw the need in real game situations, and (4) students would become more informed consumers of games.

Traditional coaching approaches, based largely on technical proficiency of players, are viewed critically by advocates of TGfU who have specific concerns related to the following limitations:

1. The widespread use of drills to teach sports techniques outside of game context.
2. The high amount of time dedicated to trying to teach skills outside of game context.
3. The low amount of time dedicated to developing game skills, and tactical and strategic knowledge within game context.
4. The low amount of time dedicated to teaching and developing game knowledge (tactics and strategies).
5. The development of a large proportion of players who believe that for one to know and perform the skills in a game is sufficient competence to be a successful player.
6. The development of a large percentage of intermediate- to high-level players with limited ability to tactically problem-solve and adapt to situations without the coaches' help. These players are too dependent on the coaches.
7. The development of a large number of players who cannot make fast and effective tactical and strategic changes during games.

8. The problem-solving actions are centralized with the coach, thereby not giving players opportunities to develop game knowledge.
9. The demand placed on players by coaches to show creativity during matches in comparison to the few opportunities available to those players to develop game play creativity in practice time.
10. A lack of player reflection on personal and team performance.

Coaches who use a traditional approach to coaching can rapidly take away a player's ability to make their own choices, replacing this with the 'coach's choice' when there is a need to fix a practice/game situation by making a tactical or strategic adjustment. Within this approach the coach retains the decision-making and problem-solving power in their own hands. Typically, such coaches are quick to criticize their players for a lack of creativity when it comes to making tactical or strategic changes, creating ways to score or preventing their opponents from scoring. However, they fail to acknowledge that they rarely allow their players to think for themselves and learn how to make effective choices in practices or game environments. Creativity is more likely to take place when the coach empowers athletes to solve their own problems (Ross and Haskins, 2013) than when coaches adopt the technical rationality approach of providing a 'definitive' answer and not considering that there may be numerous ways of outwitting an opponent.

Children and teenagers who play informal games in the park, street or backyard serve as examples of how to reflect on performance, as they often informally talk with peers about their performance, whether they win or lose, when the games are over. This informal game play environment will give them the opportunity to develop their creativity, knowledge of tactics and strategies, and will help them to gain appreciation of the game and game needs. This natural learning environment is in contrast to reductionist, over-coaching practices. Coaching for Understanding exemplifies this empowering approach.

Coaching for Understanding (CFU): TGfU as a contemporary coaching approach

TGfU has been applied to coaching in New Zealand and Australia as 'Game Sense' (Chen and Light, 2006; Evans, 2006), and in the USA, Canada and parts of Asia, sometimes under the name of 'Tactical Games Teaching' (Mitchell *et al.*, 2013). In Portugal the book *Jogos Desportivos Coletivos* (Graca and Oliveira, 1998) offers ideas for teaching games with the players as a central part of the process and emphasizes how important it is to allow players to play games in the early game learning/development process. *Jogo Possivel* (Paes, 2001) uses similar ideas in Brazil. Irrespective of the name attached to the instructional model, these approaches share the principle of the player being at the centre of the learning and development process, allowing them to participate actively in problem-solving and decision-making (Mitchell, 2005). For the purposes of this chapter we will use the term 'Coaching for Understanding (CFU)'.

Within a CFU approach, coaches design practices and modified games in order to present problems for players, allowing them time to problem-solve and make their own choices prior to finding a solution. This allocation of thinking time allows coaches to evaluate the players' abilities to make different choices and adjustments in order to achieve success. Indeed, the differences between TGfU for teaching and CFU for coaching stem from the demands of competitiveness and fast adaptation. The nature of playing to achieve success in competitive sport demands faster assessment of game needs (offensive or defensive), faster adaptation, therefore faster player-to-player, player-to-coach, and coach-to-player interactions. Inside this environment, coaches will use the same question-driven approach as PE teachers but with greater demands regarding players' psychomotor and cognitive responses. In particular, in a competitive sport environment, game assessment is constant. Players and coaches go through performance evaluation and make tactical adjustments during game play. In CFU practice settings players are encouraged to stop practices or matches as soon as they see the level of performance is not what they want it to be. If they do not stop, then coaches may need to start to mediate. General questions for players to address include:

1. Is our decision-making effective? Are we making the right choices with the ball? If not, how can it be better?
2. Are 'off-the-ball' adjustments necessary, either offensively or defensively? If so, what are the necessary adjustments?
3. Are 'on-the-ball' adjustments necessary offensively? If so, what are the necessary adjustments?
4. Is our 'transition' play effective? Do we move effectively from defence to offence and offence to defence? If not, how can it be improved?

The above questions are critical for players to ask themselves because the answers to these questions go to the core of successful individual and team performance. CFU coaches then set about trying to create practice situations where players have the autonomy to find the answers. In particular a CFU coach develops practices with the following characteristics:

- Coaches become more intentional observers. After presenting the task and goals of the practice or conditioned game, coaches become observers, not quiet observers but they hold quick feedback segments allowing time for players to take time outs in search of creating solutions to the task or problem presented.
- Coaches encourage players to be responsible. Coaches build opportunities for players to evaluate the quality of the game or practice and opportunities for players to 'make it better'.
- The use of time outs by players. Players are responsible and encouraged to use time outs and stop practice if they see the level of performance is not reaching the efficiency they want it to have. Coaches and players become partners in search of improvement in performance.

- The use of guiding questions. Practices are guided by simple guiding questions (such as those presented on page 100) that soon become part of the players' ongoing thought process.
- Decision-making has a higher priority in assessment. Choices guide on and off the ball skill selection and performance assessment. A CFU coach is always assessing how fast her/his players adapt to game needs. A CFU practice environment demands increasingly and progressively faster assessment of game needs, faster search for solutions and faster communication with teammates (if in a team sport).

To illustrate a CFU approach, in the following section of the chapter we provide two examples, first in soccer and then in volleyball.

A CFU example in soccer: coaching the concepts of possession and penetration

Soccer coaching takes a variety of forms, but national governing bodies, including the Football Association (England) (www.thefa.com/my-football/coach) and the United States Soccer Federation (www.ussoccer.com/coaching-education), have increasingly moved towards what might best be considered 'game-based' coaching approaches where the focus is on decision-making and off-the-ball movement as well as on the teaching of technique. What follows is an example of coaching the understanding of the concepts of ball possession and penetration. This example is most appropriate for players of 14 or above (depending on their technical level), playing at least in 8v8 situations where the field is of sufficient size to warrant longer passing and with enough space for through balls to be played in between defenders. Figure 7.2 outlines the games used to teach these concepts, along with the tactical and technical foci for each game. Description of these game progressions takes into account the four questions previously identified as being central to a CFU approach on page 100.

Game 1 introduces players to (or reminds them of) the importance of ball possession and maintaining their shape as a team. Players are in teams of five, with each team designating one player as a 'target player', in this case labelled To and Tx. The target player is positioned in an end zone of a playing area approximately 40 yards in length by 30 yards in width. Playing area size might vary depending on the age and ability of the players. A larger playing area provides much more time on the ball, and therefore less pressure, which would be beneficial for lower-skilled players. The size of the playing area might also depend on what the coach wants to emphasize. Initially, the goal is for each team to get the ball to its target player. A rule must be that once a target player receives the ball, he or she must give it back to the conceding team, so that each team is only attacking in one direction (i.e. one way). A progression is to then allow the scoring team to receive the ball back from the target player and attack in the opposite direction – so 'if you make it you take it!' In this case as long as a team scores they get to keep the ball and they switch the direction of play.

Conditioned game	Tactical focus (decision-making and 'off-the-ball' play)	Technical focus
Game 1 '4v4 to Target' One-way progression: make it, take it 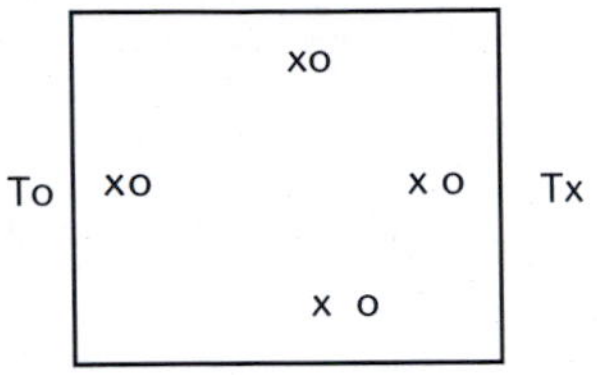 xo To xo x o Tx x o	Possession and shape Also: Transition/Turnover Pressure	Receiving skills Passing Turning
Game 2 'Corner to Corner' and 'Criss Cross' 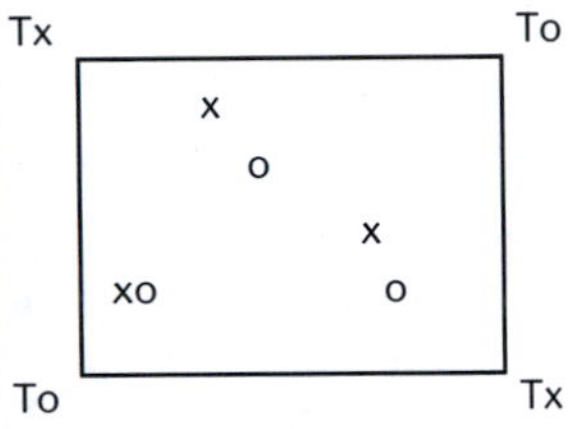 Tx To x o x xo o To Tx	Possession and shape Also: Transition Penetration using width and depth	Passing – short and long Receiving from the air Supporting distances Rhythm of play (short and long combinations)
Game 3 'Play in' – ball first 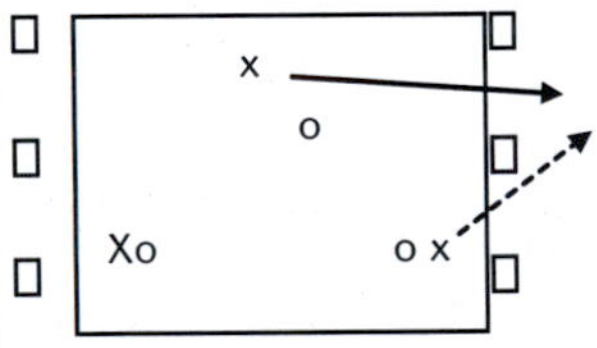 x o Xo o x ☐ = cones → = through ball --> = diagonal run	Penetration	Through ball – vertical and diagonal Diagonal and vertical runs

FIGURE 7.2 An example of a possession to penetration session in soccer

There are numerous decisions and potential adjustments to be made in Game 1, and questioning by the coach can bring these decisions to the attention of players. Questions to be asked might include:

- What do you do if there is no forward pass available?
- How can the target player help you attack?

- What shape should you try to keep as a team?
- How should you position your body to receive the ball to help you attack quickly?
- Where should your first touch go to make it easier to help you keep possession?
- How can you defend and deny possession after a score?
- How can you defend to confine the attack and make forward progress difficult?

These questions open up a range of issues related to technique or movement that might then become an appropriate focus for practice. These could include ball reception, turning with the ball, passing accuracy (probably over short distances), off-the-ball movement to create angles of support, and defensively pressuring the ball and dictating the direction of play.

Ball possession is still important in Game 2, but here the range of passing options increases which itself also brings a greater focus on penetration. The playing area can remain the same size, but now each team has two target players, one positioned at each corner with the freedom to move up to 10 yards in either direction along the line but not into the field. The goal is for each team to play from 'corner to corner'. This actually provides a longer distance over which players can pass, particularly if you allow target players to pass to each other (just one time before the ball goes back into the playing area). On a change of possession the team regaining the ball can pass to either of their target players but then that team does not score until the ball is played to the target player in the opposite corner. The game fosters similar questions to those in Game 1, but also perhaps the following:

- Which player is best positioned to play the ball to the opposite corner?
- How can your players best combine to make this easier?
- How can your team make best use of the expanded space?
- How is technique different for longer passing than for shorter?
- What techniques are necessary to receive longer passes?

One interesting change to Game 2 that really shifts the focus to the concept of penetration is to move the target players to the centre of each boundary and allow them to move anywhere along the line. So the game is now played in a 'criss-cross' pattern. Because it is a rectangular playing area, the two teams now face different problems related to shape, technique and movement, both offensively and defensively. One team is playing on a longer and narrower field while the other is playing on a shorter and wider field. In the case of the former, the attacking team will need to retain depth, and focus on trying to play the ball through the opposing team to the target player. In the case of the latter, the wider field will more likely encourage 'wing' play, particularly if the defending team sees value in compacting themselves to make it more difficult to play through them. To encourage a greater focus on movement with the ball (i.e. dribbling) a coach might remove the target players and have players score by dribbling into specific zones in either wide or central areas of the end lines. Again, this shift in playing area opens up many possible questions for the coach to ask regarding the type of individual and collective decisions and adjustments that players need to make to be successful.

In Game 3, the focus is purely on penetration and also introduces the off-side law. Figure 7.2 shows this as a three-a-side game, though this could be expanded to four-a-side or five-a-side with a corresponding increase in playing area size. To score in this game the ball must be received in the end zone behind the line of cones, but the ball must cross the line before the receiving player. Using this rule the cones actually simulate additional defenders, so the rule ensures that attacking players adhere to the off-side law and also that they have to think about finding gaps between defenders. The game, and coach questioning, can encourage players to think about the types of off-the-ball runs they should make in order to be successful, and can lead to discussion about combining diagonal runs with straight through balls or combining straight runs with diagonal through balls. Taken together these games provide an example of how the soccer coach can help his or her players understand the concepts of ball possession and penetration. Coaching is game-based and question-driven which provides many opportunities for critical thinking and player-to-player interaction in order to solve the problems presented.

A CFU example in volleyball: creating opportunities to score, creating ways of preventing your opponent from scoring

Just like in soccer, volleyball federations including the International Volleyball Federation (www.fivb.org/EN/Programmes/minivolleyball.asp), the Canada Volleyball Federation (www.volleyball.ca/content/general-info-mini-volley) and the United States Volleyball Federation (www.teamusa.org/USA-Volleyball/Features/2010/September/27/USAV-Youth-Mini-Volleyball.aspx) have been encouraging coaches to create opportunities for players to learn to play the game, develop their game knowledge as well as their on- and off-the-ball skills in a game-based approach. They have encouraged playing in courts with adapted sizes and rules which can create opportunities for learning by discovery and game adjustments. This learning process will happen more often if coaches create practices with the aim of developing players' understanding of the game.

This section of the chapter outlines examples of a CFU approach in volleyball based on the themes addressed by the four questions from the beginning of the chapter (see page 100). This questioning is designed to create opportunities and empower players to solve offensive and defensive tactical problems by themselves as they make on- and off-the-ball adjustments.

With the idea of enhancing player and team performance, examples of volleyball games will be used to demonstrate how players can develop their on- and off-the-ball skills and the ability to create opportunities to score and to create ways of preventing opponents from scoring. The effectiveness of these games is established by the use of:

- Rules to condition the offensive and defensive tactical needs of the game.
- Players' time outs called by players themselves to give them ownership in creating performance efficacy.
- Guiding questions used in time outs to help players to reflect and create possible solutions to game performance.

The game of volleyball is a game of targeting open space, in which: a) in the first ball contact players need to pass or dig to a target (the setter position), b) in the second ball contact setters need to set to a target (to a hitter position along the net), and c) in the third ball contact hitters need to attack to a target (an open space on the opponents' side). Because volleyball is a game of attacking open spaces on the opposite side of the net, players should be able to make adjustments to their on- and off-the-ball skills based on whether they are successful or not in hitting these target spaces.

Figure 7.3 illustrates two different types of games that can be modified based on age, skill level and game understanding. Game 1 shows two examples of court spaces for *co-operative games*. Game 2 shows an example of a competitive scrimmage with the goal of making tactical adjustments and developing game intelligence.

Game 1 is played on a narrowed and shortened court with the goal of maximizing opportunities for the development of defence, setting and attacking skills (techniques and transitions) by maintaining rallies. The number of rallies might depend on the level of play and players can set goals for this number themselves. Coaches need to create rules for players' rotation on and off the court (rotations can be dictated by number of trials it takes to achieve the goals or by time).

During these 'maintaining rallies' games, success will require strong positional awareness and movement from the defenders and targeting awareness from the hitters (who do need to limit power to ensure that rallies are maintained). It is by each side cooperating with each other and finding a common game rhythm that they will achieve success. The initial game format (conditions) involves two players on each side of the net and they *must* use three contacts on each side of the net, the third contact being an attack. The opposing team defence must dig the attack for it to count as a maintained rally. These game conditions help players learn to develop their understanding of several needs in the game as they work to keep the ball in play.

Playing games with the goal of maintaining the ball in play for a set number of rallies over the net will present the players with several challenges. These challenges will be related to different circumstances, such as: individual positioning (positioning related to teammate, positioning related to where the ball is coming from and going to), transitioning, jump timing, contact to the ball when defending, setting (pace, location and height) and attacking. These are some questions that could arise during the game:

- How can I improve my defensive preparation so I can defend more balls?
- Am I moving fast enough to create many chances to defend the attack?

- What do I need to fix in my setting?

  o Movement to the ball?
  o Set release?
  o Positioning when setting?

- What do my teammate and I need to do better to help us to have longer rallies?

As an example, one variation to Game 1 is to use three players on each side with a slightly larger court size and placing two players in defence, which will allow attacks with more speed to the ball and create more problems for the defenders. Another variation can be a shift from cooperation to competition with games to five points (or any other fast-scoring game).

In CFU practices it is the game variations and progressions that create needs and opportunities for players to find solutions while developing game understanding. The specific problems presented by each game format are solved through performance evaluation and strategic planning (making use of time outs and guiding questions). In a CFU practice, players need to be active problem-solvers and not merely passive listeners to coaches' instructions.

Game 2 illustrates an example of a guided game (full court, 6v6) for tactical memory and creativity development. The goal of the game is for the offence to be trained by the efforts and positioning of the defence and the defence to be trained by the creativity of the offensive system.

To train the defensive system, coaches need to ask the offence to play with specific play sets that will create the needs for the defence to make adjustments. For example, Game 2 has a very simple strategy, with team A trying to attack and score points down the line. To stop this type of attack team B has to adjust their blocking and defence to protect against the possibility of team A attacking down the line (as shown in Figure 7.3).

These are some questions that could arise during the game:

- Where is the opposing team attacking from most of the time?
- Where is their attack going to most of the time?
- How should we position our defence?
- What on-the-ball skills are important for us to use to have an efficient attack?
- What on-the-ball skills are important for us to have an efficient dig?

An important aspect of CFU practices is the concept of training one system of the game (e.g. offence) by dictating how the opposing system (i.e. defence) will play. This promotes the need for players' problem-solving, creativity and game adjustments.

Rule changes help with the idea of creating more efficiency in the attack. For example, rules such as: a) players cannot tip the ball (off speed) as an attack, or b) the last point of the rally will only count if scored with an attack or a block. These can increase offensive (deliberate) scoring intent and effectiveness when players identify

Variations of games with different size of courts, goals and number of players	Description of the positioning and game conditions
Small court used to start the defence and attack development 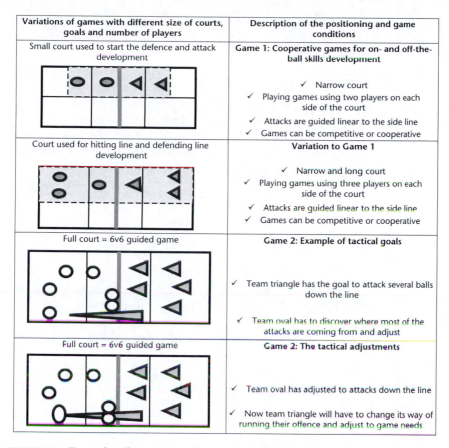	**Game 1: Cooperative games for on- and off-the-ball skills development** ✓ Narrow court ✓ Playing games using two players on each side of the court ✓ Attacks are guided linear to the side line ✓ Games can be competitive or cooperative
Court used for hitting line and defending line development	**Variation to Game 1** ✓ Narrow and long court ✓ Playing games using three players on each side of the court ✓ Attacks are guided linear to the side line ✓ Games can be competitive or cooperative
Full court = 6v6 guided game	**Game 2: Example of tactical goals** ✓ Team triangle has the goal to attack several balls down the line ✓ Team oval has to discover where most of the attacks are coming from and adjust
Full court = 6v6 guided game	**Game 2: The tactical adjustments** ✓ Team oval has adjusted to attacks down the line ✓ Now team triangle will have to change its way of running their offence and adjust to game needs

FIGURE 7.3 Example of two games for on-the-ball and off-the-ball skills and tactical knowledge development

ways to adapt their game play to the rule adjustment. In CFU practices coaches use rule changes to mimic situations that the opposing teams can bring into real competitions.

Conclusion

To conclude, Coaching for Understanding is a departure from the norm for many coaches, particularly those accustomed to highly controlled and structured environments. It takes time for coaches to feel able to allow players the autonomy of decision-making necessary for successful learning and performance improvement in a CFU environment. It also requires that coaches commit to and persevere with the approach, because discussion, asking and answering questions, calling time outs, and discussing tactics during these time outs might create an unusual amount of autonomy for many players. It might take time for players to develop comfort with these features of the approach and so it will take time for the approach to realize its benefits. However, our experiences, and those of others with whom we work, lead us to believe it to be an effective way to develop thinking and 'game intelligent' players. The governing bodies of sport and their coach education departments have a responsibility to recognize the potential of CFU in order to empower performers to develop a deeper understanding of the games they play and, therefore, to become 'game intelligent' players and ultimately analytical, reflective coaches.

To close we will reflect on some typical concerns of coaches who are in the early stages of using a CFU approach. Indeed, these concerns also represent our own past personal challenges, making it an appropriate conclusion to this chapter.

> *Concern 1:* The players are unfamiliar with problem-solving on their own. They seem to want answers, not my questions.
> *Response:* This is why it is important to talk to the players using questions instead of always telling them what to do. Persevere with questions and be patient. Continue to address the group with the big tactical idea of the game (which does not have to be complex) and encourage them to use 'players' time outs' during games or after games are over to find solutions.

> *Concern 2:* How can I improve players' on-the-ball skills in the CFU approach?
> *Response:* It is by manipulating the environment and the rules of the games that players will have the chance to do many repetitions of on-the-ball skills and off-the-ball skills (movements).

Examples in soccer:

- To help players improve their receiving touch and passing accuracy, limit them to two or three touches (depending on ability) each time they are in possession of the ball. This will force them to receive more quickly and pass more accurately (to ensure their teammates can do the same).
- To help players improve their ability to cross the ball in the air, limit all scoring to headers and volleys.

Examples in volleyball:

- To help hitters to attack with their arm extended, make the net higher and/or give them target areas to hit that are close to the baselines.
- To help the players to dig balls attacked cross court, ask the defending team to focus on eliminating the attack down the line with their block, thus opening cross court space so the cross court defender has to work harder.

> *Concern 3:* How do I use CFU for young players who have not played the game yet?

Response: This is possible if you control the environment by using appropriate field or court size. Specific to volleyball you can use more games of catch and throw, or, if the players are a little bit more advanced, use games where they need to have at least two contacts on one side of the net for them to send the ball to the other side, perhaps even allowing a fourth contact if necessary.

Concern 4: Are there a few things that I can do as a coach that will really help me develop as a CFU coach?
Response: Try the following:

- Develop your questioning skills and be patient until players feel free enough and confident enough to offer responses. Be accepting of responses.
- Be aware of your players' successes and failures and develop the ability to adjust practice situations for your players to ensure eventual success.
- Be ready to make the game more complex as soon as you see that players are developing game understanding.
- Always have one or two easy modifications to a game in case you have to make it less complex or more complex. You never know when players' execution will develop and you need to be ready to increase the level of challenge.

References

Bunker, D. and Thorpe, R. (1982) A model for the teaching of games in secondary schools. *Bulletin of Physical Education* 18(1), 5–8.

Chen, Q. and Light, R. (2006) Encouraging positive attitude toward sport through game sense in an Australian primary school. In Liu, R., Li, C. and Cruz, A. (eds) *Teaching Games for Understanding in the Asia-Pacific Region*. Hong Kong Institute of Education.

Evans, J. (2006) Capturing the essence of rugby through game sense. In Liu, R., Li, C. and Cruz, A. (eds) *Teaching Games for Understanding in the Asia-Pacific Region*. Hong Kong Institute of Education.

Graca, A. and Oliveira, J. (eds) (1998) *O ensino dos jogos desportivos coletivos*. 3rd edn. Lisboa: Universidade do Porto.

Metzler, M. (2011) *Instructional Models for Physical Education*, 3rd edn. Scottsdale, AZ: Holcombe Hathaway Publishing.

Mitchell, S. (2005) *Different Paths up the Same Mountain: Global Perspectives on Teaching Games for Understanding*. Keynote address presented at the Third International Teaching Games for Understanding conference, Hong Kong Institute of Education, Hong Kong, December 14, 2005.

Mitchell, S., Oslin, J. and Griffin, L. (2013) *Teaching Sport Concepts and Skills*, 3rd edn. Champaign, IL: Human Kinetics.

Paes, R.R. (2001) *Educação Física Escolar: o esporte como conteúdo pedagógico no ensino fundamental*. Canoas: Ed. ULBRA.

Ross, C. and Haskins, D. (2013) *Creativity in Football*. London: Sports Coach UK, National Coaching Foundation.

8

TOWARD QUALITY NOT QUANTITY IN SPORT MOTIVATION

Joan L. Duda and Jean Whitehead

What does a new coach need to know about motivation? Some would say it should be obvious: 'If you want to improve you must try harder!'

But this is not necessarily true. Certainly competitors will not normally improve without any effort, but too much effort can be counterproductive and is often misguided. Sports which rely mainly on strength and power will benefit from maximum energy expenditure after the technique has been mastered and automated, as in weight lifting. Yet in sports which require fast and accurate decision-making and fine movement control too much effort causes mistakes, as when soccer players shoot over the crossbar.

More importantly, though, to understanding sport motivation: how do competitors interpret their results and their effort? Why are athletes motivated to try and how and why does their motivation fluctuate over the course of a season, resulting in different levels of effort, which results in mixed 'success'? When does a performer feel 'successful' enough to continue, rather than to drop out? These questions will be important to coaches in terms of their awareness of motivational differences in athletes and the role they play in regard to their athletes' motivation.

Two achievement goal perspectives

One focus of this chapter is to consider what success *means* to competitors. Such a consideration relies on the application to sport of achievement goal theory (AGT) which was developed in the classroom by John Nicholls (1984; 1989) and which has common elements with the contributions of others who have also worked in educational (e.g. Ames, 1984; Dweck, 1986; Elliot, 1999) or sport (e.g. Roberts, 2013; Duda, 2001; 2005) settings. The classroom-based work has relevance for sport because (a) in all achievement contexts there is a focus on the *demonstration of ability*, and (b) two contrasting *interpretations of ability* lead to very different patterns of thoughts, feelings and actions. In order to optimise motivation, a coach needs to understand the mechanisms that underpin these contrasting outcomes.

Nicholls (1989), in particular, has focused on two different ways that athletes can judge their demonstrated competence. He referred to these two major dimensions, or goal perspectives, as *task-involvement* and *ego-involvement*. These perspectives rest on different personal *conceptions of ability* and they underpin the *evaluation of ability* in a primarily *self-referenced* or a *comparative* way. Each of these achievement goal perspectives has three different manifestations, as shown in Figure 8.1:

a) participants exhibit a transitory *goal state* at different moments of training and competition and these reflect more or less *task-* or *ego-involvement*;

b) participants acquire relatively stable *dispositional tendencies* to adopt one or the other or both goal states and these tendencies are known as *task-* and *ego-orientations*; and

c) participants are influenced by environmental conditions which they perceive to support the one and/or other goal state and these are known as *task-involving* and *ego-involving motivational climates*.

For Nicholls, the first manifestation of achievement perspectives, that is the states of *task-* and *ego-involvement*, is dependent on the *concept of ability* that a performer is using at the time. In relation to this point, we will first describe how the achievement goal perspectives change when children's conceptions of ability change.

Developmental change in goal perspectives

Most early primary schoolchildren have a *task-oriented disposition*. That is, they tend to adopt a *task-involved* mode of engaging with a task. In this goal state they do not *differentiate* between their effort, their ability and the outcome of the task. They focus simply on mastering the task itself, for example by enjoying the stimulation of a new activity, learning more about its challenges and opportunities, and using their effort to overcome the difficulties. They expect that more effort will bring more success, hence this conception of ability is predominantly *effort-based*. This

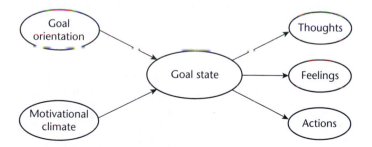

FIGURE 8.1   Some antecedents and consequences of the achievement goal state

focus on mastering the task leads them to *judge or evaluate* their performance in *self-referenced* (or *task-referenced*) ways without emphasis on the comparison of their performance to the performance of other people.

By the time they move into secondary school, however, children can *differentiate*, or distinguish between the effort they have exerted and their level of ability. That is, they can recognise that their ability puts an upper limit on their performance regardless of the effort that they put out. After this recognition they may adopt a state of *ego-involvement* in which they focus on how much ability they are demonstrating with reference to others. When strongly ego-involved, they can show ability by doing better than others (who are there performing at the same time or in reference to some norms or standards), or by achieving the same outcome as others but with much less effort than them.

This new insight can be a motivation changer and can bring negative emotions. First, it means that trying harder cannot also result in feelings of success if one's performance is not superior to others'. Children who think they do not have the ability to achieve the success they hope for can lose interest or drop out. Second, since a person's ability can only be judged when they give maximum effort, a child who does not want to expose any lack of ability to others may use only half-hearted effort so that their true ability is not evident for others to see. Adults often think that this child is not motivated, whereas the child is very highly motivated – but to avoid failure rather than achieve success.

When secondary school pupils, particularly boys, see these two implications they often undergo a change in the second manifestation of achievement goal perspectives – that of dispositional orientation. They increasingly develop an ego-oriented disposition which promotes the tendency to adopt an ego-involved mode of task engagement. However, this is not always the case. Our point is that adolescents and adults can differentiate between effort and ability and so can vary in which focus they adopt for different activities. If they are on the training ground rather than the competitive arena, or are playing a friendly game, or exploring a new activity for fun, they can be totally task-involved with limited concern for the adequacy of their ability. We will now consider how the *psychological* environment may modify the lens they use to judge their competence.

The perceived motivational climate

The third manifestation of the achievement goal perspectives is through particular features of the training and competitive environments, notably the *task-involving* and *ego-involving cues* that are perceived by the participants. Competition brings a public evaluation of valued skills and results in unambiguous judgements of success or failure, hence it creates a naturally ego-involving climate. The training ground has fewer competitive features, so it can be more prone to manifesting a task-involving climate in which the emphasis is on learning rather than performing. However, the structuring of these environments by the coach (in terms of his or her behaviours, feedback provided, nature of and criteria for evaluating performance) can manipulate the task- and ego-involving cues and have a profound influence on motivation. In essence, it is important to realise that there is a psychological environment (or motivational climate) that exists within the objective reality of training versus competitive contexts. For example, a coach who has all performers on the team feeling that they can make a contribution, encourages everyone to try hard, improve their skills, work together and persist in the face of difficulty will create a more task-involving climate than a coach who publicly criticises mistakes, gives more attention to the best performers, sets unrealistic goals and gives praise only for winning. Such coach behaviours can turn even a training ground into an ego-involving climate.

Outcomes of the two achievement perspectives

These two achievement goals (task- and ego-orientations) lead to contrasting patterns of thinking, feeling and acting. For example, reviews of research (e.g. Biddle *et al.*, 2003) show that task-orientation is associated with intrinsic motivation, enjoyment, investment, positive mood states, cooperation, endorsement of fair play and a belief that hard work leads to success. On the other hand, ego-orientation is associated with extrinsic motivation, worrying, social loafing, endorsement of cheating and a belief that ability leads to success.

Although a task-oriented perspective is more conducive to optimum long-term motivation, it is misleading to conclude that outcomes associated with ego-orientation are always negative. For one thing, the two orientations are independent of each other, so people are not necessarily high in one orientation and low in the other. They can be simultaneously high or low in either or both orientations. Hence it is a 'high-ego' athlete *who is also low in task-orientation* who will more readily show the disadvantages of ego-involvement. Someone who is high in both orientations may have an ideal profile in the long term, because when failure is encountered, the player can switch from ego- to task-orientation and focus on improvement, rather than outcome. However, in a strongly ego-involving environment, such athletes are vulnerable as well.

Another misconception is that because strongly ego-oriented athletes tend to focus on superiority and want to win, strongly task-oriented athletes do not care about the competitive outcome. It is important to remember that winning (and losing … and the occasional tie!) is inherent in competitive sport. All competitors hope to win, including task-oriented athletes! A key difference between the two perspectives is not in the desire to win, but in how competitors with different orientations interpret things when they lose, and what this does to their motivation. For example, when a highly ego-oriented athlete loses he or she frequently thinks they lost because of a lack of ability. This can be a devastating interpretation as it implies they 'just haven't got it', so their motivation decreases. Whereas, when a highly task-oriented athlete loses, he or she often thinks that they lost because of a lack of effort, so their motivation increases as they simply choose to try harder.

Perceptions of ability

Finally, a performer's emotions and behaviour depend not only on their achievement orientation, which reflects their *conception* of ability, but also on their *perceptions* of how much ability they have. Those who judge success in self-referenced terms can improve their performance whether their actual ability level is high or low, and so they can feel successful whatever their ability. However, for those who judge success in comparative terms by superiority over others, this is possible only if ability is high. For those who think their ability is too low – whether or not this is true – their motivation is lowered and they show 'maladaptive' behaviour such as dropping out, withholding effort or cheating to win.

The wider context

For simplicity, the previous material has been confined to the achievement goal theory of Nicholls. However, there are more subjective views of success than the ability-based views he studied. For example, people have goals to obtain social approval from significant others for a range of personal attributes. There are also other variables that influence goal perspectives. For example, Chapter 2 in this book discusses the role of values in a coaching philosophy. The values of a coach will influence how he or she structures the motivational climate, and the values of the young competitors will influence their goal orientation. Research (Lee *et al.*, 2008) has shown that high *status values* and low *moral values* underpin ego-orientation and the approval of cheating and gamesmanship, while high *competence values* and high *moral values* underpin task-orientation and attitudes of commitment and respect for the conventions in sport. An understanding of the dynamics of all these relationships will help a coach to provide optimal motivation for all competitors.

Another point to emphasise, drawing from Nicholl's work and related research conducted in sport and other achievement settings, is that task-involvement is indicative of optimal, higher 'quality' motivation which is likely to result in more positive outcomes. Primarily ego-involved athletes can seem highly motivated (i.e. they exhibit a high quantity of motivation) but there is an inherent vulnerability associated with this perspective. Maladaptive thoughts (e.g. 'I am only as good as my last performance'; 'my value as a person is tied to my performance'), emotions (e.g. pre-competitive anxiety, burnout), behaviours (e.g. lack of effort or trying too hard in a counter-productive manner, going with one's strengths rather than working on weaknesses) are always lurking around the corner for such athletes. This is because it is difficult if not impossible to always demonstrate superiority. Sometimes the opponent is better, and, of course in sport, we can have injuries, times when we are learning new skills and techniques, days when luck and/or the officials do not seem to be on our side, and we 'lose' and are not the best.

Beyond competence, and the importance of autonomous motivation

To understand what constitutes quality motivation, though, we need to go beyond a consideration of whether an athlete has demonstrated high or low competence and how he or she defines that competence. Another popular theory that has provided insight into variations in motivation and different patterns of engagement is Self Determination Theory (SDT; Deci and Ryan, 2000; Ryan and Deci, 2000). SDT holds that we also need to consider whether the athlete feels a sense of autonomy (voice and choice; participating in sport of their own accord) and has a respectful and caring connection with the coach and his/her teammates. If these 'basic psychological needs' are met (i.e. the needs for *competence, autonomy* and *relatedness*), SDT assumes that athletes are more likely to engage in sport for *autonomous* reasons (i.e. because they intrinsically enjoy the sport and/or because sport engagement allows the athlete to achieve personally endorsed values). If these needs are not satisfied or even are thwarted (Ryan and Deci, 2000), it is more likely that the athlete will participate because of *controlling* reasons (i.e. for extrinsic rewards, such as winning trophies, or internalised contingencies, such as playing sport to avoid the feelings of guilt that the athlete will disappoint his/her parents or coach). *Autonomous* motivation is quality motivation; this is the type of motivation that contributes to exerting effort, persevering during difficult times, optimising and enjoying one's sport engagement, and experiencing well-being and personal growth through sport (Duda and Balaguer, 2007). Those with high *controlling* motivation can appear highly motivated when they are achieving their external rewards, but this type of motivation is low in quality and predictive of a number of negative outcomes (e.g. burnout and drop out) (Balaguer *et al.*, 2012).

SDT also considers *social environmental factors* or aspects of the motivational climate which hold implications for the degree to which high- or lower-quality (autonomous or controlling, respectively) motivation will be exhibited. Specifically, it considers the degree to which coaches are more or less *autonomy supportive, socially supportive* and/or *controlling in their behaviours.* An *autonomy supportive* coach (Mageau and Vallerand, 2007) solicits input and provides meaningful options to his or her athletes in training and in relation to decisions to be made regarding competitions. *Autonomy supportive* coaches take their athletes' perspectives into account when providing advice and instruction, and they also provide a rationale (which makes sense to the athlete and is relevant) when asking their athletes to do something. A coach who is *socially supportive* demonstrates that he or she cares about and respects the athlete. Importantly, this caring and respect is not dependent on how the athlete is performing. Rather, it is more of a secure constant in the athlete's sport life. Research has indicated that more *autonomy supportive* and *socially supportive* coaching contributes to athletes feeling competent and having a sense of autonomy and belonging and connection in their sporting world (Adie *et al.*, 2012; Reinboth *et al.*, 2004; Quested *et al.*, 2013). As SDT would suggest, coach-created environments marked by high autonomy and social support also tend to promote more autonomous motivation (i.e. high-quality motivation) in the athletes who participate in such a motivational climate.

Coaches can also exhibit controlling behaviours (Bartholomew *et al.*, 2010). They can use rewards in a contingent manner (i.e. 'if you do this, you will get that!') and not allow athletes to engage in any decision-making related to their sport engagement. Coaches can speak and act in an intimidating (and even sometimes, hostile) manner and behave positively toward their athletes only when they are performing well and doing what they have been told to do. When coaches behave in this way, athletes are likely to believe they are incompetent, feel that their sense of autonomy has been actively compromised and be disengaged. As a result, controlling coaches are likely to contribute to athletes having more controlled (and fewer quality) reasons for training and competing.

An integrated approach to facilitating quality motivation

Drawing from both AGT and SDT, Duda (2013) has proposed an integrated framework that considers features of the environment held to be important across these two theoretical frameworks (see Figure 8.2). What is referred to as a more 'empowering climate' is one that is highly task-involving, autonomy supportive and socially supportive. Such an environment promotes athletes' basic needs to feel competent, and have a sense of autonomy and relatedness, and is more likely to facilitate and maintain autonomous motivation. A 'disempowering climate' is marked by ego-involving and controlling features. Disempowering coaches are more likely to diminish or even frustrate athletes' beliefs that they possess adequate ability, have

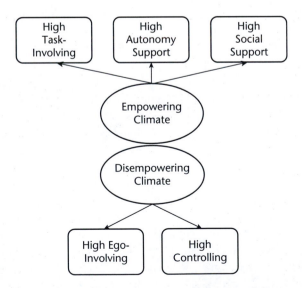

FIGURE 8.2 Components of 'empowering' and 'disempowering' climates as conceptualised by Duda (2013)

input into their own sport involvement, and feel that they are connected with others in respectful and caring ways.

Empowering Coaching™ and the 'PAPA' project

Evolving over years of research and applied work with coaches (and athletes) from different sports and representing different competitive levels, the *Empowering Coaching*™ training programme is grounded in Duda's (2013) framework. This training entails working with coaches so that they understand the principles, and can generate and, in their interactions with their athletes, effectively employ strategies which are more empowering. Activities and topics discussed within *Empowering Coaching* ™ workshops also help coaches become more aware of what constitutes more disempowering behaviours and what can be the effects and costs of such a coaching style on one's athletes (and also the coach him- or herself). The overall aim of *Empowering Coaching*™ is 'setting the stage' for athletes' sustained and optimised sport engagement that is also health conducive.

The recently completed 'PAPA' project (Promoting Adolescent Physical Activity; www.projectpapa.org) entailed tailoring the *Empowering Coaching*™ programme for grassroots football and then delivering and evaluating the training programme across five European countries (England, France, Greece, Norway and Spain) (see Duda *et al.*, 2013, for more details on the background to and protocol in PAPA). In this multi-country project, all the training materials and research measures were translated from English to the other four languages. PAPA involved almost 8,000 young footballers (ages 9–15 years) and their coaches. Across a season, comparisons were made between coaches who received the *Empowering Coaching*™ training programme (and their players) and coaches (and their players) who did not. Different methods were used in the project; for example, questionnaires administered to the players and coaches, observation of coaches and the climate they created (see Smith *et al.*, 2015), post-intervention focus groups to ascertain what coaches picked up and how they tried to change their behaviours post-training, and accelerometry with a sub-sample of players to assess objective levels of physical activity.

The findings stemming from PAPA, which is arguably the largest research trial in coach education and youth sport, will be contributing to the scientific literature and practice for many years to come. Overall, the results being generated by the project to date indicate:

a) More empowering coach behaviours over the course of the season contribute to athletes feeling more autonomously motivated, better about their sport engagement and more positive about themselves.

b) More disempowering coach behaviours, as the season progresses, are predictive of players exhibiting less quality (more controlled) motivation, reporting lower levels of enjoyment and indicating stronger intentions to drop out.

c) Participation in the *Empowering Coaching*™ training resulted in differences in how players viewed the motivational climate operating on their team and indicated desire to quit their sport. More specifically, young footballers whose coaches were trained up saw the coaching environment as less disempowering as the season progressed and reported lower dropout intentions.

d)   When assessed via observation of training sessions from the beginning of the season (pre-training) to the end, coaches who participated in the workshop were objectively less disempowering when interacting with their athletes.

Promoting quality motivation in sport: some summary comments and where to next?

Motivation is a term that is frequently used within the sport domain. We hear coaches describe particular athletes they work with as 'unmotivated'. Other athletes are lauded because they have 'a strong motivation to win'. Some coaches are referred to as outstanding 'motivators'. In this chapter, we draw from two major theories of motivation (namely, AGT and SDT) which question the utility of such popular understandings of what 'motivation' is and what athletes primarily should be motivated about. The concepts and principles stemming from AGT and SDT, and findings from sport studies based on these theories, can also enlighten coaches regarding such questions as: 'Where does "motivation" optimally come from?' and 'Who (and how) do we want to motivate athletes?'

Motivation is much more than the intensity of engagement exhibited by an athlete. That is, merely considering whether an athlete is trying hard at the moment and seemingly 'charged' or 'psyched' up tells us little about the quality of that motivation – Will the motivation be maintained? Does that level of motivation make it more likely that athletes will maximise and enjoy their sport experience? That is, when we describe athletes as being more or less motivated, this isn't informative regarding 'why' they are motivated and what makes them feel successful (or likely to feel a 'failure' as well as the likelihood of having such a negative appraisal of their sporting performance).

From AGT, and the multitude of sport studies testing its predictions, quality motivation is marked by athletes holding a strong task-orientation. As a result, they are more likely to want to strive to improve in some aspect of their 'game' or performance. Further, strongly task-oriented athletes have a more resilient sense of competence. This is because they do *not* need to (only) demonstrate superiority to feel competent (and successful).

On the other hand, and based on AGT and related research, it is clear that there are costs and risks associated with athletes being strongly and predominantly ego-oriented. Competitive sport is sometimes cruel and can be humbling. Even for the most able, it is quite a demand and source of worry to always need to be the best. In the case of largely ego-oriented athletes, there are moments when we may see them hold back effort to 'save face'. That is, they may *not* try in order to avoid looking incompetent compared to others. Or, we may see athletes with a high ego-orientation (especially if their task-orientation is low), push too much to gain superiority, resulting in overuse injuries, harm toward others via aggressive acts, compromised health due to disordered eating, the taking of performance-enhancing substances and/or cheating in other ways.

From Self Determination Theory and sport research based on this framework, the advantages of athletes being autonomously motivated are apparent. It is their sport participation after all, and when athletes engage because they enjoy and personally embrace all the good things that sport can bring to their lives, perseverance and personal growth in and through sport are likely outcomes. In contrast, controlling, extrinsic reasons for participating in sport can be 'motivating' but they do not constitute quality motivation. It is less probable that sport participation will be sustained and an all-round positive experience when athletes engage because they feel they have to (rather than want to) and/or to achieve something that is outside of the sport experience itself.

Coaches play a major role in influencing the goal orientations athletes adopt as well as the degree to which they possess autonomous and controlled motivation (Duda and Treasure, 2014). According to Duda's (2013) framework, we have a more complete awareness of coaching practices if we consider relevant dimensions of their behaviour through both an AGT and an SDT lens. At all competitive levels, we want the prevailing climate that coaches create to be more empowering (i.e. task-involving, autonomy supportive and socially supportive) and less disempowering (i.e. ego-involving and controlling). If this is the case, athletes are more likely to see themselves as competent, realise a sense of personal autonomy, and have a trusting and enabling relationship with their coach. In sport environments which are predominantly empowering, coaches provide the opportunity for athletes to motivate themselves.

REFLECTIVE QUESTIONS

At this point we would like you to pause and reflect on your own coaching. Has this chapter alerted you to any dimension of coaching that you have not considered before? Have you noticed any negative effects of more ego-involving behaviours you (or other coaches you know) may use? What are some positive benefits of more task-involving coaching that you have witnessed? What specific behaviours could you change to be more empowering and less disempowering when you interact with your athletes? For example, have you noticed any negative effects of high ego-orientation and what could you do to create a more task-involving and autonomy supportive climate?

As exemplified in the results of the PAPA project, coaches can learn to modify their behaviour to foster quality motivation and positive outcomes in their athletes with systematic and theory-grounded training. *Empowering Coaching*™ training meets these requirements and evidence exists to support the impact of this educational programme for coaches. Where to next? There are at least three important directions.

First, we would suggest the need to have training programmes, such as *Empowering Coaching*™, become an integral part of coach education. Within existing coaching award modules, the more psychology or youth sport participation focused offerings often refer to 'motivation' and how coaches need to be more 'athlete focused' and create a 'positive' environment for their athletes. However, the treatment of these important and rather complex concepts is usually quite superficial. Simple rules are presented (e.g. give more praise than negative feedback) rather than working with coaches so that they understand more about motivation and the why and how of promoting quality motivation in their athletes.

Second, there exists an errant assumption that the concepts and principles embedded in a training programme such as *Empowering Coaching*™ are relevant only to young athletes, and particularly sport participants at the recreational level. AGT and SDT are theories of human motivation and are applicable to optimising engagement in athletes from beginners to elite performers, and from those with less ability to the highly talented. The examples of or types of coach behaviours which reflect empowering and disempowering interactions from grassroots through elite level sport may vary to some degree, but the underlying motivation-related principles are the same.

Finally, the focus of this chapter has been on coaches and the motivational implications of the environment that they create. We know, however, that the coach-created climate is not the only environment impacting athletes. For example, especially in the case of younger sport participants, fathers and mothers are very important influences on athletes' sport motivation and how they judge their competence (and define success). Thus we close with a call for implementing training programmes (such as *Empowering Coaching*™) which have been tailored for parents and others who influence athletes' views on, and reasons for engaging in, sport.

References

Adie, J., Duda, J.L. and Ntoumanis, N. (2012) Perceived coach autonomy support, basic need satisfaction and the well- and ill-being of elite youth soccer players: a longitudinal investigation. *Psychology of Sport and Exercise*, 13, 51–59.

Ames, C. (1984) Competitive, co-operative, and individualistic goal structures: a cognitive-motivational analysis. In R. Ames and C. Ames (Eds), *Student Motivation. Research on Motivation in Education*, vol. 1 (pp. 117–208). New York: Academic Press.

Balaguer, I., Gonzalez, L., Castillo, I., Fabra, P., Merce, J. and Duda, J.L. (2012) Coaches' interpersonal style, basic psychological needs and well- and ill-being of young soccer players: a longitudinal analysis. *Journal of Sport Sciences*, 30(15), 1619–1629.

Bartholomew, K., Ntoumanis, N. and Thogersen-Ntoumani, C. (2010) The controlling interpersonal style in a coaching context: development and initial validation of a psychometric scale. *Journal of Sport and Exercise Psychology*, 32, 193–216.

Biddle, S.J.H., Wang, C.K.J., Kavussanu. M. and Spray, C.M. (2003) Correlates of achievement goal orientations in physical activity: a systematic view of research. *European Journal of Sports Science*, 3, 1–20.

Deci, E.L. and Ryan, R.M. (2000) The 'what' and 'why' of goal pursuits: human needs and the self-determination of behavior. *Psychological Inquiry*, 11, 319–338.

Duda, J.L. (2001) Goal perspectives research in sport: pushing the boundaries and clarifying some misunderstandings. In G.C. Roberts (Ed.), *Advances in Motivation in Sport and Exercise* (pp. 129–182). Champaign, IL: Human Kinetics.

Duda, J.L. (2005) Motivation in sport: the relevance of competence and achievement goals. In A.J. Elliot and C.S. Dweck (Eds), *Handbook of Competence and Motivation* (pp. 318–335). New York: Guildford Publications.

Duda, J.L. (2013) The conceptual and empirical foundations of *Empowering Coaching*™: setting the stage for the PAPA project. *International Journal of Sport and Exercise Psychology*, 11(4), 311–318.

Duda, J.L. and Balaguer, I. (2007) The coach-created motivational climate. In S. Jowett and D. Lavalee (Eds), *Social Psychology of Sport* (pp. 117–130). Champaign, IL: Human Kinetics.

Duda, J.L. and Treasure, D. (2014) The motivational climate, athlete motivation, and implications for the quality of sport engagement. In J. Williams and V. Krane (Eds), *Applied Sport Psychology: Personal Growth to Peak Performance*. Mountain View, CA: Mayfield.

Duda, J.L., Quested, E., Haug, E., Samdal, O., Wold, B., Balaguer, I., Castillo, I., Sarrazin, P., Papaioannou, A., Tore Ronglan, L., Hall, H. and Cruz, J. (2013) Promoting Adolescent health through an intervention aimed at improving the quality of their participation in Physical Activity (PAPA): background to the project and main trial protocol. *International Journal of Sport and Exercise Psychology*, 11(4), 319–327.

Dweck, C.S. (1986) Motivational processes affecting learning. *American Psychologist*, 41, 1040–1048.

Elliot, A.J. (1999) Approach and avoidance motivation and achievement goals. *Educational Psychologist*, 34(3), 169–189.

Lee, M.J., Whitehead, J., Ntoumanis, N. and Hatzigeorgiadis, A. (2008) Relationships among values, achievement orientations, and attitudes in youth sport. *Journal of Sport and Exercise Psychology*, 30, 588–610.

Mageau, G.A. and Vallerand, R.J. (2007) The moderating effect of passion on the relation between activity engagement and positive affect. *Motivation and Emotion*, 31, 312–321.

Nicholls, J.G. (1984) Conceptions of ability and achievement motivation. In R. Ames and C. Ames (Eds), *Research on Motivation in Education*, vol. 1, *Student motivation* (pp. 39–73). New York: Academic Press.

Nicholls, J.G. (1989) *The Competitive Ethos and Democratic Education*. Cambridge, MA: Harvard.

Quested, E., Ntoumanis, N., Viladrich, C., Haug, E., Ommundsen, Y., Van Hoye, A., Merce, J., Hall, H.K., Zourbanos, N. and Duda, J.L. (2013) Intentions to drop out of youth soccer: a test of the basic needs theory among European youth from five countries. *International Journal of Sport and Exercise Psychology*, 11, 395–407.

Reinboth, M., Duda, J.L. and Ntoumanis, N. (2004) Dimensions of coaching behaviour, need satisfaction, and the psychological and physical welfare of young athletes. *Motivation and Emotion*, 8, 297–313.

Roberts, G.C. (2013) Motivation in sport and exercise from an achievement goal theory perspective: after 30 years, where are we? In G. Roberts and D. Treasure (Eds) *Advances in Motivation in Sport and Exercise*, vol 3. Champaign, IL: Human Kinetics.

Ryan, R.M. and Deci, E.L. (2000) The darker and brighter sides of human existence: basic psychological needs as a unifying concept. *Psychological Inquiry*, 11, 319–338.

Smith, N., Tessier, D., Tzioumakis, Y., Quested, E., Appleton, P., Sarrazin, P., Papaioannou, A. and Duda, J.L. (2015) Development and validation of the Multi-dimensional Motivational Climate Observation System. *Journal of Sport and Exercise Psychology*, 37(1), 4–22.

9

ATHLETE–COACH RELATIONSHIPS

A case study from women's professional tennis

Floris Pietzsch and Heather Watson

Introduction

This chapter provides reflective observations on an athlete–coach relationship spanning more than five years within elite British tennis. It will draw upon Floris
Pietzsch's experiences as the strength and conditioning coach working alongside
Heather Watson, a high-level British tennis player. It is intended that, through
personal reflections, it will provide an understanding of some of the elements that
contribute to maintaining an effective athlete–coach relationship and which can
positively impact on performance.

   The relationship between athlete and coach is fundamental to the overall efficacy of the coach's role. As Jowett and Cockerill (2002: 16) observe,

> The effectiveness of coaches' tasks of providing technical, tactical and strategical
> instruction, as well as other tasks of planning, organizing, evaluating, directing
> and supporting depend upon the relationship between coach and athlete.

In short, to be an effective coach requires an effective relationship to be built
between athlete and coach. The case study discussed will present a harmonious
athlete–coach relationship and how this was achieved. On reflection there are critical questions that emerged that have the potential to enhance future practice. This
chapter will attempt to provide some answers to questions such as:

1.   How was the relationship built?
2.   How, as a team, did we overcome challenging issues that threatened to under-
     mine the bond between athlete and coach? Issues such as accountability of
     performance, scheduling of tournaments and overcoming differences of opin-
     ion were common and required action.

3. What lessons were learned by all parties within the team and how can knowledge of these experiences offer guidance to other coaches?
4. What does literature on psychological needs theory and the development of autonomy tell us about athlete–coach relationships?
5. How can coaches use theory to better inform their practice?

The chapter is written from the perspective of a practitioner who operated within a successful team of player, technical coach and strength and conditioning coach supported by the National Governing Body over the course of five years. These experiences will be subjected to reflective analysis in order to identify and evaluate both deliberate and implicit actions that contributed to the development of this delicate relationship. There will be an attempt to make sense of the complex nature of these interactions with reference to relevant theory from the field of social psychology. One principal aim is for the reader to use this knowledge and the applied examples to shape future contact with athletes.

The context: working with Heather Watson

Heather Watson's 2012 season offers several examples of how coaching has influenced her behaviours and performances. It is these experiences that this chapter shall draw upon to exemplify coaching processes that can be extracted and applied elsewhere. Floris Pietzsch was the strength and conditioning coach working within a small team who spent approximately 25 weeks a year alongside Heather in both training and competition periods or by providing remote support during the rest of the year. Floris was tasked with the development of her physical conditioning and to reduce the likelihood of injuries.

Finishing 2011 on a career high of being 90 in the Women's Tennis Association rankings (90WTA), and being one of only five women aged 19 or younger in the top 100, the upcoming 2012 season was full of promise and expectation. A largely successful off season training block was hampered by an injury on the very last day of the five-week block, resulting in Heather having to pull out of the first tournament of the year and reducing any potential momentum prior to the Australian Open, which began later in the month. With very little match preparation Heather's confidence was low, and it was not surprising to see her world ranking drop in the first months of the season. The injury proved a challenge for the team and it took time to overcome the disappointment of missing key tournaments. It took much longer than expected to build the performances back up to the level required to compete on the WTA tour.

From a poor start the 2012 season progressed with a high degree of success. Heather's season began with disappointment but finished with a career high ranking (49WTA) whilst also winning the Osaka Open, which ended a 24-year drought of any female British tennis player winning at the WTA tour level. Figure 9.1 illustrates how Heather's ranking began poorly but improved during the year.

The following section will present carefully considered literature that can inform the development of athlete–coach relationships along with personal insights into

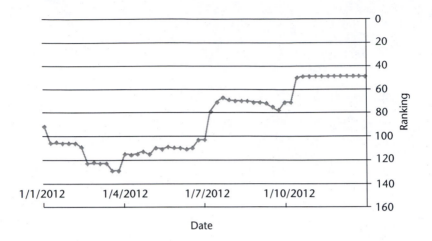

FIGURE 9.1 Heather Watson's career ranking in 2012; note the initial dip in ranking post injury before a significant win in the Miami Open propelled her ranking for the rest of the year

the application of relevant theories that contributed to an upturn in performance through the 2012 season. Included in this section are both coach and player reflections, together with some questions which are intended to encourage readers to interrogate aspects of their own practice.

Selected literature on athlete–coach relationships

Despite research within the field of athlete–coach relationships being described by Wylleman in 2000 as 'unchartered territory', there has been an increase in scholarly activity around this subject in recent years. There is research describing the varying types of social power available to coaches that might bring changes in behaviour in their athletes (Raven, 1959; 1993; 2008). In 2003 the European Federation of Sport Psychology held a special issue symposium on 'relationships in competitive sports' which aimed to encourage further research into the area. Since that time there has been significant growth in the study of theoretical concepts relating to athlete–coach relationships.

Social power

The concept of social power describes how one might be able to persuade others to follow their directions or instructions (French and Raven, 1959; Raven, 1993; 2008). Social power can be divided into six categories: legitimate, expert, informational, coercive, reward and referent. Each is now briefly considered, along with observations from the coach and athlete on the nature of their relationship.

   Legitimate power describes the natural influence a coach might have upon their athletes as the very nature of their job is to impact upon their athletes' behaviours.

The coach therefore feels that they have legitimate power to instruct athletes to perform certain tasks, but this on its own will not be enough to secure a positive coach–athlete relationship. An individual's confidence, trust and respect are not earned by simply holding a coaching role, and therefore it will be the behaviours of the coach that will decide the longevity of social power (Jones *et al.*, 2003; Potrac *et al.*, 2002). Should the athlete develop a lack of confidence in their coach's ability then legitimate power may quickly evaporate.

Expert power refers to the potential positive impact that perceived expertise may have on maintaining power in a given relationship. Generally, coaches are appointed based on their level of expertise, as this is a key ingredient to being a successful coach. Whilst the athlete maintains a positive perception of their expertise, the coach can exert influence upon the athlete's behaviour. However, this expert power can be gained and lost depending upon the coach's demonstrations, technical knowledge or win/loss record (Potrac *et al.*, 2002). Some coaches may choose not to perform demonstrations in front of their athletes if they feel inadequate, which might result in a loss of respect from their athletes.

> *Coach reflections*
>
> Reflecting back upon my six years of working within elite tennis I can see how many athlete–coach relationships failed to work. Many appointments at this level are made purely on coach reputation, which normally means reviewing the list of high-level achievers a coach has previously worked with. This may be very important experience that a coach brings to the team, and it also evidences to a certain extent the potential capability of a coach, but it does not detail the coaching style or methods preferred by that coach. These may clash with the values and expectations that the athlete may have. For example, the approach to training methods in tennis is quite varied. One coach might value a high work ethic involving early morning training sessions with long hours on the court whereas I have also observed other coaches preferring to focus more on quality and much less on training volume. The authors' recommendation is to allow for a trial period where both parties can evaluate each other's approach and create an agreed course of action.

Informational power refers to the ability to suggest a course of action based upon information that is provided. This is subtly different to expert power as it stipulates that the athlete has listened and understood the information and would proceed with a course of action based on this information (Cassidy *et al.*, 2004). For example, informing your athlete how endurance training benefits sports performance should provide them with a rationale as to why endurance training is required. It may be possible to reflect upon times where coaches have felt the need to persuade athletes to perform a technique or undertake a training session which could have been supplemented by additional information to create a bigger 'buy-in' by the athlete. Another example might be the need to provide a strong rationale as to how a drill relates to specific game play before the player includes it in their regular training regime. This is particularly useful if athletes are reluctant to fulfil the activity with the desired intensity or you feel that they are not fully committed to the task.

Coach reflections

A good example that I can draw upon in my work with Heather was her dislike of endurance training. On the court or in the gym she would be a hardworking professional but endurance training, such as running on the beach, which is something we did regularly during the gruelling training blocks during the off season, was a tough session for all of us. As a coach I had trouble motivating her to do these and to do them at the desired intensity and for Heather it simply was not an area of fitness training that she enjoyed doing. Initially, I just gave my instructions to her, providing only the necessary information to complete the session. I did not provide a specific rationale as to why we were doing certain sessions. It was not until I received feedback from Heather that I realised that she did not know why we were carrying out certain types of sessions. I think as coaches we quite often make assumptions with our athletes. I had assumed that it was perfectly clear why we were undertaking running sessions. I decided to tackle the problem by holding a short meeting to discuss the reasons behind all of my coaching strategies. Not only did it allow Heather to gain valuable information but she also learned something about training principles. It also acted as a means to our sharing our goals for our development, and we even planned targets to reach. I learnt that involving your athletes in the process can be highly valuable.

Our meeting coincided with immediate results in the tennis court posttraining blocks. A clear pattern emerged which showed that after a hard 2–3 week training period with many intense fitness sessions we saw some of her most impressive tennis performances. This provided the team with positive feedback and helped gain additional adherence from Heather.

Athlete reflections

I used to dread the morning runs! They were tough and took a really long time. As a tennis player I'm used to constant breaks and time outs between points but the morning runs really didn't give me that. We ran 4 miles 3–4 times a week and still trained as normal during the days, so I was tired a lot. Although I hated doing the sessions I valued them as I knew how much fitter they made me.

Coercive power is generally considered to be a more negative approach that a coach might utilise, and it refers to handing out punishment or negative feedback to gain the desired response from your athlete. Potrac *et al.*'s (2002) research amongst elite football coaches suggested that the occasional rebuke of athletes can sometimes be necessary, but that persistent repetitive negative communication will have a detrimental effect upon the athlete–coach relationship.

Coach reflections

This method is something that I have used previously and now try to avoid wherever possible. Stern negative feedback, used sparingly, can have a positive impact on players as it signifies a high level of displeasure which might create shock and have immediate impact. This works on the premise that players want to please their coaches and having caused some displeasure may result in some extra efforts on their part. However, when my expectation of effort or application has not been met, rather than showing my own displeasure, I would now typically put the onus on the athlete to recognise when they have fallen short of my expectations.

Reward power is something that all coaches have at their disposal, as they hold the power to provide rewards to their athletes. It may well be a tangible reward such as letting them off the last exhausting drill or having an afternoon off, but in particular it relates to the feedback and approval that many athletes value, appreciate and at times even crave from their coach (Raven, 1993). It has been suggested that the effectiveness of reward power will depend upon the athlete perceptions as to whether the reward was justified or not. Too much high praise or too frequent praise may not have much impact upon your athletes, especially if it is not fully earned.

Referent power is arguably the most important type of power that influences athlete behaviour, as it refers to the development of respect for the coach which is based on a degree of admiration. It is 'founded on an individual's identification with another person and his or her desire to be like that person' (Cassidy *et al.*, 2004: 179).

Athlete reflections

To make it as a top tennis player you have to self-motivate and push yourself. When you are on the court you are almost completely alone apart from a cheer or two from your team and that's tough to manage. However, I guess I'm like most people. Who doesn't like positive encouragement and praise? For me it is really important to get some feedback on how I'm doing. I want to know I'm doing it right and doing it well.

If I don't respect my coach then why would I work with them? Of course I want to work with someone who has similar ideas and concepts to those I have. Mutual respect is definitely needed if it's ever going to work.

Heather's comments display that respect is vitally important and support theoretical positions on athlete–coach relationships. It is clear that respect and cooperation can be achieved through good communication, which involves paying attention to athlete's ideas, feelings and feedback. As a coach we may intuitively use one method of social power more often than others without being aware of the potential consequences or benefits of each. For example, coercive power may typically be considered as having a negative influence, but it might also result in a very fast change in behaviour which in certain situations may be preferred. Likewise, the use of information power could be considered a more positive method and result in additional learning, but might require more time and effort than is available. In practice, we may find ourselves using several of the key concepts of social power within our own coaching and raising one's awareness of this could have significant benefits to both athlete and coach.

Coach reflections
In elite sport the expectation of achievement is extremely high. The coach is not held entirely accountable for the results of the player, as players should place a large emphasis on themselves. However, you may find yourself under pressure from the National Governing Body, the club, the parents, agents or the players themselves. All too often the coach is sacked due to poor results and time is a luxury that you might not have. Therefore, as a coach you need to decide where best to spend your resources of time and commitment. Do you opt for swift changes without informational power as it may be better to make short-term gains, or do you opt for the longer process which might develop the athlete's understanding for the longer term? This might result in a few tactical changes for immediate impact followed by some time dedicated to technical changes or behavioural/attitudinal changes which take considerably longer. For these reasons it's best to choose coaching strategies carefully.

REFLECTIVE QUESTIONS

1. Can you recognise how informing Heather about the rationale for endurance training helped her understand its importance to her tennis career?
2. Can you reflect upon some of your own experiences either as a coach or as an athlete and identify where legitimate, expert and information power has been apparent?
3. Can you also recognise when this has been beneficial to you as a coach?

The 3Cs model

As a consequence of Jowett and Meek's (2000) research on athlete–coach relationships, they proposed the 3Cs model. The 3Cs model highlights the importance of developing closeness, co-orientation and complementarity. Closeness refers to developing feelings of trust, respect and feeling close to your coach or athlete. Co-orientation refers to communication and developing the ability of self-disclosure and opening-up of core values and beliefs which enables feelings of closeness. Finally, complementarity refers to how well the coach and athlete engage with one another and how well they cooperate (Jowett and Cockerill, 2002). These three elements are important determinants of athletic relationships (Jowett and Meek, 2000). Feeling cared for, feeling respected and feeling valued are important to athletes and can have a positive effect upon self-confidence and, in turn, motivation (Jowett and Cockerill, 2002).

Coach reflections

Making an effort to really get to know your athlete and taking the time to learn what makes them tick will have a positive impact upon your relationship and also on your athlete's motivation. It is important to know what values and beliefs are held dear to them so you can empathise better and relate to each other more closely. These form important building blocks for long-term successful athlete–coach relationships.

When we think back to our own coaching we can probably find examples where we all too often have simply dictated the form of the training session. Typically, we see this as one of our main functions and ultimately it is our job to decide what activities our athlete should be undertaking. It is a 'we know best' way of thinking. When I first started coaching I would have constantly reverted to this type of delivery as I was extremely rigid and inexperienced with my methods. Experience has taught me that if I want an engaged, hard-working and motivated athlete they need to be involved in the process, understand why we are doing certain things and have the opportunity to contribute ideas (see Chapters 6 and 7 for examples of athlete-centred practice).

Similarly, feelings of distrust or feeling unattached, or lack of understanding, competing interests and non-committal behaviours can negatively affect your athlete–coach relationship and potentially have a negative impact upon performance. Interpersonal conflicts can represent a failure in some of the key determinants of relationships and reflect a state of imbalance between the coach and athlete. This can be described 'as experiencing discord between oneself and significant others' (Scanlan *et al.*, 1991: 112). A study by Greenleaf *et al.* (2001) found that conflicts typically arose from disagreements on training, perceived power and motivational climate.

The 3Cs model can be used to assess agreement and compatibility between coach and athlete, or stimulate conversation for relationship enhancement by identifying areas where coach and performer are not in full agreement. Figure 9.2 illustrates one hypothetical example of a comparison between an athlete's view of the coach and the coach's view of the athlete. Here we can see that there is agreement in the closeness component but a possible incompatibility or disagreement in complementarity and co-orientation. Therefore, the coach's perceptions do not match the perceptions of the athlete.

Coach reflections

We may feel that we already cater for all the needs of our athletes, that we understand our athletes well and that our athletes recognise the efforts we make for them. However, we should tread carefully when making these assumptions. It is important to have good two-way communication to ensure conflict and misunderstandings are avoided where possible. This is especially true when working with athletes for a long period of time. Through my own reflections on working with Heather, I can now see much more clearly the emotional developments any individual would make when growing from a

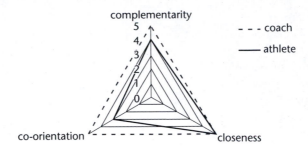

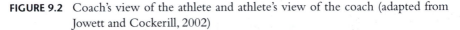

FIGURE 9.2 Coach's view of the athlete and athlete's view of the coach (adapted from Jowett and Cockerill, 2002)

junior tennis player into a seasoned professional. It would be irresponsible of me to continue talking, interacting and communicating with her in the same manner that I did when she was only 16 as a young inexperienced player, compared to a 20-year-old who is preparing for a third round at Wimbledon. My initial methods could quite easily be interpreted as controlling, patronising and restrictive to a senior player. Instead I adopted a more reciprocal method of coaching aimed at developing collaboration, joint understanding and team work.

REFLECTIVE QUESTIONS

1. Take some time to reflect upon your own athlete–coach relationship. Can you identify with the 3Cs model?
2. Can you recognise examples of closeness, co-orientation and complementarity with your athletes?
3. Consider opening a dialogue with your athletes to investigate perceptions of the athlete–coach relationship through use of the 3Cs model.

Self-determination theory

A significant determinant of a successful athlete–coach relationship is maintaining and developing our athlete's motivation and well-being. Since self-determination theory (SDT) (Deci and Ryan, 2000) has gained general acceptance as a motivational construct, there has been interest in how the social environment affects individual psychological well-being. In particular the theory suggests that coaches can create the social environment that has the 'capacity to influence the physical growth and development as well as the psychological and subjective well-being of their athletes' (Felton and Jowett, 2013: 130).

SDT is grounded in the idea that humans desire satisfaction in the three basic needs of autonomy, perceived competence and relatedness (Deci and Ryan, 2000). Autonomy refers to the need to feel empowered to make choices or take actions that are self-determined. Perceived competence refers to the need to feel capable and able in the environment. Relatedness refers to a sense of belonging to the task and being understood and connected with others (Felton and Jowett, 2013). There is evidence to suggest that an athlete's satisfaction with their relationship with a coach, along with their feelings of well-being, are enhanced by a perception that the coach is working primarily in the athlete's best interests (Lafreniere *et al.*, 2011), and therefore incorporating features of self-determination would be conducive to this.

We are motivated intrinsically to perform tasks when we possess an internal drive and enthusiasm towards the activity; 'I enjoy hitting tennis balls' is an example of this. Alternatively, extrinsic motivation is where one is driven by external rewards. These might be the outcomes of the activity, such as payment for winning a match or fulfilling a coach's instruction to gain a reward. If a behaviour is not intrinsically motivated but internalised and self-endorsed, much like the example of Heather running on the beach, then the motivation is termed self-determined. If an athlete feels pressured to fulfil a task or action through force, obligation or guilt then the motivation is termed non-self-determined. Research tells us that athletes who are either intrinsically motivated or self-determined will have a more optimal functioning (Mageau and Vallerand, 2003), greater persistence, greater concentration and will generally perform better (ibid.; Gillert *et al.*, 2010).

REFLECTIVE QUESTIONS

1. Reflect upon your own coaching experiences and identify whether your processes afford athletes an opportunity to experience autonomy, perceived competence and relatedness.
2. Can you identify when your athletes have been self-determined or intrinsically motivated and how you or the environment facilitated this?

The application of SDT to coaching practice has been the focus for a number of researchers who have found that autonomy supportive coaching practices predict improved athlete well-being (Baard *et al.*, 2004; Deci and Ryan, 2000; Blanchard *et al.*, 2009; Felton and Jowett, 2013). That is to say, coaches who strive to empower and provide free or guided autonomy environments would appear to stand a better chance of facilitating success compared to more controlling and coercive coaches. Therefore, it should always be a goal for coaches to consider incorporating autonomy whenever possible so that the athlete feels that their opinions count and matter. This view resonates with both my philosophical position and my most successful experiences in elite tennis coaching.

Research by Bartholomew *et al.* (2011) has shown that the inverse is also apparent, in that 'ill-being' can be experienced through a lack of autonomy, relatedness and competence. Therefore, the controlling coach who does not provide harmonious cooperation, joint decision-making, team cohesion or positive feedback will run the risk of developing ill-being within their athletes. This in turn has been linked to a manifestation of further more negative behaviours in the athlete, such as burnout, depression or eating disorders (Bartholomew *et al.*, 2011). Aide *et al.* (2008) found that mere perceptions of low autonomy resulted in higher reported levels of exhaustion, both physical and mental. Therefore it is feasible that a coach may actually be trying to provide a positive social environment that supports the three basic needs of SDT but an athlete is failing to recognise it. When athletes perceive that decisions are out of their control, and not self-determined (whether they actually are or not), then they can feel that their emotional and physical investment is draining.

Coach reflections

There are times when the coach and athlete do not see eye-to-eye on certain matters or difficult conversations need to take place that might test the robustness of the athlete–coach relationship. A common example involving Heather, the technical coach and myself was when deciding upon the upcoming tennis schedule, including which tournaments she should play and when the training block should take place. In tennis there are many possible choices that can be made. For the very top players it is easier as they gain entry into all the top tournaments due to ranking. Lower-ranked players face decisions such as playing a lower-ranked event which guarantees entry into the main draw, or deciding to play qualification rounds in a higher-level event.

The number of tournaments to enter, travel implications and court surface changes are other factors to consider. Flying from the USA to Australia then Asia followed by the Middle East to gain entry to the high-level tournaments is a tough assignment for a player. Add playing for your country in the Federation Cup within that time period and it is clear that somewhere along the line the elite athlete trying to maintain peak performance is going to struggle. This could link with many factors such as time zone changes, temperature/climate variables or possibly court surface changes, which are believed to be linked to increasing risks of injury. Viewed collectively it can be appreciated that scheduling becomes a hot topic within any professional tennis team. Who makes the decisions – the player, coach, parents, agent, or National Governing Body? Often there is no set method or overall decision-maker and these choices tend to be talked about and discussed at length within the team.

When relating the example of scheduling Heather's season back to SDT and the 3Cs model we considered that open communication and cooperation allowed Heather to feel some autonomy and relatedness, as her ideas and suggestions were considered by all team members. Heather therefore felt her opinions mattered and were valued, and ultimately she had the power to make the final call. An example was when Heather wanted to play two tournaments in the Middle East as they were high-profile, high-level events but the coach felt that they involved too much travelling and an alternative option was better suited. Opinions were shared from each member of the team.

Ultimately, Heather as the player made the final decision after reviewing all the opinions in detail and in this case agreed with the coach's opinion based upon his experience and judgement. Therefore, although Heather wanted to play these events she recognised that the coach had vast experience and she demonstrated her respect and trust (closeness) by following his advice. The example demonstrates good open channels of communication (co–orientation) and shared views and goals (complementarity).

Developing closeness, complementarity and co–orientation within relationships to a positive level is likely to lead to satisfaction of the basic needs of competence, autonomy and relatedness (Felton and Jowett, 2013). The notion of satisfying basic psychological needs also correlates with self-determined forms of motivation (Deci and Ryan, 2000; Mageau and Vallerand, 2003; Gillert et al., 2010), illustrating the benefits of finding ways to incorporate these principles in practice. An athlete–coach relationship which develops high levels of co–orientation, complementarity and closeness can make it easier to agree on the 'difficult' decisions inherent in coaching.

Coach reflections

When Heather was a younger junior player the relationship was significantly different to how it was when she was a seasoned professional. At the beginning the coach and the National Governing Body would dictate the schedule that she would be undertaking. This was partly due to the fact she was too young and inexperienced to make the best choices at that age, but also because it was the Governing Body which was financially contributing the most to the development of the player. As time moved on Heather became successful, and a transition period occurred whereby the internal power within the team, along with the influence of the Governing Body, underwent a transition.

It is not easy to identify when this transition begins, nor are there any guidelines on how to best manage such a transition. I do not believe we identified this natural maturation early enough and arguably failed to fully empower her as a senior professional athlete. When Heather wanted more autonomy and decision-making power we felt that on some occasions that she did not have the experience to make the best choices. As is the case with physical training the 'phasing' of autonomy and control to the athlete needs to be gauged carefully. Too little could damage relations, too much could lead to anarchy! Judging and implementing gradual delegation to the athlete, training them to use their autonomy with respect, is a significant challenge, but if successful can have significant rewards and could assist in sustaining long-term relationships.

Athlete reflections

Having spent time on the tour I have certainly learnt a lot. I now know much more about what works for me personally and what doesn't. Not everyone responds to the same way of training or structure and therefore my opinion definitely matters. It is important that coaches listen to their players' opinions and take them on board to work together.

REFLECTIVE QUESTIONS

1. Reflecting upon some of your athlete–coach relationships, can you identify how you have overcome difficulties? Were compromises made?
2. Have your athletes already started showing signs of wanting to be more autonomous?
3. What can you do to help develop autonomy for your athletes?

Conclusion

The inter-relationships of coach, athlete and support staff do invariably break down or run their course. Why this occurs can often be due to incompatibilities between the personality types, leadership styles or coaching styles (Jowett, 2003; Canary and Stafford, 1994). In the case of individual coaches working within tennis it is more typical for coaches to experience a trial period before more official contracts are exchanged, and it is the professional player who holds the power of employment. However, break-ups in successful, longer-standing athlete–coach relationships can be explained by shifting opinions or perceptions of the roles and responsibilities within the team, or when goals become conflicting rather than shared (Jowett, 2003; Canary and Stafford, 1994). It is also possible that commitments change within members of a team. It has been speculated that a significant factor in the Lendl–Murray relationship ceasing was that Lendl wanted to pursue his own ambitions.

Heather Watson's 2012 season ended with huge success as she won the WTA Japan Open in Osaka and in doing so became the first female British player to win a WTA title in 25 years. It also secured a top 50 ranking. Figure 9.1 shows the year did not go initially to plan and the team had to deal with a prolonged difficult time prior to this victory. Breaking a run of poor form is never easy but contributing to a turn of fortunes in this case was collective hard work, dedication and the strength of the athlete–coach relationship.

Athlete reflections
The event (Osaka 2012) will always be special to me. Clearly I played well but the accumulation of several hard weeks prior to the event helped me to prepare physically and mentally for the event and it resulted in everything coming together. You need a team around you nowadays in tennis and I'm grateful I have support.

In summary, the intention of this chapter is to highlight some of the key aspects contributing to a successful athlete–coach relationship. Readers are invited to relate their own coaching experiences to and work within some of the theoretical frameworks discussed here. Understanding your athletes' needs as well as their specific physical and technical requirements is paramount in developing a secure, harmonious athlete–coach relationship. Understanding what actions you can take to enhance the relationship with athletes is no less significant, and may be achieved through embedding some of the principles and considering the reflective questions presented in this chapter.

References

Adie, J., Duda, J.L. and Ntoumanis, N. (2008) Autonomy support, basic needs satisfaction and the optimal functioning of adult male and female sport participants: a test of basic needs theory. *Motivation and Emotions*, 32, 189–199.

Baard, P.P., Deci, E.L. and Ryan, R.M. (2004) Intrinsic need satisfaction: a motivational basis of performance and well-being in two work settings. *Journal of Applied Social Psychology*, 34, 2045–2068.

Bartholomew, K.J., Ntoumanis, N., Ryan, R.M., Bosch, J.A. and Thogerson-Ntoumani, C. (2011) Self-determination theory and diminished functioning: the role of interpersonal control and psychological need thwarting. *Personality and Social Psychology Bulletin*, 37, 1459–1473.

Blanchard, C.M., Amiot, C.E., Perreault, S., Vallerand, R.J. and Provencher, P. (2009) Cohesiveness, coach's interpersonal style and psychological needs: their effects on self-determination and athletes' subjective well-being. *Psychology of Sport and Exercise*, 10, 545–551.

Canary, J. and Stafford, L. (1994) *Communication and Relational Maintenance*. London: Academic Press.

Cassidy, T., Jones, R. and Potrac, P. (2004) *Understanding Sports Coaching: The social, cultural and pedagogical foundations of coaching practice*. 2nd edn. New York: Routledge.

Deci, E.L. and Ryan, R.M. (2000) The 'what' and 'why' of goal pursuits: human needs and the self determination of behaviour. *Psychological Inquiry*, 11(4), 227–268.

Felton, L. and Jowett, S. (2013) 'What do coaches do' and 'how do they relate': their effects on athletes' psychological needs and functioning. *Scandinavian Journal of Medicine and Science in Sports*, 23, 130–139.

French, J.R.P. and Raven, B. (1959) The bases of social power. In D. Cartwright and A. Zander, *Group Dynamics* (pp. 150–167). New York: Harper & Row.

Gillert, N., Vallerand, R.J., Amoura, S. and Baldes, B. (2010) Influences of coaches' autonomy support on athletes' motivation and sport performance: a test of the hierarchial model of intrinsic and extrinsic motivation. *Psychology of Sport and Exercise*, 11, 155–161.

Greanleaf, C., Gould, D. and Dienffenbach, K. (2001) Factors influencing Olympic performance: interviews with Atlanta and Nagano US Olympians. *Journal of Applied Sports Psychology*, 13, 154–184.

Jones, R.L., Armour, K.M. and Potrac, P. (2003) Constructing expert knowledge: a case study of a top-level professional soccer coach. *Sport, Education and Society*, 8(2), 213–229.

Jowett, S. (2003) When the 'honeymoon' is over: a case study of a coach–athlete dyad in crisis. *The Sport Psychologist*, 17, 444–460.

Jowett, S. and Cockerill, I. (2002) Incompatibility in the coach–athlete relationship. In Cockerill, I. *Solutions in Sport Psychology*. London: Thompson Learning.

Jowett, S. and Meek, G.A. (2000) The coach–athlete relationship in married couples: an exploratory content analysis. *The Sport Psychologist*, 14, 157–175.

Lafreniere, M.K., Jowett, S., Vallerand, R.J. and Carbonneau, N. (2011) Passion for coaching and the quality of the coach–athlete relationship: the mediating role of coaching behaviours. *Psychology of Sport and Exercise*, 12, 144–152.

Mageau, G.A. and Vallerand, R.J. (2003) The coach–athlete relationship: a motivational model. *Journal of Sports Sciences*, 21(11), 883–904.

Potrac, P., Jones, R.L. and Armour, K.M. (2002) It's about getting respect: the coaching behaviours of a top English football coach. *Sport, Education and Society*, 7(2), 183–202.

Raven, B.H. (1959) Social influence on opinion and the communication of related content. *Journal of Abnormal and Social Psychology*, 58, 119–128.

Raven, B.H. (1993) The bases of power – origins and recent developments. *Journal of Social Issues*, 49, 227–251.

Raven, B.H. (2008) The bases of power and the power interaction model of interpersonal influence. *Analysis of Social Issues and Public Policy*, 8, 1–22.

Scanlan, T.K., Stein, G.L. and Ravizza, K. (1991) An in-depth study of former elite figure skaters: III. Sources of stress. *Journal of Sport and Exercise Psychology*, 13, 105–120.

Wylleman, P. (2000) Interpersonal relationships in sport: uncharted territory in sport psychology research. *International Journal of Sport Psychology*, 31, 555–572.

SECTION 3

'What' to coach

Building on technical knowledge

The third section seeks to broaden your awareness of what to coach, presenting content knowledge that is transferable across a range of sports and goes beyond the technical and tactical.

10

INTEGRATING AND APPLYING KNOWLEDGE OF SPORT SCIENCE – 'PULLING IT ALL TOGETHER'

A case study of British Cycling

Gary Brickley

London 2012 showed that sport performance has been dramatically enhanced by scientific interventions. Looking forward to Rio in 2016, this chapter will use my substantial experience in British Cycling to underline how integrated approaches to coaching can be drawn together to aid athletes of all levels. I intend to reflect on the growth and professionalisation of coaching within British Cycling, drawing upon my own experience working within the sport. At key times throughout the chapter readers will be asked to pause and reflect on their own coaching, and to consider their own strengths and areas for development.

The British Cycling context

In 1998 I was recruited to work as a sports scientist under the British Cycling Performance Director, Peter Keen, who was a former lecturer of mine at the University of Brighton. During my undergraduate studies I watched with interest as Peter worked alongside Chris Boardman in his preparation for the Olympic Games and Tour de France in the university laboratories. I was intrigued by his attention to detail for events such as the hour record. The hour record involves a cyclist trying to travel around a track for as far as they can in one hour. Michael Hutchinson humorously writes about this in his book entitled *The Hour* (Hutchinson, 2006). To be prepared for this event you must be able to ride aerodynamically and produce a high percentage of your maximal power for the hour duration. Timing, pacing, conditioning, weather conditions, track temperature and equipment all have an influence on the final outcome. Keen's dedication to beating the record became an obsession. As a physiologist and coach to Boardman he passed on these experiences to inspire me to become a cycling coach. In 2015, the hour record was broken a number of times including when I helped Dame Sarah Storey to break the Paralympic, British and Masters hour record and just miss out on the world record at the London velodrome. Sarah completed 45.502 km, 560 m short of the 12-year-old record held by the Dutchwoman Leontien Zijlaard-van Moorsel.

In 1998 Lottery funding had just been established and British Cycling was about to go through a radical change. The building of the velodrome in Manchester was a milestone that enabled track cycling to be centralised and riders were now able to be funded by National Lottery money. Prior to the inception of Lottery funding, British Cycling had limited funds and riders relied on small amounts of sponsorship in order to fund events and equipment. Peter Keen had a vision to make Great Britain the number one cycling nation on the track. To do this the sport needed structure and a clear vision along with the right supporting personnel. Specifically, in cycling this led to professionalisation of cycling coaching and with it a scientific approach to coaching. I was fortunate enough to be part of this revolution when I was appointed exercise physiologist for British Cycling. My role included exercise testing, directing the laboratory, carrying out field testing, nutritional analysis and blood testing, as well as sitting on various management boards.

In my role I was able to meet many of the current Olympic gold medallists and work with a range of teams including the mountain bike team, track team, endurance team and Paralympic team. Peter Keen was determined to recruit coaches with a strong understanding of sports science. Simon Jones became the track endurance coach with limited coaching experience but great knowledge of the demands of the sport and possible interventions to improve performance. Simon was instrumental in the track success of the team pursuit team in Athens and at the time worked very closely with Sir Bradley Wiggins. On reflection, I had vast experience of coaching in swimming and water polo but limited coaching experience in cycling. I needed to develop my technical knowledge rapidly by gaining awareness of the demands of the sport and the various sub-disciplines of cycling.

Becoming a coach entails more than having knowledge of the discipline in question; in my case this is the physiological and nutritional demands of performance cycling. My coaching roles have placed multi-faceted demands on me which have required constant upgrading of skills and knowledge. Simon was brought into the group as an authority in track cycling. He too had to recognise his own areas for development in drawing the highest possible performance from each athlete. Our early experiences required us to be mindful of the knowledge and skills we needed to best support the athletes; more often than not their needs were unrelated to our specialist areas of knowledge. Table 10.1 is a recollection of roles that I have been required to undertake in my time with British Cycling.

I have been regularly challenged by the diversity of roles expected of a 'coach'. It is important to highlight that there is so much more to coaching than gaining a few coaching qualifications, which will often provide good in-depth knowledge of a discrete sport or discipline but neglect other vital factors. For example, learning to interact with athletes and be part of the team is an important skill that cannot be quantified. Within my role working with Paralympic athletes I would often find much of my time, when not directly with the athlete, was taken up

TABLE 10.1 The various roles of a cycling coach

- Technical coach
- Physiologist
- Nutritionist
- Talent ID
- Psychiatrist
- Publicist
- Doping control
- First aid
- Cardiologist
- External speaker
- Team manager
- Cooking
- Shopping
- Driver
- Strength and conditioning coach
- Altitude expert
- Venue reconnaissance
- Mechanic
- IT support
- Performance analyst
- Media liaison
- Counsellor
- Carer
- Writer/reporter

with the equally important task of planning and reviewing performance. Being a good listener, creating a relationship bridged by trust and mutual respect, and ensuring that outside factors do not adversely affect performance is particularly important.

TAKE A MOMENT TO REFLECT

It may be prudent for readers to pause, to interrogate their own roles and to pinpoint principles, skills and knowledge that could enhance their athletes' performance which have not been formally delivered as part of their coach education experience.

Understanding the diverse demands of the sport

To fully appreciate any sport one must consider its multi-faceted demands. For myself, this included the physical, mental, technical and mechanical aspects of cycling. This interdisciplinary approach to analysing sport was stressed by Burwitz *et al.* (1994) as being an integral part of improving performance. This section will begin to consider the diverse demands of the sport and the subsequent demands on the coach. As a coach working with cycling it is important to gain an appreciation of the demands from speaking with the athletes, but also from reviewing performances on the track, road or mountain bike course, as well as examining and keeping up to date with the latest research literature. In their book, *Performance Cycling: The Science of Success* Hopker and Jobson (2012) illustrate a number of examples of the generic physical demands of racing in cycling. However, as a coach it is important to consider each athlete as an individual case and then try to determine how to get the best out of that athlete. Athletes differ in the limitations to their performance and as a coach it is important to identify their strengths and weaknesses and construct individualised programmes. To achieve this the coach has at their disposal an abundance of technology, such as Global Positioning Systems, course profiles, power traces, heart rate monitors, wind tunnels and many other aspects that can help to determine the demands of the sport and how best to train and prepare the athlete (rider) for ultimate success. Knowledge of the demands of a sport and the technical development of key personnel are continually evolving. To improve coaching skills, continual updating is needed. It is not always a simple case of attending coaching courses but also *learning to learn* through supervised experience/mentoring, reading, research and working with diverse populations, which all can help to develop a coach's portfolio of knowledge.

Cycling events can be as short as 200 m, through to long stage races such as the Tour de France which may involve back-to-back rides of over 200 km per day. The event must be broken down into small chunks to determine the demands. The coach therefore needs to have a broad understanding of all sub-disciplines of sport science: psychology, performance analysis, physiology, sports technology. There is a requirement to understand and be able to engage with discussion that may not fall directly into their area of specialism. The following examples from my own work in cycling depict the varied demands on the coach as a block of training unfolds in the run up to competition. In these examples I have attempted to highlight the diversity of the roles I have undertaken and the breadth of demand placed on my skills and knowledge.

This chapter discusses physiological training and nutrition as my areas of discrete 'expert' knowledge. Through the following examples I hope to communicate the ways in which my skills and knowledge have evolved to meet the contemporary demands on the coach. Table 10.2 presents a summary of these diverse demands, each of which is numbered and exemplified in the following paragraphs.

The first example is being able to utilise power profile data taken from an SRM trace for a high-level athlete with cerebral palsy.

Figure 10.1 shows how power as well as technique can determine the final performance (required knowledge number 1 from Table 10.2). On the track, cadence is limited by gear selection which enables the rider to produce enough power at the start of the race but should not limit the rider's ability to maintain the cadence throughout the race (2). Energetically the initial power production is predominately from phosphocreatine stores but, as the race goes on and power production

TABLE 10.2 The diverse knowledge demands of coaching

Knowledge required

---

1. Technical
2. Tactical
3. Energetics
4. Periodisation
5. Awareness of the athlete
6. Analysis and interpretation of data
7. Understanding of specific needs of athletes
8. Technological understanding
9. Psychological considerations
10. Knowledge of the performance setting
11. Knowledge of environmental factors and their impact on performance
12. Nutrition for wellness and performance

---

reduces, there is a greater reliance on aerobic metabolism (3). Therefore in training for this event there is a need to ensure that both endurance and sprint training is covered. It is the coach's job to ensure that this training is phased correctly and the right amount of time is spent working on each aspect of the rider's performance (4). In a similar way the coach needs to be watchful for performance decrements and to find reasons and solutions where appropriate (5). Examining events of similar duration gives a useful indication of the aerobic/anaerobic contribution to the event (6) (Gastin, 2001).

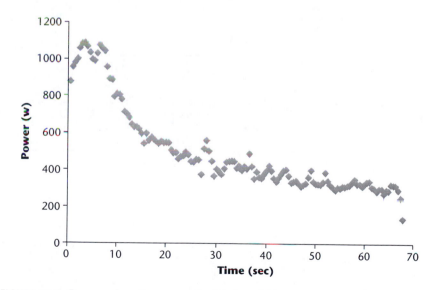

FIGURE 10.1 Power values from a cerebral palsy athlete competing in the 1 km time trial at a world championship

In the field of Paralympic sport we cannot always use world record performances from the Olympics to structure training. Working with cerebral palsy athletes and amputees I need to understand that the energetics of a sport may be relative to the performer, therefore functional limitations need to be considered (7). For example, a rider with cerebral palsy may show discrepancies between each of their legs in terms of torque production at different cadences. This has been previously demonstrated (Brickley and Gregson, 2011) and is depicted in Figure 10.2.

The graph shows that at the lower cadences the rider has large differences in torque production from each leg. This needs to be accounted for in his training and in this particular case we used an elliptical chain drive (8) to improve the rider's transmission. Once the demands of the event are understood and the limitations of the performer have been considered, a performance profile, phased performance planner, and long-term and short-term goals can be made that are specific to the rider (9). By breaking down the event to target specific aspects of it, realistic achievable targets and event-specific training can be set by the coach.

Having coached cyclists to four Paralympic Games and numerous world championships, my experience of the Paralympic Games environment can help in preparing an athlete for the most prestigious sporting event of their lives. The growth of British Cycling into one of the most successful Olympic and Paralympic sports has resulted in an increase in funding from UK Sport, which has allowed athletes and support services to grow and develop. This growth has come with an increase

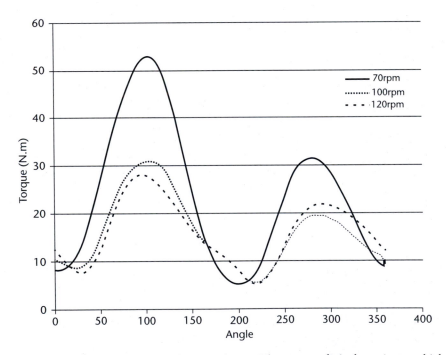

FIGURE 10.2 Torque curves at different cadences. The zero angle is the point at which the pedals are most vertical

in professionalism in coaching, which is now not limited to ex-professional riders but has a diverse mixture of sports scientists, performance analysts and research and development experts, as well as numerous coaches from grass roots, through talent identification to podium coaches. Support for athletes has grown exponentially since 1998 and the success of the Olympic and Paralympic teams has ensured that funding is maintained for another Olympic cycle.

In preparation for major championships it is important to have a good understanding of the environment, the course, accommodation and logistics, as well as making sure that the rider has the best possible opportunity to perform (10). In most cases the riders are able to do a reconnaissance of the road course, where the coach will film the rider so that they can train whilst watching the course on a video screen. A power profile can be gained to determine the optimal pacing around the course. In preparation for the Beijing 2008 Games we had to account for predicted temperatures of over 35°C and possible air pollution. To prepare for this some riders carried out heat acclimatisation in heat chambers in conditions similar to those predicted in Beijing (11). There is strong evidence that this can help in preparation for exercising in the heat (Bergeron et al., 2012). We also made sure that riders used fish oil supplements to help with the inflammation of the lungs that may have been caused by exposure to pollutants (Mickelborough et al., 2008). Assuring environmental and immune function are optimised is an important undertaking for the coach responsible for the rider (12).

In the year prior to the Beijing Games we also travelled to Australia and China to ensure that riders were used to long-haul travel and training in different time zones. We could monitor their sleep patterns using accelerometers and also determine the optimal time to arrive in a different time zone. This has been covered extensively elsewhere (Atkinson and Reilly, 1996). The attention to detail in preparation for major events has resulted in substantial success for British Cycling, and in Beijing 2008 we managed to achieve 17 Gold Medals in Paralympic cycling compared to zero in Sydney 2000.

TAKE A MOMENT TO REFLECT

In the interest of self-development you may want to consider the multiplicity of roles and knowledge requirements of your own context. You may want to interrogate your own knowledge of the sport such as the physical, technical, emotional, psychological or nutritional demands. This may extend to the required level of understanding in working with a particular group of performers (such as with disability, elderly, children) or the political or social context in which you work. Knowledge of the sport alone is seldom sufficient for high-level coaching practice. Perhaps carry out your own 'audit' of required knowledge using an example from your own work, similar to the process demonstrated in Table 10.2.

It is rightly impossible for coaches to reside within a particular discipline with no awareness or interest in the multiple faces of coaching practice. The next section will further exemplify this point through personal experiences in drawing together a multidisciplinary team to support Paracyclists.

The coach as part of the interdisciplinary team

Coaches take on many roles, as depicted in Table 10.1. This highlights the many and various roles that I have had to take on in my role as coach with the GB Paracycling Team. Although I have expertise in physiology, physical training and nutrition it is important to appreciate that the athlete is the central concern. An athlete-centred approach does offer many advantages, but also requires the athlete to take some responsibility for their actions. The more driven athletes are very good at making the most of the people around them. In my experience being empowered by the athletes and being an important cog in the wheel of their success is rewarding and motivating, but does rely on a reciprocal process between coach and athlete (Chapter 9 considers this in much greater detail).

Where other experts or specialists are available, an interdisciplinary approach may be used to assist planning, problem solving and ensuring that the athlete continues to improve. For example, an athlete may be underperforming and the support team will need to make informed decisions on how the athlete trains, recovers and progresses. Underperformance may have many causes, such as psychological factors, immune function, overtraining, poor diet, social issues, medication, to name a few; therefore a team of interdisciplinary experts may help the lead coach (Lane et al., 2014). A few of the common complexities that have faced the team at British Cycling and have required specialist input are listed below:

- Psychological support to find out what has driven the athlete when on form, alternatively what has inhibited their progress.
- Blood tests to determine if the athlete has a poor cortisol:testosterone level (Gleeson et al., 2011), which may suggest a depressed immune function.
- Monitoring heart rate or heart rate variability to ascertain whether the athlete has a depressed state of recovery (Plews et al., 2013).
- Social support systems to ensure that the individual is able to cope with stresses outside of performance in the sport.
- The use of lifestyle advisors (often employed centrally by UK Sport) to provide help to athletes with a range of personal issues.
- Consultation with a dietician or sports nutritionist to ensure that the athlete's nutritional plans meet the needs of training and competition.

British Cycling use a method called a rider development team (RDT) meeting where a number of senior managers, including the performance director, head coach, psychologist or psychiatrist, nutritionist, physiotherapist and senior coaches examine individual issues about each rider every two weeks in order to create a pathway to success or recovery. A coach represents the rider, or the rider is present at this meeting and an action plan is put into place. Meeting with people from other disciplines within cycling also helps to develop an understanding of the different approaches for improving performance. In my role as an endurance Paralympic coach, interacting with coaches from mountain biking, track sprinting as well as other endurance coaches enabled me to have a stronger understanding of the sport.

In an athlete-centred, coach–led approach the coach needs to have an awareness of the multiple aspects to the athlete they are working with. A good coach will have a good network of advisors from a number of specialist areas and, by being a good interdisciplinary coach, problems can be resolved effectively. Having championed the need for coaches to develop diverse knowledge bases, it is necessary to extend a word of caution. It is vital that the coach should know their boundaries and their limitations and when to call upon specialist support in discrete areas. Some instances require expert input that may exceed the working knowledge and training of the coach. It should not be deemed a weakness or defeatist to draw on additional support where necessary. In endeavouring to provide the best possible environment for peak performance, coaches should have a realistic expectation of themselves in providing this for their athletes. It is the filtering and sharing of knowledge and its application to the athlete that is essential to ensure continued improvements in performance.

Coaching interventions

In this section I aim to give a few examples of useful interventions that have resulted in improvements in performance and/or success. Without going into too much specific detail of the performance times and laboratory measurements, I will discuss the rationale and the coach–athlete decision-making process. Whilst it is unlikely that these specific examples will resonate with all coaches, the principle of simulating the competition environment, whether through physical, emotional or environmental means, is applicable to many contexts. In the examples below I share modes of manipulating the training to closely mimic physical and technical race conditions. In the same way coaches may use psychological tools to create an emotional or cognitive demand to recreate the performance setting, or use training to practice feeding or hydration strategies. Collectively these may all fit under the broad umbrella of simulation training.

Simulated altitude training

One aspect of endurance performance that is often used by runners, swimmers and cyclists is altitude training. Many benefits have been suggested (Millet *et al.*, 2010) and there is much debate over whether living at altitude or using an altitude simulated environment are equally effective. The following section further explores this. We have used this method before major championships and in important periods of training to create an added stimulus to training without the added damage to the body. Table 10.3 presents a typical altitude training period used in training one of the cyclists that I have worked with. Readers may wish to consider examples from their own practice where the environment may be altered to develop changes or to create an overload in challenging conditions.

When working in a controlled laboratory setting, controlling power is possible on an SRM ergometer. Where possible I try to take a blood sample for blood lactate analysis and typically this will lie around 3 mM. Having an indication of blood lactate concentration, heart rate and rating of perceived exertion (Borg, 1970) can allow for any changes in power output to be made to ensure that the rider is not working too hard or too easily. Altitude is used as a supplement to the normal training on the road or track, and in these block periods of training it can result in performance benefits for up to 10 days after the exposure and training stimulus.

It is sometimes evident that one's coaching exists in a vacuum, and to avoid being guilty of this it is important to research new ideas and methods to gain a legal competitive edge over other competitors. Coaches should consider diversifying their coaching and trying new methods in their approaches. Provided the modifications are well researched, ethically sound, measureable and challenging, this can provide a valuable edge for the athlete.

TABLE 10.3 A typical simulated altitude training period

Day	Training protocol
1	ALT 10 min at 200 W; 10 min 250 W; 10 min 230 W × 2; 10 min recovery
2	Steady 2-hours
3	ALT 10 min at 200 W; 10 min 250 W; 10 min 230 W × 2; 10 min recovery
	Early morning 2-hour ride before ALT session
4	Steady 3-hour ride less than 140 bpm
5	2-hour ride with at least 40 min around 270 W
6	ALT 10 min at 200 W; 10 min 270 W; 10 min 250 W × 2; 10 min recovery
	Plus 90 min around 200 W on road
7	2-hour road work with climbs and short hard road race efforts
8	2-hour ride with 15 min at TT pace in TT position
9	ALT 10 min at 200 W; 40 min 250 W; 10 min recovery
	2-hour steady ride PM
10	Evening 10 mile time trial
11	Easy 2-hour spin (high revs)
12	ALT 10 min at 200 W; 10 min 270 W; 10 min 250 W high revs × 2; 10 min recovery
	Plus 2-hour on road hill work PM
13	Rest day
14	ALT 10 min at 200 W; 40 min 270 W; 10 min recovery

The altitude was the equivalent to approximately 3,200 m at 14% oxygen and room temperature was maintained at 19°C. At this level of altitude the rider may potential operate at 10–20% lower power output for the same physiological stress.
Typically altitude (ALT) sessions lasted for 1 hour spread over a 2-week period with at least 6 exposures to the altitude.

Training for multiple gold medals – the case for simulation

Preparing for a major championship such as the Paralympic Games or World Championships can create several challenges for the coach and rider. In Paralympic cycling many riders will compete in more than one event. For example, in the Beijing Olympic Games, Darren Kenny was trying to achieve five gold medals and finished with four and one silver. In London Dame Sarah Storey achieved four gold medals out of the four races she competed in.

Simulation for multiple events needs to include:

1. Matching of the demands of multiple events during training
   Training can be used to simulate the racing environment in a dress rehearsal format. We have used this successfully, making sure the athletes are wearing the race clothing and using race wheels and then doing a simulated race (sometimes slightly reduced in duration). We may then try to create a similar race effort in training 2–3 days after the first event to ensure that the rider is able to put together back-to-back performances.

2. Ensuring recovery is optimised
   There are numerous recovery methods that need to be considered in high performance sport and recovery is often overlooked. Recovery needs to include relaxation, good nutrition, acute physiological recovery and other aspects such as massage that may be important. The benefits of massage are unequivocal, and having time to lie down and relax and talk with a masseur is often valued in cycling. The benefits in terms of blood flow and recovery of metabolites is still poorly understood. Depending on the nature of the event, a high protein/moderate carbohydrate recovery is used by cyclists and the carbohydrate content may be dependent on the duration and intensity of the race. There are clear benefits from consuming carbohydrate/protein 30 minutes after exercise to ensure muscle glycogen repletion (van Loon *et al.*, 2000). For the coach, optimising the time after the event is as important as the time before and during the event, if chasing multiple medals.

3. Pacing events so that the individual peaks in the final
   Pacing in and between events can ensure that the athlete can produce their best performance when needed. For example, in the preliminary rounds of qualification for the final the rider may try to ensure that they achieve a time that helps them qualify for the finals rather than break a world record in the heats. In the road race, for example, if a competitor knows that they have a strong sprint finish then they can do less work throughout the race and win the final sprint. This scenario was essential when preparing Darren Kenny at the 2008 Beijing Games. Darren won a straightforward heat in the pursuit and then had a relatively easy pursuit final. In his fifth and last event he stayed with his closest rival throughout and knew that he would win the sprint finish to secure his fourth gold in the Games.

Concluding thoughts and key messages

Having worked with a range of predominately endurance athletes in Paralympic sport, an emphasis on adopting the athlete-centred, coach-led approach to coaching appears to be warranted. Although the disability needs to be considered, it is the athlete's sporting ability and functional ability that is crucial to their performance. In Paralympic classification there has been a steady movement towards functional classification in sports such as swimming and cycling. The focus therefore should be on making the most of an individual's assets as well as addressing their weaknesses. Whilst the theory of marginal gains based on Gladwell's (2008) work has received much attention, attending to some of the large things also needs to be considered. The athlete must have the right social support, coaching support, equipment and training environment, amongst other things, to succeed in cycling performance.

Whilst my chapter has focused on success in Paralympic sport there is no reason why the coaching concepts cannot be applied to a range of other sports or situations. The principles of holistic coaching, where the athlete is at the centre, can be applied to numerous sports. Coaches should consider the gaps in their own knowledge and how to continually improve their coaching methods. Consider how different interventions may help your athlete improve their performance. Consider your own role as part of the coaching support team and think how you could improve the support for your athlete. The following are some of the key messages embedded within this chapter, and they could be used to inspire further thinking about continuing to find ways of integrating scientific knowledge into coaching.

- Understand the diverse roles of your coaching and interrogate your own strengths and areas for development.
- Understand your limitations as part of the interdisciplinary team and define where the boundaries lie within your role.
- Consider how to simulate the race or competition environment through adapting your training methods.

Coaching is a dynamic role and as a coach you need to continually advance your knowledge using a wide range of sources such as mentoring, workshops, conferences and observations. Reflect upon how you have been able to continue to develop your own knowledge and skills. Where are your needs and how can they be addressed?

References

Atkinson, G. and Reilly, T. (1996) Circadian variation in sports performance. *Sports Medicine*, 21(4): 292–312.

Bergeron, M.F, Bahr, R., Bärtsch, P., Bourdon, L., Calbet, J.A., Carlsen, K.H., Castagna, O., González-Alonso, J., Lundby, C., Maughan, R.J., Millet, G., Mountjoy, M., Racinais, S., Rasmussen, P., Singh, D.G., Subudhi, A.W., Young, A.J., Soligard, T. and Engebretsen, L. (2012) International Olympic Committee consensus statement on thermoregulatory and altitude challenges for high-level athletes. *British Journal of Sports Medicine*, 46(11): 770–779.

Borg, G. (1970) Perceived exertion as an indicator of somatic stress. *Scandinavian Journal of Rehabilitation Medicine*, 2(2): 92–99.

Brickley, G. and Gregson, H. (2011) A case study of a Paralympic cerebral palsy cyclist using torque analysis. *International Journal of Sport Science and Coaching*, 6(2): 269–272.

Burwitz, L., Moore, P.M. and Wilkinson D.M. (1994) Future directions for performance-related sports science research: an interdisciplinary approach. *Journal of Sport Sciences*, 12(1): 93–109.

Gastin, P.B. (2001) Energy system interaction and relative contribution during maximal exercise. *Sports Medicine*, 31(10): 725–741.

Gladwell, M. (2008) *Outliers: The Story of Success*. New York: Little, Brown and Company.

Gleeson, M., Bishop, N.C., Stensel, D.J., Lindley, M.R., Mastana, S.S. and Nimmo, M.A. (2011) The anti-inflammatory effects of exercise: mechanisms and implications for the prevention and treatment of disease. *Nature Reviews Immunology*, 11(9): 607–615.

Hopker, J. and Jobson, S. (2012) *Performance Cycling: The Science of Success*. London: Bloomsbury Press.

Hutchinson, M. (2006) *The Hour*. London: Yellow Jersey Press.

Lane, A.M., Godfrey R.J., Loosemore, M. and Whyte, G.P. (2014) *Case Studies in Sport Science and Medicine*. UK: CreateSpace independent publishing platform.

Mickleborough, T.D., Lindley, M.R. and Montgomery, G.S. (2008) Effect of fish oil-derived omega-3 polyunsaturated fatty acid supplementation on exercise-induced bronchoconstriction and immune function in athletes. *The Physician and Sportsmedicine*, 36(1): 11–17.

Millet, G.P., Roels, B., Schmitt, L., Woorons, X. and Richalet, J.P. (2010) Combining hypoxic methods for peak performance, *Sports Medicine*, 40(1): 1–25.

Plews, D.J., Laursen, P.B., Stanley, J., Kilding, A.E. and Buchheit, M. (2013) Training adaptation and heart rate variability in elite endurance athletes: opening the door to effective monitoring. *Sports Medicine*, 43(9): 773–781.

van Loon, L.J., Saris, W.H., Kruijshoop, M. and Wagenmakers, A.J. (2000) Maximizing postexercise muscle glycogen synthesis: carbohydrate supplementation and the application of amino acid or protein hydrolysate mixtures. *American Journal of Clinical Nutrition*, 72(1): 106–111.

11

EMBEDDING PRINCIPLES OF SPORT PSYCHOLOGY INTO COACHING PRACTICE

Case studies within professional cricket

Bill Filby, James Beale and James Wallis

The discipline of sport psychology is one of the most misunderstood and under-used support services within sport. Sport psychology is an umbrella term that is used to explain a wide variety of methods and philosophical approaches. The same objective situation may be approached in very different ways by psychologists who follow different philosophical persuasions. The case of a batsman in cricket whose performance diminishes after being 'sledged' may be approached by one psychologist through the use of a cognitive re-structuring tool, in that the psychologist would attempt to change the perception held by the batsman. Another psychologist may attempt to reduce the impact of the stimulus through a gradual increased exposure to less threatening environments in training sessions in order to make the sledging feel more normal. This approach may, for example, include sledging or other audible interference in net sessions. Whilst taking into consideration the diversity of practice, this chapter uses a general definition, defining sport psychology as:

> The study of psychological factors within sport, with the aim of developing an ever increasing understanding of how psychological factors have an impact on behaviour, across different sports and different cultures.
>
> *(Beale & Wilson, 2013: 154)*

Many coaches will recognise some of their own practices through this definition and indeed, some coaching practices are aimed at specifically impacting on the psychology of the athlete (the impact of psychological factors within sport is consistently mentioned by sports practitioners). A traditional method of encouraging athletes to 'buy-in' to sport psychology support is to ask them to quantify the proportion of their sport that is influenced by psychological factors and then ask what proportion of time they spend working on the psychological side of their sport. There is normally a huge disparity, with the proportion of influence being considerably higher than the proportion of time that athletes spend working on the psychological aspects of their sport.

There is a significant body of academic support for the notion that sports psychology has a tangible effect on both athlete perceptions and their actual performance (see Greenspan & Feltz, 1989; Vealey, 1994; Weinberg & Comar, 1994). Within sport psychology literature there is very little to suggest that any one technique is more effective than another. The consistent theme from existing literature is that the one critical factor in determining the efficacy of a psychological intervention is the relationship between the psychologist and the client. To extend this point, evidence-based studies suggest that coaches and psychologists should place most emphasis on their ability to establish an effective therapeutic alliance with athletes (Anderson *et al.*, 2004). Throughout this chapter readers should be mindful that we do not intend to provide a series of 'ready to go' interventions, but offer some guidance on principles of practice that coaches could begin to apply to their own contexts. The chapter will draw upon the experiences of two practitioners who have accumulated over 20 years of applying sport psychology principles within professional cricket. The approaches and interventions described are directly applicable to other sports and should provide the reader with clear, effective principles to begin to consider embedding sport psychology within their own coaching practice.

The next section is written by a sport psychologist who has adopted a framework for practice which is embedded in the relatively new approach of positive psychology. It begins with an overview of positive psychology and its theoretical underpinnings, before considering how the principles may be embedded into coaching practice.

Positive psychology

Positive psychology is a relatively new discipline within psychology as a whole which has its origin in the work of Seligman and Csikszentmihalyi (2000). These two authors proposed a theory that focuses on enhancing the strengths and virtues of individuals and organisations. Psychologists have traditionally focused on enabling those that are struggling to get to a point where they are able to cope. In Figure 11.1 this is represented by facilitating a shift from being in a position of weakness (−3) to a position of coping (0). However, the alternative emphasis proposed by positive psychology is on developing those that are excelling (+2) to

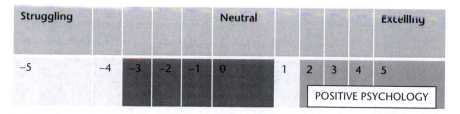

FIGURE 11.1   Human functioning and positive psychology

achieve beyond their current status (+5). By using the simple diagram and putting humans on a scale of functioning between −5 and +5 it can be seen that positive psychology looks to enable individuals, groups and organisations to move towards the excelling end of the continuum as opposed to an over-focus on managing weaknesses.

The idea of using a theoretical framework to develop techniques based on positive psychology in the sports domain is something that has considerable merit. Within sport we are often looking to enable people to achieve way beyond those who are struggling to cope, so using techniques that were initially developed to get people to a neutral rating (i.e. allowing someone with a problem to overcome that issue) appears to have only a very limited scope. In this category may be traditional interventions such as relaxation techniques or emotion regulation. The alternative principle of uti-lising theory and associated practical techniques that are specifically in place to enable people to flourish within their environment would seem far more appropriate.

Theoretical underpinning of positive psychology

Initial writing in the area of positive psychology focused on the pursuit of happiness and positive emotions. Books such as *Authentic Happiness* (Seligman, 2002) and *The How of Happiness* (Lyubomirsky, 2007) are influential examples. Current thinking, however, suggests that positive psychology is about *flourishing*, or creating an envi-ronment within which athletes can grow to fulfil their potential. This is discussed in the context of a theory of well-being known as PERMA theory (Seligman, 2011). Seligman states that the downfall of most great thinkers has been monism, whereby all human motives come down to just one (Seligman, 2011). This is evi-dent in much of the writing that has shaped our way of rationalising the driving forces behind human actions, which includes but is not limited to: a will to get power (Nietzsche), avoid anxiety (Freud) and achieve happiness (Aristotle). The PERMA theory suggests that in order to flourish it is necessary to fulfil five differ-ent human needs which are represented in the five pillars of positive psychology. Each of these pillars has three common features: they all contribute to well-being, are pursued for their own sake and are measured independently of each other. PERMA theory is illustrated by Figure 11.2.

P is for positive emotions – Positive emotions refer to items such as happiness, comfort and joy and are a cornerstone of the well-being theory and something which has a range of benefits to sports performers. Enjoyment has been recognised as having a positive impact on sports performers at both youth (Scanlan *et al.*, 1993) and elite level (Mallett & Hanrahan, 2004), as have a range of other positive emotions such as hope (Curry *et al.*, 1997), and general positive emotions (McCarthy, 2011). In addition to this, positive emotions are recognised in sport psychology theory (Hanin, 2000) and in mainstream psychology theory (Fredrickson, 1998).

E is for engagement – Engagement refers to being fully immersed in an activity to such an extent that you lose self-consciousness. This is very similar to the concept

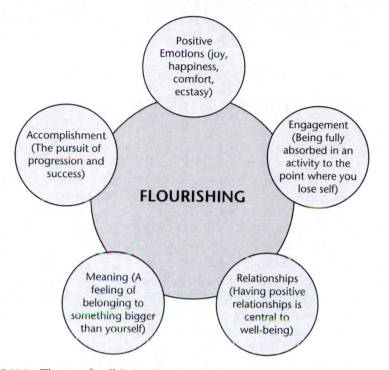

FIGURE 11.2   Theory of well-being (based on Seligman's PERMA theory, 2011)

of Flow (Jackson & Csikszentmihalyi, 1999) which has received much attention in the sport psychology literature.

R is for relationships – Positive relationships refer to prosocial experiences with other people. Seligman (2011: 20) states 'very little that is positive is solitary', suggesting that in order to flourish we need to have positive relationships with each other. Earlier in this chapter we considered the importance of the therapeutic alliance (the relationship between practitioner and client); we made the point that this was consistently demonstrated as the most important factor in how well any intervention impacted the client.

M is for meaning – Meaning refers to belonging to something that is perceived as bigger than the individual. An example of this would be spirituality, about which a small but significant body of research has emerged over recent years examining its impact within sport psychology (Watson & Nesti, 2005) and sport in general (Hamilton, 2011). The premise of this research is to enable athletes to develop a sense of perspective and draw strength from that to benefit their performance in their sport. There are frequent examples within sport where such practices could be examined within this framework. The Chicago Bulls basketball team of the 1980s and 1990s used yoga as a spiritual practice in order to try and create a sense of meaning and hence elevate the importance of 'the team' over any outstanding individuals who were part of those very successful teams.

A is for accomplishment – Accomplishment refers to progressing and succeeding (in our case within sport). Seligman suggests that in order for an individual to flourish there should exist an element of progression. Cricketers and other athletes need to see an element of progress in order to be fully satisfied.

Embedding positive psychology into coaching

Incorporating positive psychology into a professional cricket environment is challenging. A cricketer's mindset, as with any athlete, appears to be 'I will address my weaknesses in order to make me stronger'. Even at a professional level this tends to still be the case. The default setting of coaches also tends to focus on identifying and working on player weaknesses, whether technical, tactical, physical or psychological. In Figure 11.1 this may be represented by working on a weakness from −3 to 0. Applying the central principles of positive psychology would require the player and coach to focus exclusively on growing their strengths. This shift of focus can be a challenging process for both player and coach.

When asking a cricketer about their strengths and their weaknesses or what went well or badly, they almost invariably start the conversation with their weaknesses and often stumble when it comes to their strengths. Trying to get players to have an increased awareness of their strengths and what has gone well in training and match situations is often met with limited response. However, a stronger awareness of their strengths and how these are accessed and implemented in pressurised situations is extremely useful, and is not necessarily something that comes from addressing the players' weaknesses. Once a player achieves a certain level, a constant focus on their weaknesses in order to get stronger is not always as effective as focusing on how to implement their strengths or to enable a player to develop a positive focus in difficult situations.

Having introduced the underpinning principles of positive psychology, and how it deviates from traditional thinking, it may be prudent at this point for coaches to consider the following recommendations whilst reviewing their own practice:

1. During or immediately after your next coaching session, make notes on the feedback to players which have focused on addressing weaknesses. Balance this against time spent building on strengths.
2. Devise a coaching plan that deliberately prioritises attention to player strengths.
3. Having delivered this plan, reflect on player engagement, energy and performance.
4. Consider how you might build better relationships within your own coaching environment. How might you do this both between players and between players and the coaching staff?

When examining how to embed positive psychology into a sport coaching environment, the PERMA model is a useful practical theory and should enable a sports coach to have an underpinning rationale to bring creative new practices into whatever environment they are faced with. The following sections will use the five pillars of positive psychology as a framework for considering a range of practical options that have been shown to make a positive impact at group and individual levels.

Improved self-awareness and better relationships

The ancient Greek philosopher Aristotle asserted that 'knowing yourself is the beginning of all wisdom'. Modern day performance psychologists working in sport or business are familiar with the benefits of individual self-development and improved working relationships with others, through greater knowledge and understanding of preferences based on personality types. There are commercially available training programmes for practitioners to become qualified in the administration of psychometric tests such as the Myers–Briggs Type Inventory (MBTI) or the Insights profile. Depending on the environment in which you work, however, these relatively expensive options may not be available to you as a coach. Nevertheless, you can still benefit from the approach by having an understanding of the main principles. One of the main benefits provided is a common cultural language for talking about individual differences and relationship dynamics. At Sussex County Cricket Club the MBTI/Insights approach is culturally embedded and players who start on the Academy programme are introduced to the concept at an early stage. They are helped to explore their own personality type and reflect upon how it influences their behaviour individually and when working with others.

The approach is based on the theories of psychological types developed by the Swiss psychiatrist, Carl Jung. Limitation on words prevents a detailed description of the framework (see Bayne, 1995, for a review) but an entry-level consideration for coaches would be the extent to which you and your players have preferences for extroversion or for introversion. The more extrovert individual acquires energy from the outside world of other people and the environment, whereas the person with a preference for introversion is more drawn to the inner world of reflection and contemplation. This simple individual difference has significant implications for the type of coaching activity that individuals will prefer and for their interpersonal style. In combination with other influential dimensions of personality type such as practical/creative, thinking/feeling and planning/spontaneous it is possible to make a lot of progress quite quickly in terms of improved self-understanding and working relationships.

Coaches may wish to consider:

1. To what extent do you recognise different personality types in athletes that you coach? Do you adapt your style of communication to compensate for different athlete preferences?
2. Do athletes that you coach understand their own preferences? Does your coaching create opportunities for athletes to become more self-aware?
3. Contemplate a coaching approach that allows athletes to find and utilise their preferences in training and competition.

A good example of how personality preferences can influence a sporting situation is provided by the cricket batsman arriving at the crease and being greeted by their partner who has been out in the middle for a while. What does each need in terms of instructions or feedback? Would one of them like to have as much information as possible, or is a brief signal of encouragement all that is required? Similarly, what different coach inputs do different players need before performance? Theory presented to this point would suggest individualised as opposed to standardised communication. These sorts of considerations can have a critical impact on a player's confidence and mental focus and there are equivalent scenarios in all sports.

The relationship to the positive psychology framework is an interesting one in that the focus of this type of activity is to recognise preferences and differences rather than to identify strengths or weaknesses. Traditionally one of the themes is an emphasis on the idea that everyone is capable of thinking and behaving differently to suit certain situations and certain people. A positive psychology spin on MBTI would be to examine how a better understanding of personality preferences can help people to apply their strengths more effectively and to build more positive relationships with others.

The England and Wales Cricket Board has been using MBTI and Insights on its coach education programme for more than 15 years. They have been important tools used by the England team as part of the development process for individual players, coaches, and the team as a whole including support staff. On a practical level, enhanced understanding of personality-based preferences using a simple test can be useful for coaches in their everyday interactions with players. In days gone by the most perceptive coaches would have discovered such things by their own methods of man management, but it would probably have taken time. Tests like MBTI and Insights speed up the process and take it onto another level where shared self-awareness enables individuals and coaches to find the best ways of working together. Once athletes have enhanced self-awareness they are likely to be in a better position to engage in a further process of improving relationships based on a teambuilding model known as the Johari Window (Figure 11.3; Luft & Ingham, 1955).

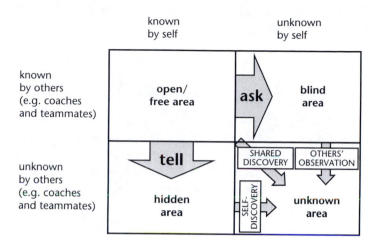

FIGURE 11.3   The Johari Window model of self-awareness and relationship building (adapted from Luft and Ingham, 1955)

The quadrants within the model expand or shrink in relation to each other as the player or coach gains more knowledge about themselves through experience, observation, feedback from others, communication and self-reflection. To operate most effectively and productively, people need to develop their 'open' area. This is the space where communication is good, with no mistrust or misunderstanding – where there is openness. Learning more about yourself through exposure to a new situation can shrink your 'unknown' area and expand your 'hidden' area. If you demonstrate or communicate this self-learning to other people, you expand your 'open' area, where people know you and you know yourself. If you ask for and take note of feedback, then things people know about you will become part of your self-knowledge, moving from your 'blind' area to your 'open' area. An understanding of this model can be advantageous to coaches and players as it highlights the extreme importance of open and honest communication and reinforces the power of disclosure and feedback in developing relationships and enhancing performance.

Here are two examples:

1.   A player gets frustrated in team meetings when asked to brainstorm ideas and just wants to get on with the task. Her fellow team members see her as impatient and disinterested. But when she explains where she is coming from, they understand her better and realise that she can still play a vital role in getting things done. In sharing self-knowledge with others, information is moved from the 'hidden' area to the 'open' area.

2.   A team are preparing for a major competition. Their coach has undertaken a great deal of analysis of the strengths of their potential opposition and has scheduled a number of meetings in which strategy will be discussed. After the first meeting, several of the players are worried that too much emphasis was placed

on their own shortcomings and that the confidence of the team will be negatively affected if the pattern is repeated in subsequent meetings. Fortunately, they enjoy a strong team environment and are able to feed their concerns back to the coach who, in turn, was able to rethink her approach to the remaining strategy meetings. This is a good example of personal growth for the coach and team through reduction of a 'blind' area and expansion of the shared 'open' area.

At this point it may be beneficial for coaches to think of a working example from their own context where expanding the open area can facilitate better relationships within a team. This may be a real or hypothetical example to illuminate some of the principles of the theory presented in this section.

Enhanced meaning within a sport context

The positive psychology framework also highlights the benefits to well-being of feeling connected to something greater than yourself as an individual. As mentioned earlier, this is often interpreted as referring to a spiritual or religious dimension but it can be equally useful when considering the importance of appreciating the wider context in which you operate. Sports coaches and players are normally part of an organisation with a structure with many people involved, and usually a history and accompanying traditions. By paying due respect to the heritage and values of the wider organisation it is possible for individuals to have a more developed sense of what is expected of them and how they can best employ their strengths to meet collective aims. The New Zealand rugby 'All Blacks' are well known for the way in which they foster their traditions, including the Haka, and have managed to imbue their famous international shirt with an almost mystical power. Many organisations, both sporting and in other domains, would love to even partially replicate the sense of reverent belonging that New Zealand rugby players experience.

As an example, at Sussex County Cricket Club the five key values for the club are well established as being: Respect, Selflessness, Honesty, Drive and Enjoyment. These values were agreed upon after a consultation process including all staff over an extended period of time. They are now fixed in the modern tradition of the club and are used in all areas of the club as a guide to strategy development, leadership and expected behaviour of team members. New members of staff and players, including all junior and Academy players, learn about the club's values as part of an induction process. The crucial aspect in the implementation of such an approach is that the values are exemplified by senior staff and that regular opportunities are taken to consider their meaning and link the values to real world activity. Academy players are especially encouraged to think of examples where application of the values is important and to recognise opportunities to develop their own personal style.

Another way in which a stronger appreciation of a wider context, and a greater strength, can be achieved is to encourage players to have a sense of historical perspective with regard to their club. Coaches and players have gone before and coaches and players will come after. At Sussex, the curator of the club museum was asked to put together a quiz called 'Who we are? Where do we come from?' in order to form the basis of a teambuilding session. Questions highlighted the long history of the club and the roles played by significant individuals, including those staff from the club who made the ultimate sacrifice in the two World Wars.

Within Essex County Cricket Club the Academy director adopts a similar approach to enhance the meaning of playing for the club to the Academy players. Players are asked to research selected past players who have represented the club and made a positive impact since the Club's formation in 1876. They are then asked to feed this information back to each other in a structured classroom based setting. The emphasis is on the club being bigger and more important than any single player, regardless of the standard of the player. This sort of perspective can be linked to the concept of 'meaning' and also to beneficial cognitive constructions regarding the relative pressures involved in sporting activity.

> Coaches may consider ways in which they can create a sense of meaning or belonging within a wider, higher context. This may utilise history, culture or spirituality to help athletes gain a sense of perspective and view their performance accordingly.

The continued pursuit of accomplishment as a pillar of flourishing

Sport psychology has made many contributions to strategies for enhancing the continued development and performance of already highly successful competitors. In terms of the 'Sussex Values' outlined above the key element is 'Drive', which is defined as being 'self-motivated to constantly strive for excellence and challenge current boundaries'. The key mental skill required in this area is that of effective self-regulation through awareness of strengths, the setting of challenging goals, self-monitoring and the willingness to accept feedback.

Players should be encouraged to have clear goals for every practice session and for every competition performance. An appropriate blend of outcome, performance and process goals has been demonstrated to have the most positive effect on player development and performance (Filby *et al.*, 1999). Process goals are especially important for guiding training and promoting full engagement with practice activity. Players must be perfectly clear about the real purpose of every training session. In cricket there are, broadly speaking, three identifiable modes of practice that have very different aims and it is vital that the coach and the player practising have shared awareness and agreement about the purpose of the current session. If the player is looking to 'develop' technically then their focus of attention and preferred activity will be quite different to when they are aiming to 'perform' tactically in a more ecologically valid practice scenario. A final legitimate aim of practice is for the player to simply want to 'feel good' mentally, in which case they will again have different requirements in terms of activity and will be using a different measure of success. A common source of player/coach misunderstanding is when the different practice modes are not sufficiently well understood and success criteria are not agreed upon.

Process goals also provide the most reliable framework for facilitating effective performance under pressure based upon absorption in the present moment to the exclusion of task–irrelevant distractions. To be effective a performance routine should ideally be based on existing habits and strengths that the player has developed naturally. However, the dangers of 'overthinking' remain ever-present, and are clearly explained by conscious processing theory (Masters, 1992), so extreme care must be taken when working on deliberately practised routines. It is particularly important to avoid part process goals that specify technical behaviour (e.g. 'arch my back at take-off') and to instead make use of simple trigger words (e.g. 'drive') that promote automatic movements. An interesting study by Cotterill *et al.* (2010) also challenged the previously accepted idea that routines have to be extremely consistent in their time duration, and highlighted that consistency in the thought process is the real key to success.

Focus on process goals could be strongly aligned to encouraging players to recognise and practice their strengths. Ask players and coaches in a group setting to discuss what they deem to be the strengths of each other. Once you have a basic appreciation from the coaching staff, team mates and the individual, begin creating challenging situations where the onus is on the player to implement those strengths. The strengths could be either cricket-skill based (e.g. the player may be able to consistently hit the top of the off stump) or psychological (e.g. the player may have an ability to stay positive in adverse conditions). Set up a scenario where each player is aware of what the other is trying to implement and then review it thoroughly to consider the impact.

Recall occasions where you have tasked athletes with achieving outcome goals as part of their criteria for success in competition. Reconsider how the goals that they are set can incorporate process and performance goals which offer complete immersion in the task and include the application of their strengths.

Facilitating athletes' goals that adhere to the bases of positive psychology are likely to create a setting in which the athlete feels more confident of success.

Promoting positive emotions as a pillar of flourishing

The positive diary in sport (PDS) (Beale & Wilson, 2013) is an adapted positive psychology tool for direct use in sport (Figure 11.4). This technique has been utilised in the field in a range of different sports and has developed from the applied

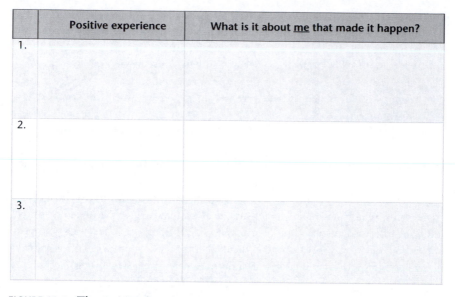

	Positive experience	What is it about <u>me</u> that made it happen?
1.		
2.		
3.		

FIGURE 11.4   The positive diary in sport

work of the second author. Within cricket this has been used in both an Academy and a professional setting. Despite its apparent simplicity this intervention can have significant outcomes as it is a practical way of engaging athletes with their strengths instead of weaknesses. Noticeable outcomes from its use have been reduced performance anxiety, greater motivation and a more positive outlook when facing challenging situations. When using this approach it is advisable to give athletes autonomy on when and where they complete the PDS to encourage adherence. As a start point, work with the player to ensure that they are able to find positive experiences even in situations where they are not immediately obvious, e.g. even when a player may have underperformed there may still be a lesson within the performance or they may have built rapport with team mates on the day – work with the player to enable them to attribute that positive experience to themselves (the desired end point is that the player takes ownership of the good things that happen).

A related tool that has been very effective within a range of settings is the 'positive frame of mind' reminder sheet. This simple but effective intervention is based on the work of Richard Butler, who used a very similar idea with Great Britain boxers in the 1990s (Butler, 1996). He recognised the benefits of athletes spending time thinking about positive aspects of their training and performance, especially in the lead up to competition. The reminder sheet is designed to be kept in a player's kit bag or pinned up on a locker or at home. The theoretical underpinning for this approach can be attributed to Bandura's model of sources of self-efficacy (Bandura, 1977) but it clearly also fits into a positive psychology formulation of the significance of positive emotions. Butler's original sheet took the form of a Union Jack and included spaces for the athlete to record:

- 'Strengths' (What do you usually do particularly well? What are you good at?)
- 'Improvements' (What improvements have you made in the last six months?)
- 'Achievements' (What are your best achievements in the last six months?)
- 'Preparation' (What aspects of preparation have gone particularly well?)
- 'Edge' (What will give you an edge over your opponent?)
- 'Previous performance' (What were the main positive aspects of your last few performances?)
- 'Goal' (What do you aim to do? Focus on process rather than outcome.)

An adapted version (Figure 11.5) simplifies the above into 'strengths', 'performances' and 'process goals'.

Part of the role of a reminder sheet is to prompt the use of positive imagery of experiences, which has been demonstrated as being useful for fostering positive emotions and performance states (Thomas *et al.*, 2011). As a coach it is really important to encourage players to properly 'bank their successes' and to make a habit of taking confidence from mental rehearsal of themselves using strengths to perform at their best.

To complete this section on promoting positive emotions of players, we briefly consider arguably the most powerful participation motive of all. The enshrining of *enjoyment* as a core value at Sussex County Cricket Club is indicative of genuine commitment to a positive approach to player development and behaviour. Coaches and players have agreed that being able to 'actively appreciate each other's differences and genuinely enjoy their own and others' success' is a vital plank of sustained flourishing as a club. Cricket is unusual in that players are required to compete under pressure on consecutive days for extended periods of time, often without much break. In this intensely competitive environment it is important for well-

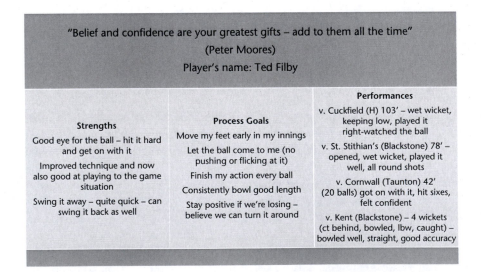

FIGURE 11.5 Example of a positive frame of mind reminder sheet

being that players are able to be authentic and true to themselves. This has tradition-ally been a stiff challenge for all, but especially for young players new to a dressing room.

In terms of promoting positive emotions in players that you coach, reflect on how you can:

1. Maximise player successes to catalyse future performance expectations.
2. Surround the athlete with reminders of their strengths in the lead up to competition.
3. Encourage 'in the moment' enjoyment of players, and encourage enjoy-ing each others' success in team settings.

Conclusion

The types of approaches explained in this chapter can go a long way towards facili-tating more positive experiences of sport for coaches and players. Most of the tech-niques and activities mentioned have the potential to affect players in all of the five pillars of positive psychology that comprise the PERMA model. The key is to apply the theory and be creative with the techniques that you use to enable players to develop in each of the areas. Throughout this chapter opportunities for coaches to consider principles in relation to their own practice are facilitated. Whilst the authors have accrued significant experience in applying these principles as sport psychology practitioners at elite level, it is felt that application of the foundations of positive psychology, using interventions outlined here, should be within the realm of the work of the coach at all levels.

References

Anderson, A.G., Knowles, Z. and Gilbourne, D. (2004) Reflective practice for sport psy-chologists: concepts, models, practical implications, and thoughts on dissemination. *Sport Psychologist*, 18(2), 188–203.

Bandura, A. (1977) Self-efficacy: toward a unifying theory of behavioral change. *Psychological Review*, 84(2), 191–215.

Bayne, R. (1995) *The Myers–Briggs Type Indicator: A critical review and practical guide*. London: Chapman and Hall.

Beale, J.T. and Wilson, M. (2013) Sport psychology, in Bayne, R. & Jinks, G. (Eds) *Applied psychology: Research training and practice*, 154–165. London: Sage Publications.

Butler, R.J. (1996) *Sports psychology in action*. Oxford: Butterworth-Heinemann.

Cotterill, S., Sanders, R. and Collins, D. (2010) Developing effective pre-performance rou-tines in golf: Why don't we ask the golfer? *Journal of Applied Sport Psychology*, 22, 51–64.

Curry, L.A., Snyder, C.R., Cook, D.L., Ruby, B.C. and Rehm, M. (1997) Role of hope in academic and sport achievement. *Journal of Personality and Social Psychology*, 73(6), 1257–1267.

Filby, W.C.D., Maynard, I.W. and Graydon, J.K. (1999) The effect of multiple-goal strategies on performance outcomes in training and competition. *Journal of Applied Sport Psychology*, 11, 230–246.

Fredrickson, B.L. (1998) Cultivated emotions: parental socialization of positive emotions and self-conscious emotions. *Psychological Inquiry*, 9(4), 279–281.

Greenspan, M.J. and Feltz, D.L. (1989) Psychological interventions with athletes in competitive situations: a review. *Sport Psychologist*, 3(3), 219–236.

Hamilton, M. (2011) Guest editor's introduction. *Journal of the Philosophy of Sport*, 38(2), 175–176.

Hanin, Y.L. (2000) *Emotions in sport*. Champaign, IL: Human Kinetics.

Jackson, S.A. and Csikszentmihalyi, M. (1999) *Flow in sports*. Champaign, IL: Human Kinetics.

Luft, J. and Ingham, H. (1955) The Johari Window, a graphic model of interpersonal awareness. *Proceedings of the Western Training Laboratory in Group Development*. Los Angeles: UCLA.

Lyubomirsky, S. (2007) *The how of happiness: A practical guide to getting the life that you want*. London: Piatkus.

McCarthy, P.J. (2011) Positive emotion in sport performance: current status and future directions. *International Review of Sport and Exercise Psychology*, 4(1), 50–69.

Mallett, C.J. and Hanrahan, S.J. (2004) Elite athletes: why does the 'fire' burn so brightly? *Psychology of Sport and Exercise*, 5(2), 183–200.

Masters, R. (1992) Knowledge, knerves, and know-how: the role of explicit versus implicit knowledge in the breakdown of a complex motor skill under pressure. *British Journal of Psychology*, 83, 343–358.

Scanlan, T.K., Carpenter, P.J., Lobel, M. and Simons, J.P. (1993) Sources of enjoyment for youth sport athletes. *Pediatric Exercise Science*, 5, 275–285.

Seligman, M.E. (2002) *Authentic happiness: Using the new positive psychology to realize your potential for lasting fulfilment*. New York: Simon and Schuster.

Seligman, M. (2011) *Flourish: A new understanding of happiness and well-being and how to achieve them*. London: Nicholas Brealey Publishing.

Seligman, M.E. and Csikszentmihalyi, M. (2000) Positive psychology: an introduction, *American Psychologist*, 55, 5–14.

Thomas, O., Lane, A. and Kingston, K. (2011) Defining and contextualizing robust sport-confidence. *Journal of Applied Sport Psychology*, 23(2), 189–208.

Vealey, R.S. (1994) Knowledge development and implementation in sport psychology: a review of the sport psychologist, 1987–1992. *Sport Psychologist*, 8(4), 331–348.

Watson, N.J. and Nesti, M. (2005) The role of spirituality in sport psychology consulting: an analysis and integrative review of literature. *Journal of Applied Sport Psychology*, 17(3), 228–239.

Weinberg, R.S. and Comar, W. (1994) The effectiveness of psychological interventions in competitive sport. *Sports Medicine*, 18(6), 406–418.

12

A VALUES-BASED APPROACH TO COACHING WITHIN SPORT FOR DEVELOPMENT PROGRAMMES

John Lambert

Introduction

Ever since sport was formally recognised as a viable and practical tool to assist in the achievement of the Millennium Development Goals (UN, 2003) we have seen a worldwide proliferation of programmes following sport for development and peace (SDP) aims (Kidd, 2008). The distinctive nature of each SDP programme is determined by its aims, the intended 'recipients', the 'agents of change' and the context. Their common characteristic is the use of sport as a vehicle to initiate social and cultural change. However, are the coaching methods that they used within these interventions appropriate to the underlying objectives, whether they are to improve community relations, health, gender equality or education? This chapter presents a coaching model that unlocks the potential of sport from its purely technocratic function to assuming a different purpose, as a medium for teaching values which are compatible with the aspirations underpinning these SDP interventions. It will explain that the sustainable behaviour change required in order to 'make a difference' to the recipients in these SDP programmes is made possible by facilitating adjustments in the value systems of those involved. If we want to bring about lasting change in attitude and behaviour we must begin by changing values.

Sport can either foster harmonious relationships or generate conflict depending on the values it is laden with. The context and the meanings attached to sport along with the teaching and learning styles used are critical to determining which values are promoted and, consequently, whether positive or negative affective and social outcomes follow. Simply getting young people together to play sport does not guarantee a favourable outcome. There are a plethora of SDP initiatives that have emerged in recent years (sportanddev.org), many of which, on close inspection, seem to have no clear curriculum or pedagogic guidelines for coaches. Consequently, this leads one to question the efficacy of the on-field activities undertaken and the extent of their community impact. Those who have called for the work of SDP programmes to be viewed through a critical lens (Coalter, 2010; 2014; Kay, 2009; Levermore, 2008) are to be commended, as many SDP projects do not stand up to robust scrutiny, but it is just as important to provide examples of good practice in this domain. The most effective SDP initiatives are characterised by clear aims, an explicit coaching programme, trained coaches and local people who feel empowered (Wallis and Lambert, 2013).

The next section will describe the development of a coaching model which has been designed to facilitate the transmission of prosocial values through sport in divided societies, and has been widely tried in the field over a period spanning ten years (Lambert, 2013a). The model is located within a theoretical framework of values structure and values change which will be explained in the third section. The Real Madrid Foundation 'Basketvalues' programme is featured in the fourth section as a pocket of good practice in teaching values through sport (Vila *et al.*, 2012). The fifth, and final, section will make a case for the widespread use of values-based coaching in SDP projects as a more appropriate alternative to the hegemonic performance culture that currently exists, and will ask readers to reflect on their own practice within community coaching.

The development of values-based coaching

Football for Peace (F4P) is a nongovernmental organisation which has operated in divided societies, such as Israel and Ireland, since 2001 and seeks to use sport as a medium through which to teach values that promote conflict prevention and peaceful co-existence. It began in Israel as a small-scale project that linked two neighbouring Jewish and Arab towns through a youth football programme. By 2011 it had grown into a large-scale grass-roots intervention involving 1,200 Arab and Jewish children and over 100 coaches from 20 municipalities from all over Israel.[1] Fifty coaches from the UK and Germany were also recruited to deliver a values-based curriculum of football activities to mixed groups of Arab and Jewish children aged 10–14.

The F4P coaching manual which guides the coaches through the programme sets out a pedagogy that uses football activities as a means to transmit the core values of F4P: respect, responsibility, equity and inclusion, trust and neutrality (Lambert, 2006; 2013a). Both the F4P values, which were chosen because they are all conducive to community cohesion, and the coaching manual were introduced in 2004 when it was decided that the project needed to do more to ensure that it was underpinned by principles that support a community relations agenda, and that a structured curriculum was required by coaches which would guide the teaching of the core values.

The development of the F4P coaching manual has been driven by an action research paradigm (McNiff and Whitehead, 2006) where feedback from the coaches on the efficacy of the pedagogic model has, over time, led to adaptations to the content and have progressively shaped its evolution. Much of the research orthodoxy in relation to values is positivist in nature but an interpretive, pluralist outlook served to inform this project, as each coach was asked about their contextual experience of values-based coaching. There are three distinctive elements to the coaching programme: the content has a values emphasis in contrast to a football skills focus; the coaching strategy is facilitative as opposed to controlling; and coaches are expected to observe and reflect on player behaviours rather than performance.

The F4P coaching model

The F4P project aims to transmit values conducive to conflict resolution and peaceful co-existence through sport, for these values to be internalised by young people and then transferred into other situations off the field. Changes in attitudes and behaviour are preceded by changes in each individual's value system, so it is reasonable to assume that sustained, tangible changes in behaviour would indicate that an initial values change has occurred (Bardi *et al.*, 2009; Bardi and Goodwin, 2011). The conceptual process for this adaptation will follow later in the chapter but first we must explore how coaches teach values through sport.

The coaching programme centres on a *facilitate–observe–reflect–reinforce* coach strategy. Learning activities which create values dilemmas are facilitated, player behaviours associated with the F4P values are observed, and these 'teachable moments' (TMs) are reflected upon during and at the end of the session, after which examples of prosocial behaviour are reinforced with praise. For example, the players referee their own games and the coach will stand back and look for behaviour which serves to make the game run fairly (TMs), for instance, a player calling a foul by his own team, and then they will reflect on that and other TMs at the end of the session. Following that, the coach would attach the tangible behaviour (fair play) to one or more of the abstract values (respect, responsibility), before reinforcing it with praise. An extension of this would then be to ask the players where the same values might be applied outside sport. The scenario might look like this: a player calls a foul by one of his team against an opponent (which is observed by the coach) – that player awards a free kick to the opponent's team – the coach highlights the TM during the post-match reflective phase – the coach reinforces the behaviour with praise and group applause – the coach asks the group which of the core F4P values it relates to (respect and responsibility) and whether any of the players can offer an example outside football where it might apply (e.g. owning up to making mistakes at home or school and taking responsibility for your actions). Put simply, the coach asks 'What?' 'So What?' 'Now What?' (Beedy, 1997) in the knowledge that contextualisation is what gives the children a rationale for their behaviour and a conviction to take it beyond the football field. Behaviours are more likely to become internalised if the children not only know what prosocial behaviour is and what it looks like but why they should behave that way.

The example of a coaching session from the F4P coaching manual presented in Table 12.1 shows how activities are designed to facilitate TMs, and the coaches are signposted to where these may emerge from the learning activity.

TABLE 12.1 An example coaching plan from the Football for Peace coaching manual

Under 14, Session 4, Dribbling skills

Activity	*Teachable moments*
Warm up	
Fox and Hen: Played in groups of 8–9. Six people hold hands to form a tight circle. One 'fox' starts outside of the circle and a 'hen' is inside. The circle must work to protect the hen from the fox by tightening the circle to create a barrier and loosening it to allow the hen to be released from the centre or enter it from outside when appropriate. The game is over when the fox tags the hen. Allow each person to experience both roles.	*Responsibility/Equity and Inclusion/Trust* Each member of the team has an important role in protecting the hen. Group bonding activity.
Head to Head: In pairs, the players balance a ball between their foreheads whilst racing each other over a set distance. If they drop the ball they must go back to the start. Progression: join up pairs and run a relay race.	*Equity and Inclusion/Neutrality/Respect* Encourage them to pair up with a partner that they do not know very well. Observe for cheating.
Technical phase	
Tag Football: Every player dribbles a ball around an area. On the coach's command the players can tag each other. You place a hand on the part of the body on which you are tagged (e.g. shoulder). When players are tagged three times and have no hands free they leave the area and have to perform a skill of the coach's choice before they can re-enter the game.	*Respect/Responsibility/Inclusion* Observe for attempts to cheat. Are the less able dribblers targeted? Offer the less technically able the chance to re-enter each game.
Kick Out: Every child dribbles a ball around the area while attempting to kick another player's ball out of the area to eliminate them. Eliminated players must make 10 ball juggles to return to the action. Progression: Eliminated players can stay in the area to help other players retain as many balls as possible or become defenders. The final game may involve no return to find a champion.	
Game phase	
Numbers Game: The players (6) in each team stand in a waiting zone and number off 1 to 6. When the coach calls out a number the players of that number from respective teams run out from the waiting zone and play 1v1 until the ball goes dead. A team score is kept.	*Respect/Responsibility/Equity and Inclusion* After one round of 1v1s, ask the players to pair up again across teams according to ability. Give them the responsibility of making the game fair.
End Zone Football: 4v4 games in 30×20 areas with the aim of dribbling the ball into a 5-yard end zone to score. Change opponents every 5/6 minutes. Progression: remove end zones and add a small central goal to shoot in and 10-yard gates to dribble through, i.e. alternative ways to score goals.	Check for adherence to the rules. Are any conflicts resolved amicably?

(Continued)

TABLE 12.1 An example coaching plan from the Football for Peace coaching manual (Continued)

Under 14, Session 4, Dribbling skills

Activity	*Teachable moments*
Cool down	
Start with *Impulse* where a small ball is thrown around the circle. The players are only allowed to speak when they have the ball. They can choose to talk about an example of football skill or of behaviour by their peers. Highlight and reinforce positive behaviour as much as good skill, showing that you value good behaviour just as much if not more than skill.	Be ready to discuss any of the core values, *Respect/Responsibility/ Equity and Inclusion Neutrality/ Trust* as they arise and relate behaviours to each value.

The notion that coaches can guide children to reflect on their behaviour and that of others, think in an abstract way in order to generalise from one experience to another, and finally to broaden their thinking to apply what they have learned to other situations is key to the transfer of values as they are generalisable across contexts (Rokeach, 1973). A player may offer to leave the field in order to allow the substitutes to gain more game time and this selfless attitude may, in turn, be applied to someone who offers to start on the bench. The value can also be applied in another context to giving up time to help an elderly neighbour. In relation to each value the coach prompts the children to ask 'What does this mean?' 'What does this look like in action?'. By transferring the learning to the outside world the coach has 'encapsulated the profound metaphors of life that lie just under the surface of the games we play' (Beedy, 1997: 114).

Teaching values through moral dilemmas

Sport, with its propensity to cause rivalry and conflict, is a prime medium through which to teach values. In spite of the aggression, cheating and even violence that can accompany sport, there are always performers who exhibit prosocial values associated with fair play. These situations offer fertile territory for behaviours which can be highlighted as TMs and the F4P manual deliberately includes activities that are competitive and create moral dilemmas.

At the end of the coaching programme in Israel each team within the project competes in the F4P Festival, a tournament in a large venue in Galilee. Whilst the structure of the competition is set by the organisers, the games are played without referees. The F4P values have previously been transmitted to the players through the coaching and the festival provides a situation where they are put to the test in a highly competitive setting. Only by giving responsibility to young people can you teach it as a value. It is ironic that typically the games run smoothly and fairly without adult intervention and that the few problems that do occur are instigated by over-zealous adult coaches.

F4P teams run their own substitutions independently of the coach, which creates the moral dilemma of whether to give your most able players more game time thus increasing the chance of winning as opposed to being equitable and inclusive by facilitating equal playing time for all. There will be those players who promote equity and inclusion through their behaviour in such situations, and they are then recognised and praised by the coach. By devolving responsibility, the coaches give the players the opportunity to show how important equity and inclusion is to them.

Coach education

Training coaches to deliver this alternative pedagogical paradigm is critical to its implementation but can be a challenging task, as coaching is traditionally located in the ideology of performance rather than in the social and affective domain (Lambert, 2013b). The F4P coach education camp brings together coaches from the UK and Israel's Arab and Jewish communities for a week-long series of off-pitch teambuilding activities and on-pitch practical coaching sessions. Those practitioners who are experienced in applying the values-based football model present exemplar coaching sessions with the new coaches. Having been subjected to the methods themselves as recipients, the novice coaches are then expected to plan and conduct an F4P session for local schoolchildren under the guidance of coach mentors. The coach educators are using similar methods to train the coaches as they are when they teach the children: reciprocity, positive feedback and reinforcement within principles of self-autonomy. At the end of the week the coaches are able to reflect and implement the values that permeate the project.

Learning theories

The F4P coaching strategies are underpinned by two learning theories. First, Social Learning theory (Bandura, 1986) which rests on rewarding and modelling good behaviour so that it is reinforced and copied, and ignoring/punishing bad behaviour. Aversive responses to antisocial behaviour are less effective than positive reinforcement of prosocial behaviour in an educational setting, so the latter is encouraged in F4P. Typically, in matches goals may be marked out with cones, leading to disputes over whether the ball went inside or outside the cone. The coach will look for children who compromise and mediate in these disputes and then praise them in order to reinforce such behaviour with the group.

Second, structural-development theory, widely used in sport interventions (Shields and Bredemeier, 1995), proposes that moral development follows moral reasoning and dialogue. To facilitate this cognitive process demands that coaches are skilled at crafting questions at an appropriate level that develop reflection, discussion and understanding. The 'cool down' in each session involves a reflective phase where players are invited to highlight TMs that they have observed in the preceding session, followed by a discussion which links that behaviour with the core values.

Both learning theories are firmly integrated into every F4P coaching session, adhering to the principle that young people learn from what the coaches say and what they do as they bring values to life.

Having described the development of values-based coaching and offered an insight into the coach behaviours that allow value transmission, it is now necessary to explain the structure of values and how changes in values systems occur.

Value theory and value change

Rokeach (1973) defined values as an individual's enduring beliefs that certain forms of behaviour, or long-term outcomes, are more personally or socially desirable than their opposing alternatives. In other words, people apply their values when deciding how they behave in pursuit of a long-term goal. Somebody, for example, may play fairly in order to gain social recognition or alternatively somebody else may cheat in order to win. As well as being criteria that people hold to guide their decisions, values are used as criteria to evaluate the behaviour of others.

The most important characteristic of values to consider when addressing value change is that individuals see certain values as more desirable than others and thus create subjectively ranked personal *value systems*. It is 'this enduring organisation of beliefs concerning preferable modes of conduct or end states of existence arranged in a continuum of relative importance' (Rokeach, 1973: 5) that must be altered if sustainable changes in attitude and behaviour are to occur. It is not sufficient just to know what values a person holds, rather what is more useful is to know the relative importance of these values to that person, as it is this that will determine their decisions and actions. Values-based coaching aims to change the value system of the participants with the intention of increasing the importance of prosocial values, such as respect, responsibility, trust and equity, in this hierarchical order.

Value structure

Extensive international studies have found that there are ten universal 'desirable' values, which are based on human needs, and form the basis of personal motivation and transcend situations (Schwartz, 1992). These are represented in Figure 12.1 as a circumplex diagram which positions conflicting values diametrically opposed to and compatible values adjacent to each other.

There are four higher order headings which categorise the values into self-enhancement and self-transcendence (concern for self versus concern for others), and openness to change, a polar opposite of conservation and stability. These will all be desirable values to some people and the most desirable for each person will influence their attitudes and behaviour accordingly.

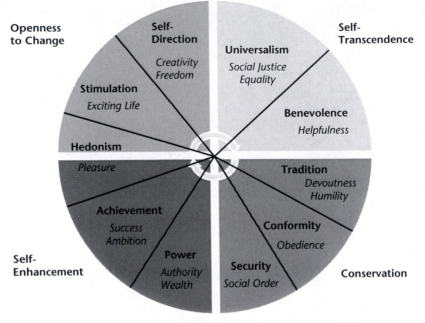

Circle Organized by Motivational Congruence and Opposition

FIGURE 12.1 A revised model of ten motivationally distinct values and their circular motivational structure (Schwartz, 1992)

Bardi and Schwartz (2013) assert that the agencies that organise interventions which seek to change value systems need to understand the dynamics of value conflict and compatibility. The reciprocal relationship between values is such that if a value increases in importance then adjacent values will become more influential. At the same time opposing values will be reduced in importance. The more important equity and inclusion (universality) are to a player, the less influence power and security will have, and the more importance liberty (self-direction) and friendship (benevolence) will assume. The F4P aims to develop peaceful co-existence through promoting equity and inclusion, friendship and openness to change in opposition to power and resistance to change. The conflicting and compatible relationships between values have underpinned the research on value change, as they mediate adjustments in the relative status of different values in a person's value system (Schwartz, 1992).

Value change

One's values are relatively stable and transcend all situations, so bringing about sustainable value change is a challenging task. Bardi and her collaborators have identified three processes that can lead to changes in a person's value system, all of which can be applied to sports interventions.

Adaptation occurs when people adapt their values to reinforcement contingencies in the environment. They may experience frustration if their dominant values are challenged and it may lead to questioning of those values, and, if this happens repeatedly, the effect may be to diminish the importance of those values (Bardi and Goodwin, 2011). The continuous recognition and reinforcement of the F4P values through reflection and praise has acted as a stimulus for value change. The young people may question their existing value systems if they continually come into conflict with those of the coach and the project. The fact that the coach values fair play more highly than winning will eventually lead to players sharing those values.

A reappraisal of values and consequent changes in attitudes can occur when dissonance exists between a person's expressed values and their actions. By coaches encouraging behaviours related to the F4P values it can lead to the children challenging some of the deep-seated values they hold which may be antagonistic to the F4P values. The resulting self-dissatisfaction and self-persuasion is known as *consistency maintenance* and can be a driver of changes in value systems. If, for example, a coach mixes the Arabs and Jews in the same teams and continually reinforces the idea that every player should be treated equally, then this may gradually erode the 'us and them' attitudes on both sides of a religious and social divide.

Joining a new group or team may lead to conflict between somebody's personal values and those salient in the group. *Group identification* is where a person adopts the values of the group even though they may differ from those they previously held important. The expectation in F4P is that Arabs and Jews work together and respect each other on an equal footing with shared team values, which may replace previously dominant values of mistrust and entrenchment, and these alternative values are then used by the children to interpret situations in a different way due to the switch in identification. A symbolic expression of group identification is the custom of the mixed Arab and Jewish teams all wearing the same shirts and being named after a European club. The Festival is played between teams with names such as Bayern Munich, Chelsea and Barcelona, and religious and racial differences are superseded by shared team values.

Teaching values through competition: the Real Madrid 'Basketvalues' programme

Aside from F4P, there are some notable examples of SDP initiatives that place values teaching at the forefront of their pedagogical programme (Vila *et al.*, 2014). The 'Basketvalues' programme (Vila *et al.*, 2012) is a grass-roots community basketball scheme run by Real Madrid Foundation (RMF) which promotes respect, self-esteem, equality, team spirit, motivation, autonomy and health through coaching and competition. Two key features of the programme are the manner in which it recognises the potential of competition for teaching

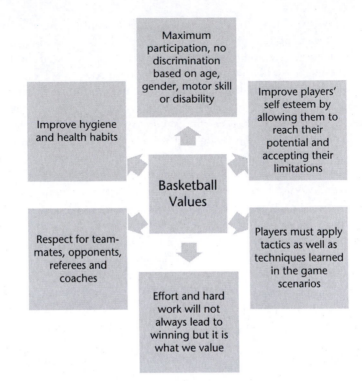

FIGURE 12.2 Adapted version of the basic objectives of the competition for beginner's basketball (Vila *et al.*, 2014)

values and the way that it integrates parents/guardians into their child's values education. Figure 12.2 illustrates how the programme uses competition to transmit values to young people through its 'Compete to share ... values' project.

The RMF Socio-Sporting Schools maximise the opportunity that competition creates for rewarding prosocial behaviour by instigating a 'white card' scheme. The 'white card' initiative has been successful as an incentive for children to model behaviour relating to their core values during competition. The children, their family or the coach can nominate individuals to receive a white card if they model the moral values that are associated with sportsmanship such as admitting to their own fouls, applauding good play from opponents, respecting the referee and encouraging other players after they make mistakes.

Families are encouraged to observe the basketball games and to identify players they think are eligible for a white card. From time to time parents are invited to join in the coaching sessions as players and experience the programme for themselves. The notion that increased involvement from families will lead to 'buy in' and reinforcement of the values in the home has been vindicated by evaluative data collected so far.

The practice of recognition and rewards for behaviour needs to be handled carefully as, when positive reinforcement takes the form of prizes, it can lead to 'artificial' motivation where extrinsic goals override intrinsic motivation. The rationale behind the choice of behaviour determines the morality of such behaviour (Shields and Bredemeier, 1995) so we must guard against children exhibiting desirable behaviour for the wrong reasons. That said, the white card is a tangible expression of the value placed on fair play by the RMF which has the support of players, coaches and families.

Both the F4P and RMF Basketvalues programmes have similar characteristics which are fundamental to values-based sport initiatives. They both:

- Use a pedagogic model which invites coaches to take a humanistic view of their role and places values teaching at the forefront of their practice.
- Create a learning environment through coach behaviours which promote the transcending values of the project (Lambert, 2013b). This climate allows young people whose value systems are taking shape to learn positive values.
- Promote a facilitative coaching style which reflects values of responsibility and equality in contrast to controlling methods which reflect power and (in)security (Cushion, 2010) – a moral coach–athlete relationship that espouses both paternalism and autonomy.
- Are underpinned by sound teaching and learning principles grounded in academic theory.

The key messages to consider

Sport is widely regarded as a cultural vehicle through which young people can be encouraged to replace anti-social with prosocial values (Lee, 2004). The efficacy of SDP programmes tasked with changing the behaviour of young people will largely depend on the interaction between the coach and the participants, which suggests that greater attention needs to be placed on the nature of what is taught and the coaching styles used in this process. On close examination, many SDP programmes apply a performance coaching paradigm which is inappropriate to their objectives, rather than coaching in the affective and social domains. There is a compelling case to be made for an accredited coach education programme to be tailored for the significant number of coaches who operate in grass-roots programmes with objectives that go beyond a narrow elitist, competitive-competence view of sport and instead seek to promote changes in behaviour through value change. This move would not only enhance the social enrichment impact of their work but also help to 'professionalise' the demographic of coaches who function towards the participation end of the performance–participation continuum, and thus raise their status.

Finally, readers who are coaching in an SDP setting are invited to address some reflective questions which will require them to consider the coaching climate in which they practise and their relationship with their participants.

Some reflective questions for coaches working in the SPD sector:

- Is the content of your coaching compatible with your aims?
- Is your coaching style suitable for achieving those aims?
- If the answer to either of the questions above is no, then how can you improve how you practise?
- What values do you transmit as a coach? Competition or inclusion? Controlling or athlete-centred? Equity or elitism?
- What values do you try to instill in your participants? And how is this achieved? Do these values link to the aims of your project?

Note

1 Football for Peace also operates a cross-border programme in Ireland with Catholic and Protestant communities.

References

Bandura, A. (1986) *Social Foundations of Thought and Action: A Social Cognitive Theory.* Englewood Cliffs, NJ: Prentice-Hall.

Bardi, A. and Goodwin, R. (2011) The dual route to value change: individual processes and cultural moderators. *Journal of Cross-cultural Psychology,* 42(2), 271–287.

Bardi, A. and Schwartz, S. (2013) How does the value structure underlie value conflict? To win fairly or win at all costs? A conceptual framework for value-change interventions in sport. In Whitehead, J., Telfer, H. and Lambert. J (eds) *Values in Youth Sport and Physical Education.* London: Routledge, pp. 137–151.

Bardi, A., Lee, J., Hofman-Towfigh, N. and Soutar, G. (2009) The structure of intra-individual value change. *Journal of Personality and Social Psychology,* 97(5), 913–929.

Beedy, J.P. (1997) *Sports Plus. Positive Learning Using Sports.* Hamilton: Project Adventure.

Coalter, F. (2010) The politics of sport for development: limited focus programmes and broad gauge problems. *International Review of the Sociology of Sport,* 31, 295–314.

Coalter, F. (2014) Sport-for-development: pessimism of the intellect, optimism of the will. In Schulenkorf, N. and Adair, D. (eds) *Sport to the Rescue: A Critical Appraisal of Sport for Development.* New York: Palgrave Macmillan, pp. 62–78.

Cushion, C. (2010) Coach behaviour. In Lyle, J. and Cushion, C. (eds) *Sports Coaching: Professionalisation and Practice.* Edinburgh: Elsevier, pp. 43–62.

Kay, T. (2009) Developing through sport: evidencing sport impacts on young people. *Sport in Society,* 12(9), 177–191.

Kidd, B. (2008) A new social movement: sport for development and peace. *Sport in Society,* 1(4), 123–138.

Lambert, J. (2006) The Football for Peace coaching manual: a values-based approach to coaching sport in a divided society. In Sugden, J. and Wallis, J. (eds) *Football for Peace? Teaching and Playing Sport for Conflict Resolution in the Middle East.* London: Meyer and Meyer, pp. 13–34.

Lambert, J. (2013a) How can we teach values through sport? Teaching values through sport in divided societies. In Whitehead, J., Telfer, H. and Lambert, J. (eds) *Values in Youth Sport and Physical Education*. London: Routledge, pp. 152–165.

Lambert, J. (2013b) How does coach behaviour change the motivational climate? The creation of a learning environment conducive to the transmission of prosocial values. In Whitehead, J., Telfer, H. and Lambert. J (eds) *Values in Youth Sport and Physical Education*. London: Routledge, pp. 166–177.

Lee, M.J. (2004) 'The importance of values in the coaching process'. In Silva, M. and Malina, R. (eds) *Children and Youth in Organized Sports*. Coimbra, Portugal: Coimbra University Press, pp. 82–94.

Levermore, R. (2008) Sport: a new engine of development? *Progress in Development Studies*, 8, 183–189.

McNiff, J. and Whitehead, J. (2006) *Action Research*. London: Sage.

Rokeach, M. (1973) *The Nature of Human Values*. New York: Free Press.

Schwartz, S.H. (1992) Universals in the context and structure of values: theoretical advances and empirical tests in 20 countries. In Zanna, M.P. (ed.) *Advances in Experimental Social Psychology*, Vol. 25. New York: Academic Press, pp. 1–65.

Shields, D. and Bredemeier, B. (1995) *Character Development and Physical Activity*. Champaign, IL: Human Kinetics.

UN (2003) *United Nations Inter-agency Task Force on Sport for Development and Peace*. New York: United Nations.

Vila, G.O., Gimenez Fuentes-Guerra, F.J., Jimenez Sanchez, A.C., Franco Martin, J., Duran Gonzalez, L.J. and Jimenez Martin, P.J. (2012) *Initiation into Basketvalues*. Madrid: MCV.

Vila, G.O., Gimenez Fuentes-Guerra, F.J., Jimenez Sanchez, A.C., Franco Martin, J., Duran Gonzalez, L.J. and Jimenez Martin, P.J. (2014) *Compete to Share … Values*. Madrid: MCV.

Wallis, J. and Lambert, J. (2013) Reflections from the field: challenges in managing agendas and expectations. In Schulenkorf, N. and Adair, D. (eds) *Sport to the Rescue: A Critical Appraisal of Sport for Development*. New York: Palgrave Macmillan, pp. 99–114.

13

IDENTIFYING AND DEVELOPING ELITE PERFORMERS

Some key considerations from a coach's perspective

Jim Lawlor and John Lambert

Coaches working towards the performance end of the participation–performance spectrum are commonly concerned with unearthing potentially gifted athletes and nurturing that latent talent so that potential is fulfilled. Those who have experience of this talent identification and development process will know, often from painful experience as coaches and/or performers, that this is a 'rocky road' fraught with value conflicts, ethical dilemmas and difficult decisions commonly based on subjective reasoning and intuition. The decisions on whether to select and retain young athletes on development programmes are often made without any empirical evidence about their physical, technical and psychological potential. Even when this evidence is at our disposal, there are differing viewpoints amongst sports scientists and coaches on which data are significant and how they are to be utilised.

Those aspiring to *become a sports coach* are likely to be confronted with a range of dilemmas relating to the selection and nurturing of young athletes and would derive benefit from gaining an insight into the key issues which permeate the talent identification and development (TID) domain. Additionally, they may appreciate being offered some guiding principles to assist them with the task of maximising the capacity of the young performers whose development they are entrusted with. To these ends, this chapter will present some important considerations for those coaches engaged in the field of TID, and embedded within this narrative are excerpts from a reflective conversation between two individuals with widespread experience within TID and coaching. Overall, the upshot is a critical discussion around some of the most germane topics that emerge from the debates around the subject. The intention is to identify salient issues that emerge from the academic research and then address these matters through a dialogue: a form of auto-ethnography which draws on the reflections of 'experts' in the field.

The reflective dialogue is between two experienced coaches and scouts who specialise in the identification of elite young players at a professional football club.

Whilst the broad topics covered were agreed prior to the discussion, the conversation is unscripted and gives the 'authentic voices' of the participants in so far as it is unedited. It is hoped that readers can recognise some of the issues as relevant within their own practice and are able to reflect on their own philosophy and practice in relation to each aspect of TID covered. Many of the points made will resonate with coaches who work within sport at all levels and can be applied to their own particular context. The discourse is not followed with any conclusions; rather, readers are left to draw their own conclusions.

Both contributors have a background in football (soccer), therefore the examples used are mainly from that sport but the principles discussed are transferable to other sports. Coaches across all sports at varying levels are required to make challenging decisions in relation to TID and the points made can be generalised across other contexts, from elite to grass-roots sport. It is appropriate to add that, whilst we are both presently employed within high-level football and chiefly focus on elite sport, this is not intended to underestimate the important role that sport at all levels can play in improving health, well-being and participation.

The concluding section presents some reflective questions which invite readers to consider their own coaching philosophy and practice with respect to TID. The purpose is for readers to consider where they are presently situated in light of the debates previously explored within the chapter and to evaluate their methods.

What is talent and giftedness? A theoretical framework

The concept of 'talent' has been widely regarded by academics to be a complex phenomenon that has been defined in a variety of ways. Consequently, coaches and other sports educators have used terms such as 'gifted', 'talented' and 'having aptitude' in an interchangeable way without a clear understanding of their meaning. Some of the most effective reviews of literature in this area are those that use Gagné's Differentiated Model of Giftedness and Talent (DMGT) as a theoretical framework to make sense of a dynamic and multidimensional process which is influenced by genetic and environmental variables (Tranckle and Cushion, 2006; Vaeyens et al., 2008). With the aim of clarifying the terminology and offering a coherent model for TID, this chapter will draw upon the work of Gagné and specifically his DMGT paradigm (Gagné, 2000). Gagné's model classifies four domains of natural ability or giftedness (intellectual, creative, socio-affective and sensori/motor) and seven talent fields (academic, arts, business, leisure, social action, sport and technology). Figure 13.1 gives a modified version of his model which is specific to those elements that relate to sport. This adaptation simplifies the model and makes it relevant to the content of the chapter, whilst retaining its central theoretical premise.

Gagné described *giftedness* as 'the possession of untrained and spontaneously expressed natural abilities within one ability domain which places the child in the top 10% of their age peers' (Gagné, 2000: 67). This definition identifies *giftedness* as the 'raw material' at the start of a development process. Gagné locates *talent* at the other end of the continuum as 'mastery of systematically developed abilities and knowledge in one field of human activity which places the child's achievement within at least the upper 10% of age peers who are actively in that field' (Gagné, 2000: 67).

Figure 13.1 illustrates the relationship between the three *catalysts*, environmental influence, interpersonal variables and chance, and their effect on the *developmental process* from natural ability to sport-specific talent. All three catalysts can have a positive and negative effect on both selection for development programmes and the athlete's personal 'learning journey' that follows. The catalyst of chance may impact on the other variables: natural ability through genetic endowment, environmental circumstances including home background and intrapersonal dispositions such as health.

At this point it feels appropriate to encourage caution amongst coaches of athletes at grass-roots level who may interpret the DMGT model as a rationale to focus their efforts on the 'top 10%' of their athletes. This may lead to this group of athletes thinking they need to put in less effort as they are 'gifted'. Another consequence may be that the rest will see no point in continuing to train. We would guard against the notion that coaches are 'prospectors for gold' and encourage you to develop a growth mindset (Dweck and Leggett, 1988) in all of your young players.

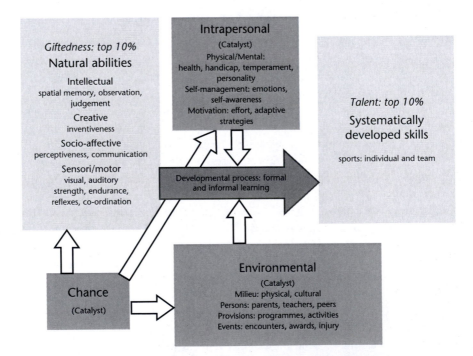

FIGURE 13.1   An adapted version of Gagné's differentiated model of giftedness and talent which specifically relates to sport

Environmental influence: identifying potential rather than performance

The importance of the environmental situation within which a young athlete exists and the level of its effect on the TID process is difficult to measure due to the complexity of the context within which each person lives and the number of influences they are subjected to. However, it is a widely held view amongst academics and practitioners that a young athlete's background and surroundings play a part in their progression in sport (Horton, 2012). Parents can be supportive of their son/daughter's sporting development (e.g. by facilitating coaching opportunities or providing the conditions conducive to their physical development, such as a healthy diet), or, on the other hand, some parents may have a negative influence on their child's motivation (e.g. by placing so much pressure on their child too early to win that sport ceases to be fun). Teachers can inspire young people to gravitate towards certain sports by providing a positive experience of that sport at an early age. The locality in which a child grows up may have a tradition of developing elite players in a particular sport and the local coaching infrastructure may reflect that, or, conversely, a child may be gifted in a specific activity but there is no opportunity to nurture those aptitudes as they lack access to organised coaching close by. Potential, in the form of the natural abilities as Gagné terms them, may not be realised in the form of tangible skill or physical competencies if positive environmental catalysts have been limited, or negative catalysts have been prevalent in a young person's life.

The implications of environment for TID and coaching are that those given responsibility for selecting and developing young athletes need to take into account potential and not just performance. Performance is often easy to measure and is therefore used as an indicator of potential. This can be a misleading criterion for selection as it normally only identifies those that have had a disproportionate level of support relative to other children, or those that have grown the most or matured the quickest. Of significance here is a coach's awareness of the relative age effect where some players have the advantage of being born earlier in the sporting year and are therefore older and bigger relative to their peers. Studies into the relative age effect have been conducted in numerous sports including football (Helsen et al., 2005; Dundink, 1994), cricket (Edwards, 1994) and baseball (Thompson, et al., 1991), all reporting a disproportionate number of professional players being born in the first months of the year.

Spotting potential is a more challenging task. This requires coaches to look beyond the obvious performance measures and make informed predictions of player potential. An example scenario would be that player A started to play competitive football a few years later than player B and has received less coaching. They both demonstrate a similar level of technical proficiency. In this case player A may be considered to have greater potential and this may be taken into account and reflected in a coach's judgement of that player. The capacity to learn and the speed at which a young sportsperson improves has been identified by researchers as a more reliable indicator of potential than a taking a 'performance snapshot' of that individual at one point in their development as a young athlete (Gagné, 2000).

JIM: Age is only important as it is the way in which football is organised. It provides a benchmark but we should be looking at whether their physical and cognitive behaviour is typical of a player of that age. Are they ready to play up an age group?

JOHN: So we are talking about their level of maturation? Early developers?

JIM: Not necessarily. Their mentality is probably more important than their physical profile. Do they have a love of the game, an appetite to play? Do they have a hunger to practice and improve? And are they quick learners? Always ready for the next challenge?

JOHN: I once saw that intrinsic motivation several years ago in a 9-year-old at a football project that I was working on in London in the Easter holidays. Unforgettable! The desire to be the best was there for all to see ... and that lad went on to captain England.

Intrapersonal characteristics: the identification of a wide range of competencies in addition to skills specific to the sport

An overemphasis on the technical, tactical and physical skills specific to any sport can limit the identification of potential. Whilst these skills are undeniably important, an excessive emphasis on them can obscure other competencies that hold vital clues in predicting player potential. Adopting a broader approach requires significant consideration of some of the personal, social and emotional competencies that often go unnoticed but make an important contribution to potential and longer-term performance. Gagné lists these as intrapersonal catalysts, and they include characteristics that are recognised as being part of the profile of a successful athlete: intrinsic motivation, adaptive strategies, self-awareness, positive values and stable temperament.

Taking the ability to use adaptive strategies and self-awareness as sporting assets, most coaches have known athletes who do not progress as expected due to an inability to find coping strategies to deal with the inevitable disappointments and problems that come their way. They may suffer a serious injury, or not gain selection for an elite squad due to a dip in form, or suffer a run of poor results, or come into social conflict with team mates and/or the coach. Conversely, sport is an arena where there have been many examples of triumph over adversity by performers who have the necessary psychological attributes to deal with setbacks. Whatever the psychological 'trough' that they are confronted with, they require personal coping strategies and mental resilience to get through it.

The motivational problems that ego-oriented individuals who are driven by extrinsic rewards can have when they are confronted with 'perceived failure' are discussed in Chapter 8. Athletes who are intrinsically motivated are more able to get through these 'troughs' as they tend not to judge themselves solely on short–term outcomes and are not 'derailed' by disappointing results. As Michael Jordan so succinctly put it, 'to win big you have got to be prepared to lose big'. To identify the intrapersonal traits of a potential elite performer in the behaviour and attitudes of a young athlete can be a challenging task. However, a young sportsperson who relishes a challenge, increases effort following failure, respects their team mates and the coach, enjoys competitive situations and practises hard possesses most of the intrapersonal characteristics needed to reach a high level.

JOHN: It is said by some to take 10,000 hours of deliberate practice to become an elite sportsperson. It takes a special person to have the desire to accumulate that volume of practice. How can you maintain the motivation of players to practise at the required level? … apart from the extrinsic rewards, of course!

JIM: The motivation to improve comes from them. It is inherent in the individual and is dependent on them how much the club can influence this. Motivation is affected by their role, how much game time they are getting, enjoyment, success of the group and recognition, such as international call ups.

JOHN: So, they are motivated by intrinsic reward rather than financial?

JIM: Most top professional players are driven by fear of failure. They are very self-critical and would hate to fall short of the level that *they* feel is acceptable, let alone the coach. When all the practice hours have been put in they are building up to the stage when they can perform at their top level and this gives them supreme confidence. It equates to going into an exam with all the knowledge at your disposal. There was almost a feeling of certainty when Ronaldo stepped up to take a free kick. This belief is developed through sustained practice over a long time.

Prioritising long-term development over short-term success

Due to the dynamic and multidimensional nature of sport talent, practitioners and researchers have found that the process of selecting performers for development programmes at a young age can be problematic (Baker, 2012). Traditional models of talent identification, based on measuring physiological, physical, anthropometric (body size and shape) or technical variables within age groups, tend to exclude late maturing athletes as well as those from an environment where there has been a lack of training and coaching. Adolescents who possess the required characteristics for success in adult sport will not necessarily retain these attributes through maturation. Evidence-based TID programmes suggest that the qualities necessary for success in top-level sport do not emerge until late in adolescence. Despite this evidence, professional sport still invests considerable resources into identifying 'talented athletes' at an early age. There are two reasons for this: a) it allows them to accelerate the development process for that group, and b) they can focus available resources on a relatively small number of young people.

There may be a rationale for early identification and selection for sports such as gymnastics where peak performance comes at a young age. However, the reliability of predicting the success of a performer 10 years in the future has been widely challenged for most sports. Youth sport programmes that over-prioritise performance rather than learning will produce athletes who miss fundamental development experiences which they require to progress in their sport. Physically advanced players may dominate the play at under-11 level but they should be advised not to rely solely on speed and strength as they move along the developmental pathway. They will need to develop their technical and tactical skills in readiness for a later stage when they are up against the late-developing children, who at a young age have had to rely on developing their skills, and who by 16 have caught up in terms of physical maturation. Relying on performance measures at an early age may also conceal significant weaknesses in early developers that could hinder later development. The early developer may well struggle to make the step up from youth to senior level due to a prior reliance on physical strength when progressing through their developmental process.

> JOHN: I feel that many coaches of youth teams do not give players enough time to develop, especially those who are slower to mature physically. They are too obsessed with winning to take a long-term developmental view of coaching. I hear about under-10 coaches with fixtures at our club that seem only interested in the result. I now support the notion of long-term athlete development but cringe when I look back at my early days as a youth coach and sometimes I didn't use the bench players for fear of weakening the team and losing.
>
> JIM: Youth coaches are not put under pressure for results at our club. They might put themselves under pressure. You cannot get away from football being a game of winning and losing. The youth coach's role is to create the conditions where players can develop. Results are good for morale and sometimes show progress but there are clubs that put too much emphasis on them at youth level. Over the last few years small, technical players have emerged as being very successful, especially in attacking positions. The enlightened coaches spot this trend and allow time for this type of player to flourish.

The challenge is to create an environment at youth level where the main emphasis is on development rather than winning. A manifestation of this may be that the coach avoids the temptation to always select the most physically and technically advanced players in key positions in the team. Coaches should also consider developing styles of play that will underpin longer-term success as opposed to tactics that will deliver immediate results. For example, youth football teams that are encouraged to build attacks through each 'third' of the pitch are more likely to concede possession in dangerous areas, but ultimately will produce players who are comfortable manipulating the ball in tight areas.

Identifying giftedness: possibility vs actuality

Early selection of young athletes for development programmes on the basis of performance against a set of physical criteria, although extensively used, has been described as 'talent elimination' as it may discourage individuals with potential from participation in sport. This process, often being subject to discrimination along economic and maturation lines as it fails to take into account any lack of playing experience and adolescent growth, is both flawed on ethical grounds and has questionable reliability and validity (Bailey *et al.*, 2011). By contrast, Gagné held the view that the gifts that any individual possesses would be likely to show up in different tasks in the form of *accelerated learning*: their rate and aptitude for learning within a domain. This interpretation of giftedness would suggest a need to resist the imperative to cut development squads at early age groups and leave the door open for the late developer.

Although potential in 'closed' skill sports like rowing and athletics field events can be predicted by identifying a relatively small number of attributes, within the more 'open' activities, such as team ball sports, endowed giftedness consists of multiple components and elite performance can be achieved in ways specific to an individual through a combinations of assets unique to them. *Compensation phenomenon* is where an athlete may be deficient in one key attribute but this is compensated by their strengths in other areas (Williams and Ericsson, 2005). We can all think of footballers who lack speed but compensate with their perceptual awareness or of others who are small in stature but compensate with their tenacity. Again, early de-selection on the basis of one deficiency is likely to lead to some young athletes being unwisely rejected.

JOHN: Most research on talent ID focuses on scientific testing to measure physical capacity and cognitive ability. Where do you stand on this?

JIM: Physical tests on 15 and 16 year olds are done to predict long-term physical outcomes and they use scans to forecast growth ... which has its uses in certain contexts. But it is not a legitimate reason to de-select a player. I still think that their motivation to reach the top is the key.

JOHN: So what other criteria are important to look for in elite young players? The sport scientists rate endurance, speed and perceptual awareness as determining characteristics in an elite sportsperson.

> *JIM:* Yes, those attributes are important along with the ability to manipulate the ball in a tight space and then to move the ball over varying distances. The psychological adjustment to playing in a larger space and the increased endurance required can be very challenging for some boys. They need to move from 5-a-side to 7, then 9 then 11 gradually, but that step up is critical to their development.
>
> *JOHN:* So, what sets those young players with star quality apart? What special characteristics do they have?
>
> *JIM:* You look at how they affect the game … their impact. It is easy to see a special talent. They have individual technique that is way above average. They will be above average in terms of speed of decision-making and game understanding. Their strengths will be so great that they may compensate for an obvious weakness such as lack of physical stature.

The effect of chance as a catalyst

The importance of chance as an influencing factor in the development of young athletes should be acknowledged. The old saying states that, 'You can choose your friends but you can't choose your relatives'; but this is arguably only partly true. Whilst it is undeniable that each one of us is born with a genetic profile linked closely to that of our parents, we also grow up in the surroundings and are educated in the school of our parents' choice. Not only the family that a young person is born into but also the environment in which they live, including the peer groups that they are subjected to, can have a critical effect on their early developmental years; 'presocialisation' (Donnelly and Young, 1988) is an effect over which they have little control.

The effect of chance on intrapersonal catalysts can be seen when we consider injury. Many athletes have had promising careers blighted by injury and, although the risks can be reduced by adopting certain training methods and playing styles, no athlete can perform to a maximum level without risking injury. There are examples in all elite sport of athletes, most notably boxers, who have overcome either a difficult upbringing or misfortune (or both) to get to the top of their sport and are stronger for it. Their natural ability and intrapersonal attributes (resilience, adaptability and motivation) have allowed them to conquer their circumstances and have often brought an added 'edge' to their performance. Whilst chance as a catalyst can be influenced by coach and athlete behaviour, it is by definition a variable that is difficult to predict.

> *JOHN:* The route to the top in all sport can be a hazardous road with inevitable 'downs' alongside the 'ups'. How does the club protect and support young players in this respect?

JIM: As in life, there are diminishing levels of support as people advance in age. Aside from the coach, the young players have a club welfare officer to offer support and help. He knows the players' backgrounds and needs. As players grow as a person they are rightly expected to develop increasing independence. Senior professionals are, to a large extent, expected to stand on their own two feet. There are 55 pros here from 17 different countries. Some foreign players find it difficult to adapt to the weather, the food and the physicality of the British game. If a player is not playing it can be a difficult period for them. The challenge for the coaching staff is to get each player's focus on practice, performance and recovery, and to minimise other distractions. The manager and coaches nowadays need a wide skill set.

The developmental process: nurturing young athletes – the balance between play, practice and competition

A variety of models of athlete development have been advanced by academics and sports educationalists, all of which try to make sense of the factors that impact on the process and identify how they interact (Bailey *et al.*, 2011). Cote (1999) presented three phases as stages in the development of an athlete: the sampling phase (where children at 6–12 years play a range of sports for fun and develop their fundamental movement skills), the specialising phase (when 13–15 year olds begin to focus on specific sports and are still largely motivated by enjoyment) and the investment years (when they get to 16+ and begin to commit to one sport by developing skills and strategies linked to competitive performance through *deliberate practice*).

Deliberate practice is to engage in learning activity that is designed to improve performance, requires effort and is not necessarily enjoyable (Baker and Young, 2014). *Deliberate play*, on the other hand, covers sporting pursuits that are modified versions of the standard rules, can be played in adaptable contexts and allow children to experiment with different skills and tactics. The development of intrinsic motivation through *deliberate play* is regarded by Cote *et al.* (2007) as being of importance to adherence to a sport, especially in the first two stages of development. These periods of informal play at an early age are where creativity is cultivated, as there is the freedom to try things without the risk of negative feedback from adults and where the pressures of competition are either low or zero. Whilst it is necessary for athletes to access coaching during the development stages, an over-exposure to formal coaching and competition in the sampling and early specialising years may limit creativity and may reduce intrinsic motivation.

> JIM: I believe that development of technical skill is largely organic rather than manufactured. As society in Western Europe and North America becomes more affluent, sport becomes just one of many social choices and the effect is that young people have a whole range of pastimes and the level of practice in a specialist sport is diluted. In South America, Africa, parts of the Far East and Eastern Europe football is still the dream for young boys. They sleep with the ball so it is there when they wake up. These regions are where most of the technically gifted are coming from.

The type of coaching that these young children are subjected to is crucial; coaches who employ methods that empower players through self-determination and enhance perceived ability (Abbott and Collins, 2004) will 'free up' the athletes to 'express themselves' and promote creativity, whereas coaches who adopt controlling methods and focus solely on winning will stifle flair and may well experience high drop-out rates from their performers due to low levels of enjoyment.

Young players in team sports are frequently guided by coaches into always playing in a certain position in the team or encouraged to play within a prescribed tactical plan that they must adhere to. This 'over-coaching' approach can be detrimental to the long-term developmental interest of the players (Ford et al., 2010). Facilitating learning activities where players are required to solve their own tactical problems has been referred to as 'benign neglect', as it can lead to benefits to the performer in terms of enhanced game understanding.

As they evolve, team sports are increasingly demanding technical and tactical versatility from their players which requires them to play in a number of positions and be able to adapt to the tactical preferences of each of the coaches that they may work under. A young footballer who has developed technically, physically, mentally and tactically will be able to take a change of position and different coaching strategy in their stride; this adaptability may also prolong their career.

Cote (1999) draws attention to *critical incidents* as often being the main reason that young people choose to specialise in one sport. These are when 'positive value' is associated with an experience in that activity. For example, gaining enjoyment through a regular game in the local park with friends or attending a fun and rewarding programme of coaching. It is reasonable to assume that critical incidents are more likely to occur in deliberate play settings than formal, structured instruction sessions.

According to Walters and Gardner (1986) athletes are more likely to commit to a sport after a *crystallizing experience* which initially, for young children, may take the form of the pleasure gained from a sensorimotor experience, e.g. feeling success in consistently juggling a football or hitting a tennis ball against a wall. Again, it is important that young athletes have the opportunity to gain such experiences through activities that are informal and self-determined (Deci and Ryan, 2000).

At a later stage in the development process a child may well experience a *refining crystallizing experience* which will further draw them towards a particular sport, such as finding a sport that 'comes easy' and developing an identity as a gifted performer. Typically, this is the stage in which deliberate practice will become a feature of their life but it should not be at the expense of deliberate play.

JOHN: Can we end by looking to the future. How do you see football and coaching developing in the next 10 years?

JIM: There will be a move towards quicker, more technical players in attacking positions and there will be even more emphasis on maintaining possession. Players will need to be intelligent and versatile as systems of play will change between games and even within games. They will be expected to interchange positions. Players will need a full repertoire of skills as defenders will need to attack effectively and use the ball well. Of course, attacking players will need good defending skills.

JOHN: What implications does this have for coaching methods? How do we develop these technical, creative, 'flair' players?

JIM: We need to regress rather than progress. By that I mean … in recent years we have put emphasis on coaching qualifications, coaching manuals, organised practice … but there needs to be more free play.

JOHN: When we were youth players there was very little coaching available yet there were plenty of players around with high-quality technical ability. Every team had a good dribbler who modelled themselves on George Best. It's a cliché, but they learned their skills by playing in the park or their backyard.

JIM: Coaches should question themselves before intervening on the coaching field. They should ask, 'Why am I intervening here? Is it a question of discipline? Is there a problem with the practice? Or should I just stand back and observe to see whether the players can learn for themselves?' This 'discovery' method should be encouraged. Yes, step in if they really need guidance but the best way to learn is to solve their own problems.

JOHN: That way we are going to develop 'thinking' players, able to adapt to tactical problems.

JIM: If we want to develop the next generation of players with 'football intelligence' … players who can be captains … and then coaches, then they need the freedom to make decisions for themselves rather than the coach prescribing everything they do.

To summarise, this chapter is not aiming to provide a comprehensive guide to TID but to address some of the critical issues that coaches are confronted with, and it offers some insight into each of these using applied examples. From the outset the difficulties associated with both identifying and nurturing talent in sport in terms of practical, theoretical and ethical considerations have been acknowledged. The key points to consider for coaches empowered to tackle this challenging task are:

- To take into account the specific components of the sport and its position along the closed–open continuum when deciding the most effective methods for identifying young athletes for development programmes.
- To consider potential alongside performance when making these selections.
- To understand that giftedness in the form of accelerated learning may not show up until late in adolescence.
- To consider 'intrapersonal characteristics' such as intrinsic motivation alongside obvious technical, tactical and physical attributes as indicators of potential.
- To guard against 'over-coaching' and allow young athletes some autonomy to develop individual techniques, versatility and creativity naturally through deliberate play.

The 'experts' in the area of TID will continue to judge talent through performance and their subjective view will rightly be valued. Nevertheless, there is an increasing body of research and expertise in this field which coaches and coach educators should be aware of and engage with, so that practice can be based on evidence rather than merely tradition, intuition and hunches. After all, we have a responsibility to every young athlete in our care at all levels to offer them the most fulfilling sporting experience that they can possibly have.

Interrogating your own philosophy and practice: some questions to prompt self-analysis

This final section includes questions which are designed to engage the reader in a reflective process and invite them to consolidate their own thoughts on the issues highlighted in the chapter.

It is now appropriate to ask you, the reader, to reflect on your own views about talent identification and the process of developing young athletes by presenting questions aimed at provoking introspective thought. For each question, you are asked to think carefully about your response, give a rationale for that response and ask yourself what that response says about your philosophy and practice. There is no right or wrong answer. You can apply each question to your particular sport and context, and consider the possible reaction of the players and significant others to your responses and how you might deal with that.

- What criteria do you use to select players for your (development) squads? Do you look beyond physical, technical and tactical attributes?
- Do you take into account a player's previous sporting and environmental background when selecting players for your (development) squad or are judgements made solely on present 'performance'?

- How important are height, strength and power in determining whether young players should be selected for your (development) squad? Would you reject a player who lacks in one or more of these areas but has advanced technical ability?
- Intrinsic motivation, resilience, self-awareness and a desire to improve are regarded as being part of the profile of a successful athlete. What do you do as a coach to develop these attributes in your players?
- What is the ratio of deliberate practice, deliberate play and competition in your coaching sessions? Are you confident that the ratio is right for the age group you are coaching?
- What do you do as a coach to actively promote 'creativity' from players in your squad? How could you do more to encourage individual flair in your performers?

References

Abbott, A. and Collins, D. (2004) Eliminating the dichotomy between theory and practice in talent and development: considering the role of psychology. *Journal of Sport Sciences*, 22, 395–408.

Bailey, R., Toms, M., Collins, D., Ford, P., Macnamara, A. and Pearce, G. (2011) Models of young player development in sport. In Stafford, I. (ed.) *Coaching Children in Sport*, pp. 38–57. Abingdon: Routledge.

Baker, J. (2012) Do genes predict potential? Genetic factors and athletic success. In Baker, J., Cobley, S. and Schorer, J. (eds) *Talent Identification and Development in Sport: International Perspectives*, pp. 39–51. London: Routledge.

Baker, J. and Young, B. (2014) 20 years later: deliberate practice and the development of expertise in sport. *International Review of Sport and Exercise Psychology*, 7(1), 135–157.

Cote, J. (1999) The influence of the family in the development of talent in sport. *The Sport Psychologist*, 13, 395–417.

Cote, J., Baker, J. and Abernethy, B. (2007) Practice and play in the development of sport expertise. In Tenenbaum, G. and Eklund, R. (eds) *Handbook of Sport Psychology*. Hoboken, NJ: Wiley.

Deci, E.L. and Ryan, R.M. (2000) Self-determination theory and the facilitation of intrinsic motivation, social development, and well-being. *American Psychologist*, 55, 68–78.

Donnelly, P. and Young, K. (1988) The construction and confirmation of identity in sports subcultures. *Sociology of Sport Journal*, 5, 223–240.

Dudink, A. (1994) Birth date and sporting success. *Nature*, 368, 592.

Dweck, C.S. and Leggett, E.L. (1988) A social-cognitive approach to motivation and personality. *Psychological Review*, 95(2), 256–273.

Edwards, S. (1994) Born too late to win? *Nature*, 370, 186.

Ford, P., Yates, I. and Williams, M. (2010) An analysis of practice activities and instructional behaviours used by youth coaches during practice: exploring the link between science and application. *Journal of Sport Sciences*, 28(5), 483–495.

Gagné, F. (2000) Understanding the complete choreography of talent development through the DMGT-based analysis. In Heller, K. (ed.) *International Handbook of Giftedness and Talent*, pp. 67–79. Oxford: Elsevier.

Helsen, W.F., Van Winckel, J. and Williams, M.A. (2005) The relative age effect in youth soccer across Europe. *Journal of Sports Sciences*, 23(6), 629–636.

Horton, S. (2012) Environmental influences on early development in sports experts. In Baker, J., Cobley, S. and Schorer, J. (eds) *Talent Identification and Development in Sport: International Perspectives*, pp. 39–51. London: Routledge.

Thompson, A., Barnsley, R. and Stebelsky, G. (1991) 'Born to play ball': the relative age effect and major league baseball. *Sociology of Sport Journal*, 8, 146–151.

Tranckle, P. and Cushion, C. (2006) Rethinking giftedness and talent in sport. *Quest*, 58, 265–282.

Vaeyens, R., Lenoir, M., Williams, M. and Philippaerts, R. (2008) Talent identification and development programmes in sport. *Sports Medicine*, 35, 703–718.

Walters, J. and Gardner, H. (1986) The crystallising experience: discovering an intellectual gift. In Sternberg, R. and Davidson, J. (eds) *Concepts of Giftedness*, pp. 306–331. New York: Cambridge University Press.

Williams, A. and Ericsson, K. (2005) Perceptual-cognitive expertise in sport: some considerations when applying the expert performance approach. *Human Movement Science*, 24(3), 283–307.

CONCLUDING THOUGHTS AND FUTURE DIRECTIONS

James Wallis and John Lambert

We began this text with two short statements concerning our own personal experiences of setting out on the road to becoming a sports coach. Our own journeys between then and now have been littered with implicit and explicit learning episodes that, upon reflection, have shaped our philosophies and informed how we coach. The most recent of these moments have come in the editing of this book, in particular reading, digesting, contemplating and applying contributions from each of the authors, which has added to our learning process as coach educators. We are grateful to each contributor for this sharing of experience and their willingness to be openly reflective about their own practice in order to enlighten readers about their specialist areas and demonstrate how even the most experienced and accomplished coaches encounter problems and dilemmas along the way. It has been our intention for coaches at all levels to be open to the prospect of this book guiding, assisting, informing or confirming their practice. Whilst by no means exhaustive, this short plenary draws together four of the more substantive themes that have emerged from the narrative, all of which can be viewed as key concerns for the future development of sport coaching.

Using theory to underpin practice

Coaches derive knowledge of how to practise from various sources, most notably through observing and working alongside other coaches with more experience (Cushion and Jones, 2001; Gilbert and Trudel, 2001) who can demonstrate 'how things should be done' (Lyle, 1999). There is considerable merit to the cascading of knowledge, experience and 'wisdom' to new recruits to the coaching fraternity, not least the value of serving an apprenticeship of observation (Lortie, 1975) and benefiting from the 'wealth of knowledge' possessed by good coaches (Cushion *et al.*, 2003: 225).

There are, however, significant limitations in an over-reliance on this as a dominant means of coach education and development. Adoption of traditionally and contextually accepted practice, without exposure to analysis and critique, risks creating a regime of truth which is stagnant and limiting. This form of cultural reproduction of coaching has been considered as being shaped by coaches' own personal biographies within the sport and their coaching is 'both the product and manifestation of a personally experienced involvement within the coaching process' (Cushion *et al.*, 2003: 219.). Coaches tend to rely too heavily on emulation of other coaches or on specific traditions held within the sport or context, as opposed to the application of evidence-based practice (Williams and Hodges, 2005). In keeping with this it has been consistently reported that there is, at best, a 'time-lag' between research findings and their application to coaching and to coach education processes (Farrow *et al.*, 2008; Ford *et al.*, 2010). It should be pointed out that some research has its limitations, which is alluded to below, but a 'profession' that embraces a culture where there is a willingness to review one's practice on the basis of new research is more likely to develop and improve. That is not to say that coaches should accept that their previous practice has been 'wrong' or misguided, but based on the best knowledge available at the time. For example, the teaching games for understanding model (Bunker and Thorpe, 1982), originally developed in the1980s, has been regularly developed, applied and reviewed (Griffin *et al.*, 2006; Kirk and MacPhail, 2002). It is currently undergoing a recent resurgence in popularity within coaching. As knowledge moves on, practice must keep pace.

In the interest of balance it would be inappropriate and counter-productive to simply dismiss the cultural norms which have been built up over years, often generations, of coaching. In the same way it would be equally inappropriate to recommend blind acceptance of all of the most recent research findings, which may have limited range, scope or ecological applicability given that they frequently emanate from laboratory-based as opposed to field-based settings. The message being presented in this text is that coaches should make informed, conscious decisions concerning their coaching, as opposed to automatic acceptance of received wisdom which may not have stood the test of time, in meeting the evolving demands of many sports. We propose a more concerted attempt to assimilate scientific, sociological and pedagogic research with the best of the accumulated wisdom from specific contexts in finding the 'right' way to support athletes, relative to the sport, the individual and the context. Coaches may consider using alternative and diverse approaches as recommended by more recent research findings and texts such as this. They may seek further guidance or advice on new ideas in their field through workshops, further study or mentoring, with National Governing Body (NGB) coach education structures leading the way. The important point is that whichever ways that a coach decides to gain content and pedagogic knowledge, it is advisable that they are open-minded and do not dismiss others because they work differently.

Bringing theory to life

We, the editors of this book, consider ourselves practitioner-academics. We hope that this is reflected in the way in which the book is presented, as a practical resource underpinned by reflection and application of theoretical concepts. There is growing evidence of the inclusion of theoretical concepts in coach education programmes in certain sports. Concepts such as LTAD (long term athlete development), deliberate practice, relative age effect, holistic coaching and periodisation are increasingly well recognised and commonly included in coaching vernacular. Less evident is a clear understanding of how to bring the theory to life by integrating it into practical coaching. Youth sport contexts for example, may claim to model a LTAD 'philosophy' but then contradict this with inequitable team selections, over-prioritization of outcomes and early specialisation in the formative years. This example shows one case where theory may be spoken about, but with little appreciation of how it is brought to life and applied for the good of the players. Similar examples may exist where coaches are presented with sufficient knowledge to engage in an informed discussion, but this is not underpinned with sufficient awareness of how to embed the concepts into practice. For example: What does a task-orientated environment look like in athletics? How can cricket drills be more holistic and less one-dimensionally technocratic? How can training be made more self-determined for athletes? What does values-based coaching look like in the field? Knowing theory and applying theory should go together for coaches, as should supplying theory and demonstrating theory for coach educators.

Reviewing our own biographies, and those of many of those with whom we have worked, it is evident that a significant amount of coaching is underpinned by coach intuition rather than any formal process of engaging with research evidence. In essence, 'thinking coaches' may instinctively practise in a way that seems right at the time, and find later that it is supported by research evidence. Coaches may intuitively offer autonomy or athlete voice in decision–making, resonating with self-determination, or reconstruct a task to make it more appealing to all performers, in keeping with threads of motivational climate or goal orientations. Examples such as this should confirm to coaches the efficacy of their interventions, build their confidence in trusting their intuition and confirm that their work can be substantiated by theory. Whether educating coaches to apply relevant theory to their practice, or to appreciate and recognise theory which validates their practice, it is intended that this text will encourage further narrowing of the theory–practice gap that coaching must continue to find ways to bridge.

The multi-dimensional nature of coaching

The vast majority of coaches take up the role for philanthropic reasons. They want to 'make a difference' by creating a compelling learning environment for their athlete(s) and thus contributing to the sport that they once enjoyed playing. This desire to 'give something back' to their beloved sport is a laudable starting point but in itself is not enough. A coach, unlike an athlete, assumes significant responsibility for those in their care as soon as they put the tracksuit on. It is incumbent on them to first understand then demonstrate the multi-faceted skill set which the role requires, including many of the competencies covered in this book. To gain the necessary content and pedagogic knowledge and, just as importantly, apply it in practice, they need to take part in coach education programmes that recognise the multi-dimensional role of a coach. Seminal work on teacher knowledge by Shulman (1987), later applied to physical education by Metzler (2005), listed 11 knowledge bases required by physical education teachers. These areas extend the content knowledge that continues to dominate traditional coach education processes, and include: knowledge of learners, the context, learning theories, developmental appropriateness, emotional climate and equity. These areas are all featured in detail within this text. It is our contention that coaching should follow a similar pathway in 'phasing up' the required knowledge and coach education programmes.

'Bad coaching' is worse than no coaching at all. It can dampen enthusiasm, limit enjoyment, stifle creativity and lead to athlete drop out. This text aims to help empower coaches at all levels to fulfil their role in its widest sense and, as a result, make them more likely to be 'good' coaches who inspire their athletes to reach their potential and develop a passion for sport. The need for coaches to take a holistic approach to their work and adopt a humanistic relationship with the athlete has been highlighted throughout this book (for example, see Chapters 6 and 7). The application of technical skills is critical to all sports but to solely focus on this element of coaching to the exclusion of others is to fail to fully recognise the responsibilities of the coach. By unlocking the potential of sport, beyond its purely technocratic aims (Laker, 2000) we emphasise the coaching of the person within the sport and not just the sport.

Continuing to learn to become a coach

A recurring theme within this book is to communicate to readers the never-ending quest to *become a sports coach*. Whilst subjecting oneself to NGB coach education programmes and subsequently gaining accreditation will provide valuable basic grounding as well as allow access to higher-level remunerated coaching, it would be myopic to think that these courses offer the only way to raise competence levels and, more importantly, that arriving at a certain benchmark signifies that one has 'made it' as a sports coach. Sports coaches, as well as the bodies responsible for coach education, should adopt an outward-facing perspective, whilst reviewing their own methods through a critical lens in order to avoid the static, out-of-date and limiting practice that has inhibited the progress of some sports in the UK. Sport coaching is dynamic, ever-changing and increasingly demanding. Pedagogic research, sport science and technological advances within sport are moving at an unprecedented rate, and it is the obligation of anyone using the name 'coach', or anyone tasked with providing 'coach education' to make attempts to critique their practice and, where necessary, to assimilate new knowledge into their work.

This book is not designed to be a 'how to' guide. The title alludes to a social process – a *becoming*, which has no end. It is designed to provoke introspection, cognition and ultimately enhanced action for coaches, at all levels, to move forward through constant iteration between practice and theory. It is intended to inspire questioning and creativity amongst coaches and to encourage interrogation of why, how and what to coach in a constructive and productive way. The recurring reflective strand, weaved throughout the text, is intended to kick start this process and to illuminate new ways of thinking and acting within coaching practice. It is these processes which we feel will uphold the integrity of coaching in a professional era, and should even be criteria used to distinguish the sport coach from the sport leader, trainer, administrator or manager.

Professionalisation – making the transition

Having established that it is the responsibility of coaches and coach educators to continue to evolve their practice as coaching ventures towards a new era, it is pertinent to ask: how close is coaching to being regarded as a profession? There is increased expectation on sport to deliver social, political, health or economic goals, with the part played by coaches being fundamental to these aspirations. Sport continues to hold increasing significance in many contexts worldwide, whether for performance, health or community development. This presents challenges to the governance of coaching, the education of the next generation of coaches and the continued (re)education of existing coaches.

The UK coaching community is currently waiting to see how far coaching has progressed since it outlined its ambitious intentions in the *UK Coaching Framework* (2009) (see section on 'The UK coaching context' in the introduction of this book). It will be interesting to review the findings of the evaluation post-2016, as this will indicate progress achieved against strategic action areas, which will, in turn, demonstrate the areas in which the professionalisation of coaching has made headway and where progress has been less apparent.

Readers may consider which challenges confronting coaching are most relevant to their own particular context. However, it is hoped that within the scope of this book, as well as providing you with food for thought and guidance, we have offered reassurance that your practice has strengths that can be built upon. Finally, the most important message that *Becoming a Sports Coach* conveys is that the role brings with it great responsibility. Some coaches do not realise how important they are to the people in their care or to significant others involved in the coaching setting. A coach's words and actions can inspire or deflate, motivate or demotivate, create joy or anger. Deploy this responsibility with great care and, whilst striving for continual self-improvement, do not forget to enjoy your work and convey a passion for sport to your athletes.

References

Bunker, D. and Thorpe, R. (1982) A model for the teaching of games in the secondary school. *Bulletin of Physical Education*, 10, 9–16.

Cushion, C.J. and Jones, R.L. (2001) A systematic observation of professional top-level youth soccer coaches. *Journal of Sport Behaviour*, 24, 354–376.

Cushion, C.J, Armour, K.M. and Jones, R.L. (2003) Coach education and continuing professional development: experience and learning to coach. *Quest*, 55(3), 215–230.

Farrow, D., Baker, J. and McMahon, C. (2008) *Developing Sports Expertise: Researchers and coaches put theory into practice*. London: Routledge.

Ford, P.R., Yates, I. and Williams, M. (2010) An analysis of practice activities and instructional behaviours used by youth soccer coaches during practice: exploring the link between science and application. *Journal of Sports Sciences*, 28(5), 483–495.

Gilbert, W. and Trudel, P. (2001) Learning to coach through experience: reflection in model youth sport coaches. *Journal of Teaching in Physical Education*, 21, 16–34.

Griffin, L.L., Oslin, J.L. and Mitchell, S.A. (2006) *Teaching Sports Concepts and Skills: A tactical games approach*. Champaign, IL: Human Kinetics.

Kirk, D. and MacPhail, A. (2002) Teaching games for understanding and situated learning: rethinking the Bunker–Thorpe model. *Journal of Teaching in Physical Education*, 21, 177–192.

Laker, A. (2000) *Beyond the Boundaries of Physical Education: Educating young people for citizenship and social responsibility*. London: Routledge.

Lortie, D. (1975) *Schoolteacher: A sociological study*. Chicago: The University of Chicago Press.

Lyle, J.W.B. (1999) The coaching process: principles and practice. In Cross, N. and Lyle, J. (Eds) *The Coaching Process: Principles and practice for sport* (pp. 1–24). Oxford: Butterworth-Heinemann.

Metzler, M. (2005) *Instructional Models for Physical Education*. Boston: MA, Allyn and Bacon.

Shulman, L.S (1987) Knowledge and teaching: foundations of the new reform. *Harvard Educational Review*, 57, 1–22.

Williams, A.M. and Hodges, N.J. (2005) Practice, instruction and skill acquisition: challenging tradition. *Journal of Sports Sciences*, 23, 637–650.

INDEX

whole-heartedness 18
whole self, consideration of 19
Wiggins, Sir Bradley 140
Wilson, M. 152
winning, over-emphasis on 28, 32, 40, 84, 89, 94, 113, 186–7, 190
women in coaching 75–6
Women's Sport and Fitness Foundation (WSFF) 34

Women's Tennis Association (WTA) 123, 134
Woodman, L. 4
Wylleman, P. 124

Youth Sport Trust 70

Zijlaard-van Moorsel, Leontien 140